Yoruba Philosophy and the Seeds of Enlightenment

Advancing Yoruba Philosophy

Yemi D. Prince
(Yemi D. Ogunyemi)

Vernon Series in Philosophy

VERNON PRESS

Copyright © 2019 Yemi D. Prince (Yemi D. Ogunyemi)

All rights reserved. No part of this publication may be reproduced, stored in a retrieval system, or transmitted in any form or by any means, electronic, mechanical, photocopying, recording, or otherwise, without the prior permission of Vernon Art and Science Inc.

www.vernonpress.com

In the Americas:
Vernon Press
1000 N West Street,
Suite 1200, Wilmington,
Delaware 19801
United States

In the rest of the world:
Vernon Press
C/Sancti Espiritu 17,
Malaga, 29006
Spain

Series in Philosophy

Library of Congress Control Number: 2017952895

ISBN: 978-1-62273-482-5

Product and company names mentioned in this work are the trademarks of their respective owners. While every care has been taken in preparing this work, neither the authors nor Vernon Art and Science Inc. may be held responsible for any loss or damage caused or alleged to be caused directly or indirectly by the information contained in it.

Every effort has been made to trace all copyright holders, but if any have been inadvertently overlooked the publisher will be pleased to include any necessary credits in any subsequent reprint or edition.

Map of Yoruba-land

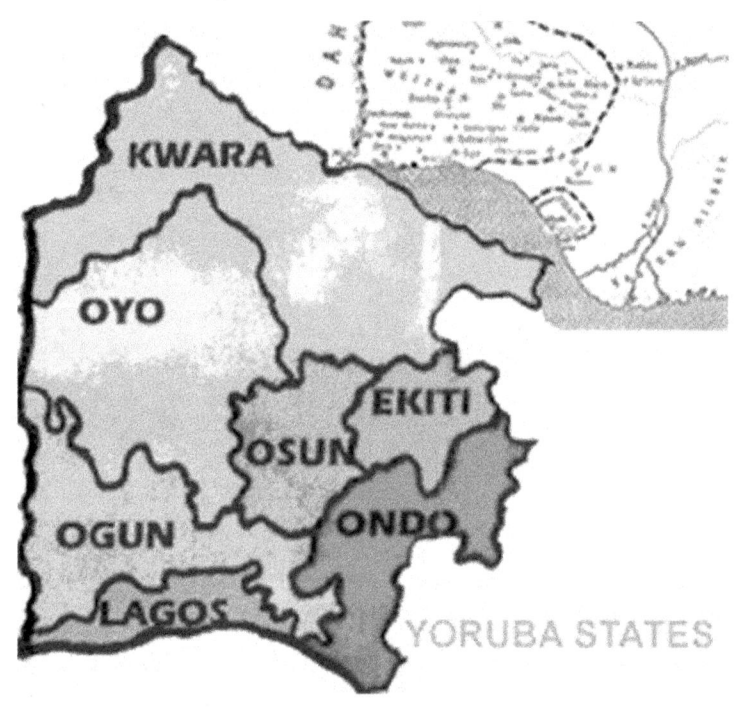

Symbol of Yoruba Philosophy

Y=Yoruba

P=Philosophy

O=Head (Ori)

The figure bearing Head and Philosophy represents philosopher-king
Oduduwa, seated couchant.

To Prince Omoneye Ogunyemi
The youngest blood
Who departed
Without crossing
The Bridge

Dedicated to Chief Obafemi Awolowo (the Best President Nigeria never had) for his vision and magnanimity was the upshot of the scholarship that his administration awarded me (and other children in Western Nigeria) to complete my Primary School Education.

And to Chief Susanne Wenger and Professor Ulli Beier for sacrificing their time and faculties (ori) to promoting/projecting the aesthetics of the Yoruba arts and culture, and for being instrumental to the mainstay of the Oshogbo School of Arts Movement.

Poetic Birthday

Born in 01-01-01 betwixt Mortality and Immortality. That was when the age, a number, meant nothing to me but immortality.

Shedding Light

Folk Philosophy: A folk philosophy (as applied to Yoruba philosophy) is the cultural philosophy of a people depicting their cardinal virtues such as love, justice, temperance, valour, honour, honesty, morality, prudence and fortitude.

Yoruba Philosophy: Yoruba philosophy is a narrative, cultural, folk or literary philosophy explicating and pointing to the knowledge of the causes and nature of things affecting the corporeal and the spiritual universe

Literary Philosophy: Literary philosophy is the blending of philosophy with religion (autochthonous religion in the case of Yoruba) and literature.

The Demythologized Deities/Divinities: The demythologized Yoruba Divinities are the divinities (often called pedigrees/ancestors) who have contributed immensely to the meaning and life-building of the Yoruba people. Their imaginative and real presence in Yoruba life have made themselves relevant in Yoruba folk philosophy. These Divinities (amongst others) include Divinity-Philosopher King Oduduwa, Divinity-Philosopher Obatala, Divinity-Philosopher Ogun, Divinity-Philosopher Sango, Divinity-Philosopher Oshun, Divinity-Philosopher Oya, Divinity-Philosopher Olokun, Divinity-Philosopher Orunmila, Divinity-Philosopher Sopona, Divinity-Philosopher Yemoja, Divinity-Philosopher Esu, Divinity-Philosopher Oshosi.

Yemi D. Prince, PhD: (Yemi D. Ogunyemi)
(Literary Philosopher)

Table of Contents

Preamble — *xv*

The Conspectus — *xix*

Preface — *xxiii*

Introduction — *xxv*

Chapter 1	**Yoruba Philosophy in the Beginning**	1
Chapter 2	**The Kernel of Yoruba Philosophy**	7
Chapter 3	**Oduduwa's Leadership Philosophy**	11
Chapter 4	**The Power of Words and Love**	15
Chapter 5	**Some Hints in Teaching Yoruba Philosophy**	17
Chapter 6	**The Philosophy of Sacrifice**	21
Chapter 7	**Head, the Philosophy of the Body**	23
Chapter 8	**A Typical Yoruba Narrative Philosophy**	27
Chapter 9	**Diviners as Philosophers**	29
Chapter 10	**Artistic Expression of Yoruba Philosophy**	31
Chapter 11	**The Metaphysical Divinities**	33
Chapter 12	**The Ontological Journey to the Atlantic Yoruba**	43
Chapter 13	**The Theory of Narrative, Literary or Folk Philosophy**	61

Chapter 14	Vicissitudes of Yoruba Philosophy	125
Chapter 15	The Sociology of Yoruba Philosophy	127
Chapter 16	The Symbolism of Oshogbo School of Arts Movement	129
Chapter 17	The Political Philosophy of Chief Awo (1909-1987)	131
Chapter 18	The Sublimity of Fagunwa's Philosophy (1903-1963)	135
Chapter 19	The Royalties and the Yoruba Thought	137
Chapter 20	The Import of Ijapa's Philosophy	143
Chapter 21	Yoruba Philosophy of Happiness	149
Chapter 22	A New Dawn—Part One	157
Chapter 23	A New Dawn—Part Two	161
Chapter 24	The Way to Enlightenment	167
Chapter 25	The Effects of Psychology on Yoruba Thought	173
Chapter 26	The Characteristics of Yoruba Pragmatism	177
Chapter 27	The Effects of Paradoxes on Yoruba Philosophy	179
Chapter 28	The Impacts of Proverbs on Yoruba Thought	183
Chapter 29	The Philosophical Aphorisms	187
Chapter 30	The Colourful House of Ethics	193
Chapter 31	The Religion-Philosophy of Samuel Ajayi Crowther (1807-1891)	199
Chapter 32	Philosophy of Yoruba Language	205

Conclusion   *209*

Selected Bibliography 217

References 219

Index 223

Preamble

"Yoruba Philosophy" is a commonplace phrase in the literary, religious, historical, sociological, archaeological and anthropological circles. Broadly, it designates the thoughts of Divinity-Philosophers in ancient Yoruba land. The research on ancient philosophers lets us know that Olofin Adimula Oduduwa is the pioneer of Yoruba philosophy. Thus Olofin Adimula Oduduwa remains the centre or pivot of the ancient and oral and contemporary Yoruba philosophy.

The present or the on-going discussion and study commenced in 19th century with the works of Bishop (Dr.) Ajayi Crowther (1807-1891). From this discussion and study, we will know what we need to know and comprehend about Yoruba philosophy.

The Conspectus

Chapter One: Yoruba Philosophy in the Beginning: This chapter shows the vortex of uncertainties during the proto-history of Ile-Ife and how Oduduwa discreetly used his faculty/head (ori) to put things in order, taking cognizance of the natural virtues. This chapter let us know that Philosophy, the act of reasoning is antecedent to religion.

Chapter Two: The Kernel of Yoruba Philosophy: This shows the trichotomic quintessence of Yoruba culture, embodying philosophy, religion and literature.

Chapter Three: A Leadership Philosophy: Here it is shown to the world that the ability to lead is the ability to understand and consider the opinions of others, young and old, as contained in Yoruba ethical values. Comprehension and reasoning should start at an early stage.

Chapter Four: The Power of Words: Either in an oral culture or in a written culture, this chapter lets us know how words have become a sine qua non in our daily life.

Chapter Five: Some Hints in Teaching Yoruba Philosophy: This chapter pinpoints some fundamental topics while teaching Yoruba philosophy as an academic subject.

Chapter Six: The Philosophy of Sacrifice: This shows how creatures are being sacrificed by the sacrificers on a daily basis. In short, there are sacrificers and the sacrificed. That the world is a whirligig is incontrovertible.

Chapter Seven: Head, the Philosophy of the Body: This chapter depicts the head as the captain, the definition and the substrate onto which other parts of the body are answerable to.

Chapter Eight: A Typical Yoruba Narrative Philosophy: This lets us know a classical narrative about how an ostrich lost his flight feathers when he did not properly carry his head (ori). Consequently, he became a flightless bird.

Chapter Nine: Diviners as Philosophers: This chapter lets us know that there are traits of philosophy in a diviner, as there are traits of divination in a philosopher. What is common to both diviner and philosopher is the knowledge and the truth. They are perpetual seekers. Both of them seek knowledge and truth. This is their principal goal.

Chapter Ten: Artistic Expression of Yoruba Philosophy: This chapter sheds lights on how sculptural artists had worked hard and expressed themselves spiritually and corporeally like philosophers. In proto-history, they formed different Art Guilds in Ile-Ife, which could be likened to our Cultural Schools of Philosophy, today.

Chapter Eleven: The Metaphysical Divinities: Spearheaded by Oduduwa, this chapter supplies the chronology of the ten Yoruba philosophers who opened the door to the Yoruba Book of Enlightenment and prepared them for the act of reasoning.

Chapter Twelve: The Ontological Journey to the Atlantic Yoruba: This chapter lets us know how one of the children of Oduduwa journeyed to the southern part of Yorubaland and founded the Atlantic Yoruba.

Chapter Thirteen: The Theory of Narrative Philosophy: The theory of narrative philosophy is an explicit conspectus about the narrative philosophy, as expounded by Mi Rivera, who went around the world as a raconteur, telling and collecting old and new stories.

Chapter Fourteen: Vicissitudes of Yoruba Philosophy: This chapter seeks to pinpoint the up and down about the Yoruba Philosophy.

Chapter Fifteen: The Sociology of Yoruba Philosophy: This chapter essays to shed light upon the country and urban philosophy.

Chapter Sixteen: Symbolisms of Yoruba Thought: What are the symbolisms of Yoruba philosophy? This chapter seeks to answer the question.

Chapter Seventeen: The Import of Chief Awo's Philosophy: This chapter sheds light on Chief Awo's political philosophy, who is today remembered as the President Nigeria never had.

Chapter Eighteen: The Sublimity of Fagunwa's Metaphysics: This chapter brings to light D.O. Fagunwa, the first folk philosopher in post oral culture Yorubaland.

Chapter Nineteen: The Royalties and the Yoruba Thought: This concerns itself with the king and his royal family. It helps us understand the role played by the king regarding folk/cultural philosophy. Natural virtues are at the disposal of the royalties.

Chapter Twenty: The Import of Ijapa's Philosophy: This chapter reveals how Ijapa is the greatest folk/narrative philosopher the Yorubaland ever knows.

Chapter Twenty-One: Yoruba Philosophy of Happiness: This shows the path to the philosophy of happiness as it relates to the Yoruba people.

Chapter Twenty-Two: The New Dawn—Part One: Shows the Movement towards African/Cultural Enlightenment during the second half of the 20th century.

Chapter Twenty-Three: The New Dawn—Part Two: This chapter manifests the stages of Cultural Movement in respect of Enlightenment.

Chapter Twenty-Four: The Way to Enlightenment: This chapter names four luminaries (Fagunwa, Crowther, Johnson and Soyinka) who have contributed largely to the Way of Enlightenment.

Chapter Twenty-Five: The Effects of Psychology on Yoruba Thought: This chapter manifests how psychology/divination works in tandem with philosophy.

Chapter Twenty-Six: The Characteristics of Yoruba Pragmatism: What are the characteristics of Yoruba pragmatism? This chapter sheds light on them.

Chapter Twenty-Seven: The Effects of Paradoxes on Yoruba Philosophy: Here Yoruba philosophy shows some effects of paradoxes.

Chapter Twenty-Eight: The Impacts of Proverbs on Yoruba Thought: Proverbs are very common when it comes to the act of reasoning. This chapter expatiates on some.

Chapter Twenty-Nine: The Philosophical Aphorisms: This chapter enumerates some of the common-place philosophical aphorisms. It helps one to comprehend the fact that Yoruba land is rich in maxims, proverbs and sayings which are often the precincts of the keepers of traditions.

Chapter Thirty: The Colorful House of Ethics: Here some ethical values and cardinal virtues of the land are made known.

Chapter Thirty-One: The Religion-Philosophy of Samuel Ajayi Crowther (1807-1891): This chapter relates and illustrates how Bishop (Dr.) Samuel Ajayi Crowther showed his passion for religion and folk philosophy before and after his consecration in 1864.

Chapter Thirty-Two: Philosophy of Yoruba Language: This chapter speaks to Philosophy of Language in general and of Yoruba in particular. It lets us know that language philosophers always seek to understand the way language represents reality.

Preface

Yemi D. Ogunyemi's *Yoruba Philosophy and the seeds of Enlightenment* is a masterpiece that developed in a phenomenal, stage-like process, thereby capturing the essence of the importance of a taste that would make for a thorough understanding that Yorubaland has enough love and wisdom, foundational to possessing a philosophy in its own right.

A former research fellow of Harvard University, Yemi D. Ogunyemi (whose literary/pen name is Yemi D. Prince) has thrilled many a reader with his numerous literary works. His works – particularly this present book – are no doubt imbued with creativity in the realm of rare originality and ingenuity.

The head (**Ori**) that assumes a spiritually-distinguished status among the Yoruba is literally portrayed in this book. Indeed, **Ori** is synonymous with the Creator, referred to as Creator-Philosopher Olodumare. He is the greatest philosopher that ever lived. The assumption by Oduduwa and his contemporaries that Olodumare was also the creator of the contents of world is in line with the belief system of other religions, since all other religions basically believe in the Almighty God, given different names in the context of the various languages and dialects associated with them. Because God is not visible, the medium of supplications is a necessity. The disconnect, however, arises where, since humans are created in the image of God, dependence on His creation as gods/goddesses is utterly disdained by God, the Supreme Being and the Maker of heaven and earth.

The important hallmarks of this book graphically consist in the dichotomy between worshipers and worship buildings (namely shrines, temples, etc.); between masculine and feminine elements; and the absence of limitation of God solely to a particular religion, regardless of its name. Thus, there is only one God: worshipers differ in their varying modes of worship. Even among the Yoruba, specialization is the order of the day, with, for instance, Orunmila specializing in psychology, thereby interpreting the nature of an individual's **Ori** and its destiny, which is heavenly orchestrated.

Philosophy, in this context, is less leaned upon, though philosophy is generally antecedent to religion itself.

The periods of cultural, enlightenment movement divided into four – when Ile-Ife was rich in aesthetic terracotta, the amalgamation of Nigeria and the preceding period, the nationalist movement, the arts and literary movements, coupled with the emergence of renowned writer-playwrights – give this book a sharper focus. Interestingly enough, the role of Afrocentric scholars and intellectuals in the realm of African Cultural Philosophy readily fits in with these phenomenal episodes.

Of fascinating research significance is the fact that the ancient Yorubaland propagated the knowledge of its worldviews on cosmogony, cosmology, love, and morality via the medium of sculpting and carving. This has paved the way for historiography in which oral tradition is a centerpiece. The sculpting and carving existed in lieu of publication. Having been accorded a literary, modern flavor, this book easily lends itself to be of use for students and the general public, particularly those whose unsolicited encouragement motivated the author to work on it and get it published. Indeed, its cultural, philosophical, literary, and didactic significance as a vibrant, enlightening mechanism cannot be overemphasized.

Joshua Adekunle Awosan, Ph.D.

Introduction

Ever since The Artist-Philosophers in Yoruba-land and We Should All Be Philosophers were both published in 2016, ever since The Covenant of the Earth and Introduction to Yoruba Philosophy, Religion and Literature were published in 1991 and 1998, respectively, some students and members of the public wanted to know when I would be writing a book, a full-fledged book on Yoruba Philosophy. First, I began to cudgel my brains in order to comprehend the body of love and wisdom (the Book of Enlightenment/Ifa-Ife Divine Divination) which has aided and sustained the lives of the Yoruba people for hundreds of years. It is incumbent on me to commence to define and define again and again that body of love and wisdom, as other faiths are wedging it apart. Second, I beseeched the divine intervention which every faith-believer does, to guard and guide me on the project, a task that must be done, knowing full well that Yoruba philosophy cannot stand alone without a prop from religion and literature. But I know that the project is worth carrying out if only to give credit to recent researches and advances in the theory of folk/cultural or narrative philosophy.

After a number of years, I recognized that I was faced with two challenges—the challenges as to how to expound to the proto-history philosophy and the current challenge, growing fruitlessly ever since the Yoruba land became a literate milieu. At these two challenges, my heart rejoiced exceedingly, realizing that I would never again run away from my reality just because I have found a comfort zone. The time to scratch my head: the time to take the bull by the horns and the serpent by the tail has come.

How this will defy the conventional wisdom is the news that a new child has been born, born to drag philosophy from the back burner to the front burner and let it breathe freely like religion.

Happily enough, the research that led to the publication of **The Oral Traditions in Ile-Ife** in 2010, lets me know that the head/faculty (ori) is the substrate onto which other parts of the body are answerable. Other parts of the body are answerable to the head because Yoruba narrative/folk philosophy is a body of **love and wisdom.** Additionally, it gave me an added confidence when the Ifa-Ife Divination (the body of **love and wisdom or knowledge**) is being recognized worldwide as ***the Book of Enlightenment.***

Yet another Gordian knot crept in like a blessing in disguise, as the search for the appropriate title of the book was proving difficult to me to find. I started by entitling it Cultural Enlightenment, which could have touched on the Cultural Enlightenment of the Yoruba People and the Political awakening sweeping throughout the African continent in the 1960s. However, after writing three thirds of the manuscript, I change the title to **Yoruba Philosophy and the Seeds of Enlightenment.** (The word, seeds, contained in the title is what everyone must taste in order to comprehend that Yorubaland has enough **love and wisdom** to lay the foundation of its present, as the seeds of its philosophy are being planted). This must be the final title, I said to myself. **Chapter Twenty-Two** and **Chapter Twenty-Three** shed some iridescent light on my initial proposed title of the book.

The head (the good head) and its essence appear in every spoken and unspoken word of the Yoruba people. To them and for them, the head is the definition of the entire body. It is the foundation of the house, the taproot and the source of reasoning for other parts of the body. Every thinker knows how vital the head is to the body and philosopher Bertrand Russell must have put that import into its right perspective when he once said, "To understand an age, or a nation, we must understand its philosophy, and to understand its philosophy, we must ourselves be in some degree philosophers."

Can one understand an age, or a nation without (ori) head? This is not possible as long as we invite rationality to play a part, an active part for that matter. And we must see why this is not possible as emphasized and explicated in chapter seven and chapter twenty-two that shows that the head (**ori**) is the most important and definable destiny man possesses. As shown in chapter one, during the proto-history Yoruba it is the head that made the divinities recognize their respectful and philosophical responsibilities. During the modern times, the essence of the head made it possible for Herbert Macaulay to found the first political party in the united Nigeria. It is the head that made it possible for Chief Awo to become the first premier of the Western Nigeria. It is the head that made Queen Funmilayo Ransome-Kuti to show a dynamic leadership in respect of the Women's Rights in the 1950s. It is the head that makes Wole Soyinka the avant-garde writer and the winner of Nobel Prize for literature in 1986. It is the head that makes the former President Olusegun Obasanjo the first ex-president-farmer in Africa. It is the head that makes Governor Fashionable of Lagos State an exceptional governor in West Africa. It is the head that makes Ijapa the best invisible folklorist and folk philosopher in the land. The fact is vivid as the whorls on the palms. The vividness is that there is nothing, practically nothing, a Yoruba person can do or achieve without a head, as there is nothing he or she can do without the Creator-philosopher Olodumare/Olorun. Oftentimes, it is said that without the head, there will be no Book of Enlightenment and without the Book of Enlightenment, Ile-Ife could not have existed. And without Ile-Ife, there could not have been a race called the Yoruba people. The rationale of what the Book of Enlightenment stands for, by courtesy of (ori) head, seems to be endless.

Yoruba Philosophy and the Seeds of Enlightenment is thus an attempt to depict with felicity that philosophy and religion have stopped butting each other. Each has carved its own identity. In other words, the stranglehold of religion over philosophy has been loosened. While watching it loosening, step by step, my soul was filled with trepidation but I was lucky to reason it out of fear. The book is about Yoruba philosophy which is essentially narrative, explicating and pointing to the knowledge of the causes and nature of things, affecting the corporeal and the spiritual universe and its wellness. I have now fully accepted the invitation by the students and the general public to postulate that which is fundamental on Yoruba folk philosophy, otherwise referred to as the cultural/folk or simply narrative philosophy. For all intents and purposes and for what it is worth, I will stick to the nitty-gritty: that is, there will be no complicated or jargonized words. Except a few double entendres, there will be no tongue-twisting words or phrases, no learned quotations or references to obsolete theories. But it must be understood that Yoruba culture, by its encyclopaedic nature, speaks to many areas of social sciences and the Humanities.

Reflecting on how the world has changed during the last one hundred years, Steven Pinker, in his book, *The Blank Slate*, said, as paraphrased that the world is changing and systematically too. There is potential mood everywhere, noting that most Victorian gentlemen would be amazed to see how things are changing around the world, not least among the African-American public intellectuals, and how industrial plants are springing up in Bangalore, India. Writer Pinker went further to say that both men and women are now able and capable of realizing their full potential in life.

On the score that the book, when published, would be of great use and benefit to the general public, the university students and the academics, the path towards the enlightenment is now lit and people of both sexes and all races are cognitively treading it.

Furthermore, it is important to understand that the ancient Yoruba land propagated the knowledge of its worldviews—cosmogony, cosmology, love, morality—philosophy in sculpting and carving. Like the present, it was/is a commonplace to find a sculptor, a potter, a carver or a weaver in every family in Yoruba land.

Chapter 1

Yoruba Philosophy in the Beginning

Those who desire to reach, and keep their places at the top in any calling must be prepared to do so the hard way.

By Philosopher Obafemi Awolowo

The Genesis of the Act of Reasoning: There were so many phenomena in the beginning that one may be compelled and impelled to transpose Ile-Ife for Oduduwa and Oduduwa for Ile-Ife. Oduduwa, the theanthropic founder of the beginning and the proto-history had been sent on a mission to the earth to philosophize and put a face (with **love and wisdom)** on the surface of the earth in order to make the earth liveable for him and for those coming after him. What he took as the explanation for the phenomena and the reason for their existence played well on his mind as teleology. He would not let the eon be lost without a mark. He had to make a homey mark for the sake of mankind, explicating the necessity and the use of natural virtues, pitted against priori knowledge. Making use of his faculty/head (ori), did he succeed in making Ile-Ife a liveable place of peace and happiness? The following shows how the phenomena started to work in his favour.

Granted that philosophy is the act of reasoning and arriving at a logical conclusion, it does stand to reason that the beginning of man was emblazoned with reasoning, including love and wisdom. These acts of reasoning, could be found in reflections, chanting, divining, tales, epigrams, proverbs, prophesies and metaphorical allegories.

Motivated by the love of Nature, and the seven attributes of natural virtues—love, prudence, justice, temperance, honour, valour and fortitude, our ancestors, the keepers of traditions, spearheaded by Divinity-Philosopher Oduduwa, could revel in all the above for hours without referring to anything but the act of reasoning—philosophy in form of narrative poetry and narrative philosophies.

They realized that philosophy is imbued with love and proper application of words. This was after they had all savoured the seeds of enlightenment (growing from day to day), brought to the land by Divinity-Philosopher Oduduwa. They could find words in the body of every creature: words from which stories are revealed and related. Their consequential discussions, based on reasoning or argumentation opened their minds and hearts to the contents of the world and the great Creator-Philosopher Olodumare whom they assumed to be the Creator of the contents of the world. As a matter of fact, Oduduwa and his contemporaries did not only assume Olodumare to be the Creator of the contents of the world, they knew Olodumare is the greatest Creator-philosopher that ever lived—reverential, visible and untouchable. Sometimes, their discussions would end in noisy arguments and diatribes whenever anyone of them attempted to impose his argumentation upon the rest.

Ontologically, our ancestors took cognizance of things around them as we do today. They saw changes in man—from the years of innocence till old age. They observed changes also in animals, birds, fishes, insects, flowering plants and seasons. Everything has a life to live and a destiny to obey. Everything moves in a circle. They were delighted and indeed enchanted by life's rich tapestry. The sun, the moon, the stars are causes for wonderment to them. More often than not, they were speechless—lost in what they saw but could not understand. Their discussions were also based on mysteries and phantasmagorias. In some cases, they assumed that the things they could see were less in number than the things they could not see or perceive. The world and the contents of the world are mysterious. Each creature is a mystery. Everything they imagined or touched was a source of inspiration, emboldening them to continue their act of reasoning because they were cognizant of the fact that reasoning embraces a wide field of knowledge. They came across phenomenal things that marvelled them in the day as they came across phenomenal things that marvelled them in the night. A clear perception of the true world seemed to have dawned on them. From what they saw from the colourful coats of animals, from the plumage, from the flowers in their variegated, dazzling, amazing colours and from the different hues of fishes and insects and so many other phenomena, they came to an inference, rather reluctantly that Nature is a nonpareil artist whose work must have started for days and nights before consummation.

In their ontogenetic observations, they discovered that the Supreme Being has created masculine and feminine things in order to balance each other. Positive and negative phenomena are created from which they drew their conclusions that the world is flooded with the aesthetic contradictions. It was no secret to them that everything has a reason for its creation. Everything is useful and beautiful. However, they realized that the beautiful world will not stop man from passing away. They saw the phenomenal births of creatures and they witnessed their demises. But they theorized that death is not the end of life. By way of cognition, they believed in life after death. Life is a journey, starting from a point on a circle and coming back to the same point on a circle.

Divinity-Philosopher Oduduwa's followers were cooperative and thoughtful of everything they saw. He was a good leader with an aura of holiness. Although he could not have been able to lead without a good ori—head, as evidenced in chapters seven, eleven, and twenty-two of this book. We must but enunciate that they were constantly in danger of the wild creatures. But they were able to master any ugly situation due to the law of self-preservation (in conjunction with transcendental unity) which was always on their side. As they were gradually moving from their pristine status to self-realization and semi-civilization, they were overwhelmed by reflective and ruminative dreams. Sooner than expected, they could not divest themselves of the notion that man, in the near future, would become the wisest creature on earth, as he would emerge the most thievish creature on the surface of the earth. Today, their reflective and ruminative dreams seem to have come to pass as almost every door in Yoruba land must have a padlock in order to prevent a thievish nonentity from entering it.

Assuming his responsibility as a flagship, let's hug the scenario that Oduduwa must have uttered the following: "Olodumare, our Creator is an inscrutable thinker of unlimited words and ideas. He is the greatest philosopher in heaven and on earth. Every divine creature of Creator-Philosopher Olodumare is a thinker who must make use of his head—ori. We are the divine creatures of Creator-Philosopher Olodumare. Therefore we are thinkers who are making use of our heads."

Philosophy of Religion: Which I may also refer to as the **Birth of Religion.** During the birth of religion, came the nine attributes of Yoruba cardinal virtues—love, honesty, honour, temperance, prudence, justice, morality, valour and fortitude. Sooner than expected, cosmogony and cosmology under the watch and aegis of Divinity-Philosopher Oduduwa became the kernel of their discussions and reasoning. As their minds were occupied with curiosities and phenomena about the world and its Creator, it became manifest that the theory describing the natural order of the universe as well as the origin of the universe was born. Philosophy had given birth to religion. The transition was smooth and gradual. It was a reflection rather than a reflex. There was no conflict between reason and passion. Philosophy had taken its rightful place under the act of reasoning, and passion had liaised with religion. A new epoch in their lives had begun. Their discussions and reasoning had opened their minds and hearts to the need to reverence the Supreme Being. They would now begin to reverence Creator-Philosopher Olodumare by way of thanking him, by way of beseeching him and by way of asking him to spare their lives and accept their votive sacrifices. Soon, sacrifices were plentiful as they saw the need to pray to the Creator-Philosopher Olodumare during their special meetings in huts and open places.

Step by step, their social meetings had become as consequential as their philosophical meetings. As time matured and passed by, they commenced to build houses—shrines and temples, designed for meeting in the name of worshipping the Supreme Sky Being, the absolute Creator of heaven and earth. In their shrines and temples, their hearts longed for answers to unravel the mysteries surrounding them, through cosmogony and cosmology, with the help of the Creator, who must be a spiritual power, and who must be worshipped through intermediaries. He is the Creator of all these awesome phenomenal things, who alone, is capable, knowledgeable of opening their faculties to the world beyond the compass of their imagination. The thought that their minds must be enlightened when the reason taxed their exhausted brains by the unseen power made them believe in worshipping the Creator every day, the invisible Creator, in whose image they are created. Sooner than expected, their minds had parachuted them to yet another level of imagination. Divinations and votive sacrifices and ritual performances became a commonplace. Step by step, the act of reasoning has given birth to an act of worshipping the sole Sky Supreme Being, the Maker of heaven and earth, the source of kismet, the Giver and Taker of Life, who would later be called and addressed as Olodumare or Olorun, blessed with hundreds of intermediaries who are duty-bound to be answerable to him in various degrees and circumstances. But from all accounts, and as far as the Book of Enlightenment can testify, Olodumare/Olorun is essentially a ***Creator-Philosopher of an immeasurable status.*** Thus it will be wrong to associate him with a particular religion. Because of his power of reasoning, because of his ubiquity, because of his omnipotence, omniscience, omnipresence, plus the fact that he is worthy of reverence, mankind has no choice but to thank, praise, honour and worship/reverence him. This is not short of what Yoruba people and the rest of the world call religion.

The supra sheds light on the beginning of Yoruba culture and its attributes—natural and cardinal, as embodied in folk/cultural philosophy, religion and folk tales. They are embodied in Ifa-Ife Divination, known as the tripartite Book of Enlightenment in Yoruba land and in Diaspora.

Yoruba philosophy is a witness of two epochs. The first epoch is an epoch-making history in cosmology and mythology. This is also an epoch-making history in oral philosophy in oral culture during which time Oduduwa was the sole philosopher, the head, the Bringer of Light, and a prominent thinker. He theorized about the visible and invisible worlds, reminiscing about the cosmology, cosmogony, and the mythological creatures in the visible and invisible worlds.

Like Oduduwa, Orunmila also concerns himself with cosmogony and cosmology and the mythological creatures in the visible and invisible worlds. Divinity-philosopher Orunmila did excel as a diviner, epitomizing wisdom and idealism. But he is more of psychology than philosopher. He is the cultivator of divination, ambitions and desires and the interpreter of ori (head) and its destiny.

The second epoch is the epoch of metaphysical philosophy. This commenced in the 19th century when the Yoruba land was becoming literate through the diligence and pragmatism of Dr. Bishop Ajayi Crowther, the first Anglican Bishop.

Although religion is often considered first in Yoruba culture, nonetheless, it is philosophy, the thought of man and the reasoning of the mind that actually leads the faculty/head (ori) to the creation and the practice of religion. Thus, philosophy is antecedent to religion. This begs the question in totality. The act of reasoning (philosophy) has succeeded in putting Yoruba in touch with God by means of supplications. And the act of reverencing Creator-Philosopher Olodumare becomes religion.

Today, the academic and the non-academic people are becoming more and more interested in Yoruba philosophy. Thus more and more researches are being carried out on Yoruba philosophy, as more and more books are being written on it—embossing its mark and advancing its research amongst non-African thinkers in colleges and universities and political scientists around the world who are beginning to open their doors to other cultures, widening their views.

One thing to remember is that Yoruba philosophy (the body of **love and wisdom**) is mainly a narrative philosophy, explicating and pointing to the knowledge of the causes and the nature of things, affecting the corporeal and the spiritual universe and its wellness. Yoruba people have hundreds of syllogisms and philosophical aphorisms and lore, and they believe that any lore that widens people's horizons and presents food for thought is the beginning of philosophy.

Life is a whirligig. And man's philosophy of happiness is found or evidently apparent in the whirligig of time, inasmuch as man is answerable to his five senses—sight, hearing, smell, taste and touch, as he grows every day to make a mark in the world.

It is a plausible scenario to believe that philosopher Oduduwa will continue to remain number one on the list of Yoruba ancient thinkers. Like his symbiotic contemporaries, he is not an additive inverse who is added to a real number that is expected to produce or result into zero.

The Legacy of Oduduwa: Like Divinity-Philosopher Orunmila, he pioneered of Yoruba idealism and realism. He is the father of Yoruba philosophy and the Bringer of Light. Oduduwa succeeded in letting Yoruba people appreciate the fact that **ori,** the head, is the most organized part of the body, the definition of the body and the substrate unto which other parts of the body are answerable. He expounded that there would be a continuum between spiritual and the corporeal worlds. Each consists of its own organization, the realm of enlightenment and a force beyond the compass of human mind. (But that force seems not to be incomprehensible beyond the compass of human mind, as Steven Pinker argues in his book "How the Mind Works").

Chapter 2

The Kernel of Yoruba Philosophy

The ethics of real life, the experiences of our ancients, the love of wisdom of our Elders, are present in my investigation, displayed humanistically with a novel metaphysical sublimity, roofed under spirituality and absolute enlightenment.

   Yoruba culture is a trichotomy of mini-pyramids. It is a trichotomy because it has three segments or three pyramids which are based on philosophy, religion and literature, respectively. These three fundamental pyramids have fashioned themselves into a single pyramid of indivisibility. On the top rung of the pyramid seats philosophy as an act of reasoning, followed by religion and literature. This is the finding of my previous research and it is not the position held by other researchers and writers who postulate that religion is the first order of its quiddities. Religion is born because philosophy as an act of reasoning allows itself to leak into religion. Retrospectively, religion had once side-lined and overshadowed philosophy of consciousness until philosophy of religion started to build places of worship, such as groves, shrines, temples and churches. Years after those places of worship were constructed, religion became the cornerstone of the Yoruba culture. Consequently, philosophy tapers into a prose idyll, forming a series of paradigm shifts, otherwise called narrative philosophies.

   From the paradigm shifts, emerged literature, bringing together the auras of the oral and written culture of both the past and the present. Thus philosophy and religion in their earthly kindred become the witnesses and the players of the social order, the composition of their beginning and end, of the days and nights, of the whims and caprices; all coming together and expatiating on the rhetoric of literature that derives its fundamentals and its ingredients of pleasures from the Attic salt of the post-oral culture.

   Yoruba culture also represents three of our fingers. Unlike the first representation, the middle finger is the philosophy as an act of reason; religion is the ring finger; the index finger is the literature. The middle finger, sandwiched between the ring finger and the index finger, is the longest of the three. Thus philosophy exercises once again its antecedent position.

It stands to reason and to perorate that if you cannot find Yoruba culture in your compound, it is likely you discover it elsewhere in the world, representing a pyramid. And if all those places refuse to cooperate consciously and epistemically, open your palm-fingers before a mirror and discover your culture as close as a distance betwixt your lips and your nose.

Are they not the same fingers holding the mirror that are used while climbing and finding your way to the top of the pyramid in search of trichotomy? Yes, they are. If indeed they are, no culture can do without philosophy, religion and literature, as no culture can do without fingers, regardless of the paradigm shifts, now the embodiment of rhetoric politics.

If you spread your palm-fingers, you will find out that you will make a pyramid out of it, as soon as you imagine that your wrist will form the base of your personal pyramid. The reason and argument for seeking truth and knowledge is right here.

Comparing an exogenous pyramid to a personal pyramid, you will take yourself far away from any labyrinthine alley of discomfiture. Again, we cannot deny the fact that we are on the right track where reason will definitely prevail.

Reason, standing pedagogically, on a pedestal table, will therefore be the fruit of your contentment. The aesthetics of the empire and the romantic corridor of the hermeneutics is no more. However, the fact that man is a tetrad savours the sensibility that without Oduduwa, the father of Yoruba philosophy, the protagonist, the principal player; Ile-Ife could not have evolved. The upshot is that Yoruba land and its triplicity could not have been created. Yoruba land is a letter and so it was created, for no letter can be created without a thought.

Again, as opinionated by most believers in Yoruba philosophy, it is the religion which has put the Yoruba people in touch with God as the Law has put the Hebrews in touch with Yahweh. Conversely, there are some theorists who are reminiscing that it is the philosophy which has put Yoruba in touch with Olodumare as the Law has put the Hebrews in touch with the Tetragrammaton.

If culture is the totality of man, the *agbada* and the dashiki or the *buba* we wear today cannot but be a part of that totality. As the philosophy is the designer of nature, so also it is the tailor of mankind, the diviner of all cultures. To deduce that culture is found in philosophy is to move into a territory that is unknown to known parametric base that presents its challenges to the author. It is not uncommon to find minds common-sensing and common-reasoning differently on the same rational view. A time has come to develop Yoruba philosophy which will be relevant to contemporary life.

We perceive the realm of philosophy as we perceive the innards of poetry, every day. How can one liken philosophy? To what can one liken it?

In this day and age, we can liken philosophy in part to a modicum of water dangling under a faucet, dropping to fill the thirsty lips of religion and literature.

In Yoruba land, religion concerns itself with that which transcends the unknown, the natural, the expected, the extra-ordinary, the supernatural, the spiritual wellness; seen as sacred and mysterious—all associating and liaising themselves with Olodumare, the omniscient one, calling in question the eternity of oral literature.

Is religion practiced by the Yoruba people as a result of faith and reverence to Olodumare, thrust upon them by the apocalypse of God himself?

Are the philosophers losing faith in religion because they look to philosophy to provide them with some independent way of attaining religious truths? Do religion and philosophy come to the same pitched area of conclusion that reality is spiritual?

The reality of Ogun and Orisa-nla (two of the most powerful divinities in Yoruba pantheon) is a testimony against idealism, bringing to the front-burner a vivid view of Ifa-Ife, the Book of Enlightenment which helps to explicate and helps to point to the knowledge of the causes and the nature of things, affecting the corporeal and the spiritual universe—and its wellness.

Is religion the first order of things? Or is it Philosophy? This is what my research is all about—trying to find out which one of the two came first during the act of reasoning in the beginning. Literature (poetry and folktales) will ultimately serve as an epilogue on finding out which one precedes the other. Literature on deriving its fundamentals from the Attic salt of the pre-and post oral culture is a consummation of what religion and philosophy have bequeathed to Yoruba land. Mustn't we heave a sigh of relief that the stranglehold of religion over philosophy is no more? Religion has ceased pushing philosophy to the back burner.

With the principles and the dimensions of a nod, born as a result of the act of reasoning, one can easily infer that philosophy is both the pride of the morning and the pride of place.

Chapter 3

Oduduwa's Leadership Philosophy

Oduduwa's teachings and pronouncements were aphoristic, delightful, varied and often than not argumentative. Pedagogically, he lets us know that every person whose idea is fruitful, helpful and educational is a teacher. Merging ancient teachings with the present, let's ponder over his teaching philosophy. Today, every family in Yoruba land adheres to some of his aphoristic teachings. As the pioneer of the Yoruba idealism and realism and the father of Yoruba philosophy, he had successfully passed down from the oral culture to the written, his leadership philosophy. His teaching philosophy is a sine qua non, educationally. His leadership philosophy has been the guiding principle for Bishop (Dr.) Ajayi Crowther (1807-1891), D.O. Fagunwa (1903-1963), Chief Obafemi Awolowo (1909-1987) and many scions of the land who believe that the leadership and educational philosophy should begin at a young age at home, just as charity begins at home.

As school or college education, which is an extension of family or home education will be a continuous process till the end of one's life, so also leadership traits, once imparted to, in infancy, will be part and parcel of one's personality until one pays the debt of nature. Certainly, there are leadership trainings which one may acquire as one becomes an adult but the one, ingrained in one's head or constitution from infancy, is more natural, telling and fundamental than the one which is acquired in adulthood.

It is a general concept that college education should be a natural linchpin between the teacher and the students. The teacher should invariably be dedicated: should be dynamic, innovative, inspirational and creative. He or she should make sure that his or her "research file" is up-to-date in order to ensure confidence, progress and to promote curiosities of the students in particular, and of the school in general.

According to Yoruba Philosophy, if a leader is able to establish his/her developmental cum experimental philosophy, members of the community will inherit a leadership role.

As embraced by many in Yoruba land, a leadership philosophy, in a position of responsibilities is to manage to maintain a leadership role (in spite of any opposition), for the ability to lead is the ability to consider the opinions of the young and old, while making a decision affecting one and all.

Furthermore, an educational philosophy is remarkable and should help to improve informal education which is as important as the formal or traditional education. The folk philosophers do believe that the younger generation (including some in the older bracket) needs an ethical, educational system in which it should endeavour to develop its faculties and not the faculties of others. They should invariably be optimistic—always seeing the bright side of life or things.

Also, educationally, and ethically, a leader must be prepared at anytime to support, encourage and advise both the strong and the weak, especially those who are psychologically weak, so much so that by the time they leave college/university, they would see themselves as resolute, enthusiastic, promising and responsible leaders, not only to their communities but also to the world.

Personal Maxim: It is not the imposing school building that matters but also what the leadership or the teachers have to offer to the students, and the students to the world.

Reasoning at Early Age: The path to a sound education depends on a sound reasoning. If reasoning is not sound enough, or if it fails to be genuine, education will be dismal or catastrophic. If reasoning or Creative Thinking prevails, education in the hands of our education experts will be a success and everyone will have a cause to smile, and to be proud and to be happy. The philosophy of education is like the saying which lets us know that charity begins at home. What do I mean by this? What I mean is that the home education or training is very important as our children are preparing themselves for campus education. Home is the first place where the act of reasoning should take root. Home is the first place where parents should teach their children the act of reasoning. A child who gets involved in the act of reasoning will excel in its learning and eventually become a good leader with a sound philosophy.

We do not want to treat this chapter as though we are teaching a class of psychology, or a class of creative writing in which understanding and comprehension is very essential for the class.

However, we may want to pay more attention to our kids as they are moving from one stage of development to the other. Let's take a hard look at the following five areas which a kid needs and which are linked with understanding and comprehension skills.

Firstly, Verbal Reasoning: A child needs verbal reasoning, for verbal reasoning is the understanding and full-fledged reasoning, using concepts imbued with words. The main purpose of verbal reasoning is to evaluate the ability to think constructively and perceptively.

Secondly, Quantitative Aptitude: The quantitative Aptitude test measures the numerical ability and accuracy in mathematical calculations. The knowledge of addition, subtraction and multiplication is very crucial in this respect, in every stage of a child's development.

Thirdly, Vocational Aptitude: This is an eye-opener for every child. It helps the child in his/her way to finding the best vocational choice.

Fourthly, Comprehensive Mathematics: A child needs comprehensive mathematics, as it enhances his/her ability, especially in self-evaluation.

Fifthly, Comprehensive English Language: Some language proficiency assessment must be developed in this respect. Children should be taught the value of listening and answering simple questions. They should be taught how to compose short and simple sentences and stories. The act of reasoning is a gift. Every child should be a recipient of that gift.

A child who is groomed in those five areas above, will not only be exceptionally brilliant but will also become a good philosopher whose faculty (ori) will never let him/her down. A good book on reasoning will surely encourage students to reflect on the process of critical thinking, as well as to practise thinking skills.

Chapter 4

The Power of Words and Love

Let's look at the power and the quintessence of the words with a view to capturing and recalling the minds and perceptions of our ancient philosophers. Since the creation of Ile-Ife, Yoruba people have always asserted that we should treat with care every word like a wholesome egg, adding that as one cannot make whole a dropped-and-broken egg, so also one cannot make vanish a spoken word.

> **The Words:** I deal with words
> I am a dealer vis-à-vis lover of words
> I let the words deal with me
> And I get a crunching clout for doing so
> That eventually turns into clapping
> Our dealings are friendly
> They are reciprocal too
> The words have taken liberty with me
> I've taken liberty with letters in the words
> The words cannot do without me
> And I cannot do without the words
> The words and user of the words
> Are interdependent
> The words and the user are indispensable
> I dwell in the bucolic domain of the words
> There are many words here
> I left only when darkling came
> Surrendering myself to a catnap
> That rudely charmed me
> And lulled me to my bucolic but divine domain
> Here I regaled on my sweet dreams.
>
> There is no philosophy without words
> Words are the shimmers of the moon
> That fillip philosophers into reflection.
>
> Every character (iwa) is praiseworthy
> Manners are relative to character

Therefore, manners are praiseworthy.
These are the words of Pa Ogunyemi
(Major premise and minor premise)
As I was growing to have a handle
On Yoruba philosophy, cognizant that
Imagination is the mother of living
I find myself always on the laps of imagination
I imagine how to be
The cynosure in whatever I do, write or say
I imagine how to sleep good
And dream sweetest
I imagine how to become a king
I imagine how to help my subjects
I imagine how to become a president
I imagine how to help my fellow citizens
Imagination is the mother of living.

An Interview in 1995: The import of this interview is that it is one of the seeds of enlightenment in my search and research to advance Yoruba philosophy. The search for the seeds of enlightenment started in 1983 and culminated into ***The Literary Philosophy for the Year 2000,*** first published in 1991 and republished in 2014. Additionally, the interview is a veritable reflection on my work—fiction and nonfiction which today has found a literary cum philosophical name known as literary philosophy, a novel reality blending philosophy with literature and religion.

Daniel B. King, the Editor, Diaspora Press of America, was my interviewer: His interview helps me elucidate the quiddities regarding the folk philosophy in general and Yoruba philosophy in particular. As stated in Shedding Light on page 2, a Folk Philosophy (as applied to Yoruba philosophy) is the cultural philosophy of a people depicting their cardinal virtues such as love, morality, honour, honesty, temperance, bravery, justice, prudence and fortitude. Within that context is Yoruba Philosophy which is a narrative, cultural, folk or literary philosophy explicating and pointing to the knowledge of the causes and the nature of things affecting the corporeal and the spiritual universe.

Talking of the power of words and love; a literary philosopher whose story has the power to heal corporeally and spiritually must have possessed the spiritual wellness that will make him believe that man can live as long as he can overcome common illnesses which can be healed by the power of the word.

Chapter 5

Some Hints in Teaching Yoruba Philosophy

Ifa-Ife or Ifalogy, is the tripartite Book of Enlightenment, comprising philosophy, religion and literature. Its narrative philosophy explicates and points to the knowledge of the causes and the nature of things, affecting the corporeal and the spiritual universe—and its wellness.

The cut-throat hunt after material acquisition has limited man's power towards spiritual science. Thus his way to enlightenment or inner development is handicapped. Thusly, man is unable to tell, for example, what would happen tomorrow. Nor has he the power to rebuke a mere nagging of headache.

Teaching Yoruba Philosophy can be very enlightening, interesting and exciting. It can be very enlightening, interesting and exciting because it embraces many elements of Yoruba autochthonous religion, a symphony in which Creator-Philosopher Olodumare is seen in all things and in which he, the supreme Creator is depicted and acts as the Alpha and Omega in all things visible and invisible. The outline below is offered for the teaching of Yoruba Philosophy. And it cannot be done in isolation from its literary quintessence and its spiritual wellness. The outline below is a beginner course but it is equally ideal for the scholarly world and the general public.

Week One: The students will be introduced to philosophy as the act of reasoning and arriving at a logical conclusion. It is the heart of wisdom, craving for truth. Understanding that head (ori) is the definition of the body, the substrate onto which other parts of the body is answerable. The students will learn about personal development and moral integrity as an integral part of enlightenment.

Week Two: The function of the body: its waking: its sleeping.

Week Three: The search for inner peace, based on love and moral development.

Week Four: A hunt for good health and spiritual development.

Week Five: The Desire of the mind and soul.

Week Six: The birth and the purpose of life. The role played by character as an ethical value.

Week Seven: Philosophy as the brainchild of religion.

Week Eight: Drive towards a goal, placing Creator-Philosopher Olodumare as the Creator, the motor and the driver and the Author of Life.

Week Nine: Experiential philosophy: the right use of intellect. The proper use of the mind and emotions, conflated with experiences.

Week Ten: The holy gourd, the source of material, spiritual and mystic benefits, and *ase* the ultimate crown of one's desires in conformity with Creator-Philosopher Olodumare's propensity to immortality, his rules and regulations.

Week Eleven: The import of aphorisms, proverbs or euphemisms. Quite a number of Yoruba narratives end with aphorisms, proverbs or euphemisms.

Week Twelve: The quintessence of Yoruba major and minor premises. The period for this beginner course is by no means limited to twelve weeks. It all depends on the teacher. Let's take a quick look at the following—Weeks Thirteen and Fourteen:

Week Thirteen: Understanding Yoruba principal moral attributes as contained in cardinal virtues—justice, prudence, love, valour, honour, morality, honesty, temperance and fortitude.

Weeks Fourteen: Explaining the difference and similarity between the cardinal virtues and the natural virtues. Shedding light upon the proto-history and the post oral seven natural virtues—justice, valour, honour, love, temperance, prudence and fortitude, is essential.

*All the living persons must pass away and be reborn again.
I am a living person.
Therefore, I must pass away and be reborn again.

*All the even numbers such as 4, 6, 980, 2112 are divisible.
Six is an even number.
Therefore, six is divisible.

*All the Yoruba names have meanings
You are Yoruba.
Therefore, your name must have a meaning.

*All the index fingers are pointing to Oduduwa dynasty and the Staff of Creation in the holy city of Ile-Ife.

Without putting out my hand from my pocket, I observe that my index finger is pointing to Oduduwa dynasty and the Staff of Creation in the holy city of Ile-Ife.
Therefore, I must have some royal blood in my veins that signifies my kin.

It must always be remembered that a student of Yoruba philosophy must know a little bit of Yoruba religion and Yoruba literature in order to have a broad, if not complete, knowledge of Yoruba cultural philosophy.

Chapter 6

The Philosophy of Sacrifice

Every animate creature is both a sacrificer and a sacrificed. That is, every animate creature offers up sacrifices, as well as being offered as a sacrifice. Life itself is a sacrifice, for a life is given to a child after the woman must have sacrificed herself to carrying the fetal child. Life, looking at it from the four corners of the world, is awash with contradictions. Life is a struggle. Every day, we hustle for something to kill and sacrifice for our stomachs. Every day, Death waits for the right time to kill and sacrifice us for its own pleasure and destiny. Life is inundated with amazing contradictions which we observe as they occur in circles. For example, earth is the contradiction of heaven. Day is the contradiction of Night. So when we give, we are supposed to receive. When we lie, we will be lied to. When we kill, we will be killed. The simple saying that *what goes round must come around*, or *what goes up must come down*, is as truth as truth can be.

When asking for something to be done for you: when praying for something to happen in your favour, is a kind of sacrifice. Offering up a sacrifice this way, is regarded an abstract sacrifice or an invisible offering. All our wishes, every day, every week, every month, every year, are a kind of sacrifice.

But if you elect to offer up a sacrifice to your deities, to your ancestors, to your Creator, making use of a ram or lamb, then, it is only then your sacrifice will be seen as visible, and touchable.

Every day, we, human beings sacrifice food for our stomachs. Every day we ask or beseech God to do something for us. A sacrifice like this, invisible and untouchable, is hardly regarded as the sacrifice we know. But, it is a sacrifice.

Every day, other inanimate creatures such as a goat, a whale, an eagle, an ant, sacrifice foods for their stomachs. Thus human beings as well as other creatures that need food to live are sacrificers or offerers of sacrifices. Life is eternal, so it seems, for man and other creatures. But Death can, and it does stop any creature at any time. And whenever this happens, Death becomes the sacrificer of us. Death has offered us up as a sacrifice. We must demise like other things which have died as food-sacrifices that have gone down our gorges to our stomachs.

This is a short account of how Koro, a seasoned and sharp-shooting hunter set out after offering up a prayer as his sacrifice to Olodumare. A few yards into a glade, that is nestled in the splendid savannah forest, where bucolic philosophers often question the rationale behind the beauty in its abstract state, where serenity, tranquillity and something akin to paradise, has generated to the biblical paradise, he met a group of big cats, sitting in a pride. He aimed at one of them. As he wanted to pull the trigger, a voice roared, "Please stop. Please stop in the name of my kingdom in this paradisiacal glade."

"Who are you?" asked Koro, the hunter.
"I am the Lion, the king of the Beasts."
"But I need to eat. My stomach is empty. I need to kill and sacrifice a meat for it."
"We are peace lovers and as a king, I don't want any of my subjects to be killed and sacrificed for your need. I will advise you to go further to the north of this glade where you will find gnus and buffaloes."
"But why are you afraid of being killed and offered up as a sacrifice, for if I am not taking you out today, some other hunter will do it."
"I want this pride to stay together a little longer. I don't want to miss anyone of them now. And I am so grateful that you are able to understand my plea, cooperatively. Thank you very much for showing me the milk of human kindness in you."

Koro left for the north. Two minutes before getting there, he saw gnus, impalas, gazelles, buffaloes and giraffes, playing and enjoying the company of each other. Aiming at a group of impalas, he fired and killed two of them, simultaneously. He got home, a happy man.

A month later, Koro discovered that the king of the Beasts had lost one of his subjects to a hunter who had not listened to his plea.

In sum and substance, all the animate creatures, in which man is the most carnivorous and the most powerful, cannot live beyond their destiny. Their destiny is to die in the graveyard of the Death's palm. Death is the ultimate immolator/killer of all the animate creatures. There is no exception. The folk/moral philosophers and the metaphysical philosophers including the natural philosophers cannot agree less.

Chapter 7

Head, the Philosophy of the Body

Each part of the body is important. It is important because each part depends on each other. But head (ori) is regarded as the definition, the captain of the body. It is the substrate onto which other parts of the body are answerable. Other parts of the body look up to the head as the children look up to the village-head. The head is also said to be the director of the body, for the rest of the body will be helpless, or even useless without the chapter and verse from the head.

Can the head then be said to be the philosophy of the body? Yes, is the answer? Inasmuch as the philosophy is the act of reasoning that nudges a meaningful and logical conclusion, the head, the captain/director of the body can be *arrested* and *charged* to be the philosophy of the body.

Let's quickly illustrate the importance or the indispensability of the head with the following. It happened many years ago when the head decided to go on a trip in search of terracotta. On getting to a glade beautified by daisies, the head commenced to build a pyramid from a deposit of terracotta. Within a span of five hours, the pyramid was half-complete. The head asked his immediate associates—the eyes, the ears, the nose and the tongue to climb the pyramid to the summit before completion. But the hands, teaming up with the legs, said to the head that they had to put a finishing touch to the pyramid before they attempted to climb it. The head acquiesced. So the hands spent some hours solidifying the pyramid until it is concrete enough to withstand any inclement weather.

Since that day, the hands have been on the same par with the eyes, the ears, the nose and the tongue, even if they are not attached to the head.

It is a fact, which is beyond sufficient arguments to say that the eyes, the ears, the nose, the mouth-tongue are the agents of the head and they loyally perform their duties without fail.

"*Head is the live-wire of man,*" said Pa Ogunyemi, the author's father. If this is true, it must also be true to expound that man's head is the most developed, compared to the heads of other creatures. Man's head has developed so much that man is the sole creature who is able to make clothes and cover his erstwhile naked head and body with clothes.

> See this, an instance. A man was walking with his legs wobbling west and east. Two men saw him and asked why he was walking like that, he said, "Men, do not blame my legs. Blame he that is mightier than my legs."
> "Who is he that is mightier than your legs?"
> "He who is mightier than my legs is the head."

Yet there is another instance in which the head shows that he is the boss or the action-phenomenon of the body. In a distant town, behind seven rises, known as Reason, there was a paragon of beauty. She was so pretty that people simply called her Paragon.

The head was looking for a woman to marry. The body was looking for a woman to marry. Now, there are two men looking for women to marry. It must be made clear that they did not know each other. When they heard that there was a paragon of beauty in Reason, each one of them thought he had a chance to marry her.

One bright day, the body set out. He reached Reason as the paragon of beauty and her parents were having their delicious lunch. Paragon's parents asked him to join them. He did and he commenced to demolish the lunch. As he was enjoying himself with ball-round dainty morsels, all of a sudden, the head entered and told Paragon's parents that he was interested in their daughter.

Shrieking out like a wounded kangaroo, the body let Paragon's parents know that he also had interest in their daughter. But Paragon's parents let him know that because his first choice is food, they could do nothing but to allow the head to marry Paragon. As the body was going home well-fed but crestfallen, he said that he had been hoodwinked just because he is a tall person from a land of tall people going to marry in a land of short people. However, what he did and experienced signifies the head to be the wisest part of the human body. The head is the philosophy of the body because it has the absolute capability to reason for itself and for the rest of the body. The act of reason is the philosophy. Therefore philosophy is the head which is the source of our reasoning. Therefore, without placing non sequitur upon clarity, the head is the captain of the body. As long as man has a head, philosophy should not be treated as an abstract. Philosophy in its different branches is a daily living experience.

In sum, without courting complexities, we must infer that the head is the determiner of our destiny. It is the custodian of what we would become and what we could not become in life. Because the head knows our destiny, as our destiny knows the head, it is very easy to see that an auspicious destiny brings good and eudemonia to man in a lifetime, while an inauspicious destiny leads to the opposite. If a head is very auspicious, and spiritual, there is hope for his resurrection whenever he pays his debt to nature.

Just in: This is another snippet from Pa Ogunyemi, "From a metaphysical or mythological land, we invariably hear from our ancients that there are people with one or no legs. There are people with one or no hands, and yet they are alive and kicking. But head is the sole part of the body that one can lose and never can live."

Chapter 8

A Typical Yoruba Narrative Philosophy

Koo-Ostrich and Ka-Eagle used to be close friends many, many years ago. They had flown to the southern and northern hemisphere on many occasions in search of foods and pleasure. The eastern and the western parts of the planet were not unknown to them. The contours of the heavenly bodies were familiar to them. In short, the two of them ruled the world as the kings of the feathered creatures.

One bright sunny day, they decided to go to River Oshun to have a swim. No sooner they reached the eastern part of the river than it started to rain—in drizzles. This was attended by a rainbow that stretched from the eastern to the western skies. It was unusual panoply that made every creature think of flying and got lost in the invisibility of eternity.

As Ka-Eagle plunged into the river, Koo-Ostrich began to remove its flight feathers, smiling and telling Ka-Eagle that he would prefer to swim without his flight feathers. As soon as he had plucked out all his flight feathers, except his contour feather, he jumped into the river and he commenced to swim and, diving like his friend, Ka-Eagle. Exceedingly, did they enjoy themselves, as they swam from upstream to downstream and vice versa.

All of a sudden, the drizzles turned into a downpour, pouring torrentially. In no time at all, the banks of the Oshun River were swollen with water and Koo-Ostrich's flight feathers were washed away by the torrential rain.

After three hours of swimming and enjoying themselves to the maximum, they got out of the water. But to Koo-Ostrich's amazement, conflated with a hay of confusion and paroxysm of nervousness, his flight feathers were nowhere to be found. His flight feathers had been washed away by the torrential rain. After searching for the feathers for almost a score and fifteen minutes, around and beyond the coppices of the grains of paradise and divi-divis that beautified the banks of the river, he gave up the search.

"I am finished as a bird. Shall I ask divine Oshun to help me?" said Koo-Ostrich in a tearful voice.

"You don't need the divinity. Listen to these major and minor premises: All the birds are bi-footed and have gizzards. You are booted and you have a gizzard. Therefore, you are still a bird even if you are no longer able to fly. Another syllogism is this: All the feathered creatures are designed by our Divinity to lay eggs. You are a feathered creature. Therefore, you are designed to lay eggs."

Since that day, Koo-Ostrich has become a flightless bird but he is given the gift (courtesy of divine Oshun) of being the fastest-running bird in the entire universe.

Chapter 9

Diviners as Philosophers

As we have noted in chapter one, the Yoruba people concerned themselves very much with the act of reasoning to the extent that they nearly became obsessed with the nitty-gritty of reasoning. They invariably regarded Nature as their sublime domain. Nature is a reasoner, giving man everything man needs. By all accounts, they are very circumspect people who love to concern themselves with a lot of things—big and small—visible and invisible.

Can the diviners regard themselves as philosophers? Wait a minute; let's put the question in another way. Can the world regard diviners as philosophers? Additionally, do diviners reason and observe things like philosophers? The answer to all the questions is a monosyllabic yes. Diviners and philosophers are reasoners. They enjoy the act of reasoning. What is most common to them is that they both seek wisdom and truth. That this is their main goal or objective is incontrovertible. The only difference between a diviner and a philosopher is that a diviner might need a board of divination from time to time, while seeking the much-needed knowledge and truth, whereas a philosopher needs nothing but his head (ori) which is exactly what a diviner also needs. A head is a sine qua non for both a philosopher and a diviner. But nowadays, not every diviner needs a board of divination. Many a diviner can find the knowledge and truth without a board of divination, as long as he/she possesses a head which is destined to seek and discover the unknown.

This is a skit about a philosopher and a diviner who saw a house burning during a downpour attended by a frightening lightning. After the house had been reduced to ashes, they were invited to attend a meeting of the keepers of traditions. During the course of the meeting, they were asked to explain what might have caused the burning of the house. None of them could provide an answer. Then the keepers of traditions adjured them to find the answer, willy-nilly. Both of them left for a glade in search of the answer, where they slept for two nights. As the third night was beginning to announce itself, they separated from each other. The diviner went to the east of the glade. The philosopher went to the west of the glade. But they met each other on a forked path as the day was dawning. Here they met another diviner telling them that the house must have been razed to the ground by a lightning bolt. The answer has been found and the case put to rest.

There are two schools of thought who have never come to a conclusion of unity whenever the discourse on diviners and philosophers becomes topical. One school believes or assumes that it is easier for a diviner to become a philosopher than a philosopher to become a diviner. But the other school would counter that statement by saying that it is easier for a philosopher to become a diviner than a diviner to become a philosopher. Only the head, (ori) would be in a better position to put the argumentation of the two schools of thought to rest—conclusively—logically. Nonetheless, both schools believe in a life rich in knowledge and truth. Therefore both of them are seekers of a life emblazoned with knowledge and truth.

Chapter 10

Artistic Expression of Yoruba Philosophy

It is often said that in every Yoruba compound, there is a weaver, a potter, a carver, a dyer or a sculptor. This was true during the oral culture. It may not be true today, but it is true for the author's compound where his father was a sculptor and his mother a weaver. Why is it that there is so much love of weaving and sculpturing in Yoruba land? The answer is this, very simple. The Yoruba people believe that anything they touch is either a story or a symbolist poem which they can translate into a weaving or a sculptural emblem. Also, they believe that Ogun, the primary Artist-Philosopher, has blessed the land to be the primary colony of art and artists. We must also remember that Oduduwa, the founder and the primogenitor of the Yoruba land was a natural philosopher cum diviner who had instructed the Yoruba people to always make a symbolic mark on the surface of the earth.

Furthermore, it is crucial to understand that the ancient or the proto Yoruba land propagated the knowledge of its worldviews—cosmogony, cosmology, love, morality—philosophy in sculpturing and carving. Like the present, it was/is a commonplace to find a sculptor, a potter, a carver or a weaver in every family in Yoruba land.

Since time immemorial, the Yoruba are prolific sculptural artists, famous for their magnificent and sometimes nonpareil terracotta works throughout the world, from the 9th to 14th centuries.

Sculptural Schools of Philosophy: In his book, "The Oral Traditions in Ile-Ife," the author refers to the terracotta artists of the 9th to 14th centuries as the founders of the Art Guilds, otherwise known as the Cultural Schools of Philosophy, which today can and will be likened to many of Europe's old institutions of learning which were originally set up as religious bodies. These guilds/cultural schools of philosophy may well be some of the oldest non-Abrahamic African centres of learning to remain as viable entities in contemporary world.

The ever-present emotion of an artist in his/her work and the aesthetics of his/her work have always marvelled a philosopher, giving him or her a kind of mind at peace. Sometimes a philosopher may feel jealous of a prolific sculptural artist, knowing full well that the sculptural artist has acquired his wisdom and knowledge solely from his milieu, and without a formal education, in a modern sense. While the jewels and the colours of words are the precint or the domain of a philosopher, the emotion of an artist as displayed in his/her palpable work (such as Ife bronze head, terracotta head and the philosophical mask), plus the touch or feel of that reality makes every mortal give a regal nod of celebration, felicity and appreciation. An aesthetic appeal is sales appeal, according to the opinion of the connoisseurs of good taste.

Chapter 11

The Metaphysical Divinities

What do we mean by metaphysical divinities? By metaphysical divinities, we mean the Yoruba divinities that philosophically concern themselves with the knowledge of the causes and the nature of things, affecting the corporal and the spiritual universe. We may have succeeded in answering the question, for it is more difficult to give a definition of a word than to give an illustration of its use. In particular, this chapter will deal with eleven of the most consequential metaphysical divinities in the land who are well up in natural and cardinal virtues. They are Obatala, Orunmila, Sango, Ogun, Olokun, Oya, Oshun, Esu, Yemoja, Sopona and Oshosi. All of them have contributed to Yoruba philosophy from the proto-history to this day. Each one of them had played a philosophical role before combining that role with religion for which philosophy is antecedent to. And all of them are regarded as theanthropic and have contributed to the meaning and wellness of Yoruba land. Sitting at the high table and discoursing with these eleven demythologized Divinity-Philosophers is Divinity-Philosopher King Oduduwa who is equally well up in natural and cardinal virtues of the land, as pitted against priori knowledge.

Some people will say, "Leave those divinities alone. They are speculative philosophers without former training. They cannot see. What do you need them for? They are dead and have been swept away by winds and can only be glorified as anachronisms." But it is proper to let such people know that Yoruba people cannot succumb to passion alone without reflection in the first place, and reflection is a limb in the act of reasoning. This is why they have to stick to their beginning and the divine men and women of consequence that brought splendour to their existence. Within that context, each epoch has its own distinctiveness. As credited to Oduduwa, *"a generation comes, a generation goes."* As propounded by Karl Marx, and as does Ollman (1976) each stage in history creates its own distinctive needs in men and with the passing to the next stage these needs disappear, along with their owners, to be replaced by new people and new needs."

Oduduwa: Prior to treating these divinities, one by one, we must consider Oduduwa, the primogenitor, the founder of Ile-Ife and the father of Yoruba moral cum narrative philosophy. King Oduduwa was a transcendentalist, a great reasoner/thinker who planted the seeds of enlightenment and brought light to Yoruba land. His love for words is rooted in his exposition of the universe, focussing on cosmogony and cosmology. He theorized about the visible and invisible worlds, reminiscing about the quintessence of the sculptural arts and how his children would utilize them to express themselves, from day to day, making use of their faculties/heads (ori). This is the main reason the Yoruba land is a land of artists and artworks. While sending his children to found the historical and philosophical towns and cities, he intuited in them a sense of perfection. Additionally, he reminded them of their creative mission and their obligation to build Art Guilds as a mark of their happiness and readiness to serve mankind. These Art Guilds could be likened to our today's Schools of Philosophy.

From the timelessness to the present, no one can say precisely how Oduduwa acquired his gourd and seeds of knowledge and wisdom to build Ile-Ife. During those days of timelessness, there were many things which one can not comprehend. We must simply confine them to the realm of proto-history and let the aeon become their contemporary, otherwise their transposition.

How philosopher Odudwa navigated himself out of the timelessness remains a mystery that stands to be demystified. However, we must be reminded that he had an excellent head upon his shoulders, for without a good head, he could not have been able to navigate himself to the light and build a *"living city,"* a dwelling place which later becomes a *"sculptural city."*

Some schools of thought have expounded that Oduduwa was not only a moral philosopher but also a kind of prophet. A powerful man, a theanthropic being, one could have expected him to have a future in his voice. It is not unlikely to assume that Oduduwa must have predicted all the unfortunate happenings in Ile-Ife, notably that of Queen Moremi and the circumstances that led to the sacrifice of her only begotten son, Oluorogbo. The belligerence amongst the Yoruba city-states and the eventual fall of the Oyo Empire, plus the occupation of Ilorin are sad as they are unfortunate occurrences that Oduduwa must have forewarned his people. But his people unheeded his warning, we must perorate.

The most nagging question which Oduduwa was unable to answer convincingly is about life and death. What he had told his fellow philosophers is that life is a journey that never ends. He compared life to a tree that loses its leaves during a particularly harsh weather or season and regains its leaves when the weather or season is friendly or favourable again. So also is the life of man, who will die whenever he is faced with something more than what he can bear or endure. He comes back again like the leaves of a tree whenever the condition is favourable for him to grow and live.

Is Oduduwa a myth or a reality? The answer will be an overwhelming and ear-tearing no. Oduduwa is a reality so far as Creator-philosopher Olodumare is a reality. Oduduwa's theory lets us know that there is good and bad in the world. If ever his theory can be proved wrong, that will elucidate the fact that he is a myth. As our research has indicated, Divinity-Philosopher Oduduwa is the greatest Yoruba philosopher that is known to Yoruba people since the creation of the holy city of Ile-Ife. It seems he will forever remain the greatest. He is the founder of the Yoruba ancient homeland-kingdom. Here is the father of the proto-Yoruba philosophy. As long as Ile-Ife exists, it will be more than certain that Divinity-Philosopher Oduduwa is a reality and not a myth. There is no doubt that Divinity-Philosopher Oduduwa's name is the first name on the list of the inductees into the Divine Hall of the Yoruba pantheon.

Obatala/Orisa-Nla: We know much about Obatala (who is otherwise called Orisha-Nla), as one of the founders of Yoruba religion but little is known about him as one of the thinkers that ever lived or imagined to have lived. Despite his drunkenness that led to his demotion by Creator-Philosopher Olodumare, Obatala is one of the great Divinity-Philosophers during the days of creating the world in general and Ile-Ife in particular. He partook in the seeds of enlightenment and understands the human anatomy.

Can we say or suggest that Obatala is a myth or reality? We can say that philosopher Obatala is a reality. But we cannot say that he is a myth. Why? Because it is philosopher Obatala who has the faculty (ori) to mould the human body out of clay before giving it to Creator-philosopher Olodumare who breathes life into the body. And so, a human being is made. Divinity-Philosopher Obatala/Orisa-Nla is arguably number two on the list of the inductees into the Divine Hall of the Yoruba pantheon.

Orunmila: Like Obatala, Orunmila is associated with Yoruba faith and realism. But before the making of Yoruba religion, Orunmila worked with his people having being inspired by Creator-Philosopher Olodumare as a philosopher cum psychologist, projecting **IFA** Divination as the Body of Knowledge, containing many fields of human interests. He was so good a psychologist that proto-history Yoruba is not and cannot be complete without him. As he is versed in divination, so is he versed in telegnosis and psychology and philosophy of destiny, as we shall read in chapter twenty-five. He lets us know that there are 256 Odu Ifa, explicating that each Odu contains 800 stories. All together, there is a total of 204,800 stories in what is referred to as the Book of Enlightenment. He was the first naturalistic psychologist to know that mankind needs corporeal and spiritual healing. Thus he received "ase" from Creator-Philosopher Olodumare that whoever used his herbs properly shall be healed diametrically. Due to his divine power, he knew the exact time of the exact day of the exact year when one is due to pay one's debt to nature. Also, it should be proper to know that Divinity-Philosopher Orunmila was versed in analytical philosophy, the only one in all ancient Yoruba philosophers.

Let's share the seven ethical paradigms from his body of **love and wisdom** as contained in the Book of Enlightenment. They will also be found in The Colourful House of Ethics, on Chapter Thirty of this book. They are the following:

   *Respect your parents and Elders
   *Love yourself in order to love others, for Divine Divination is love and wisdom
   *Do no harm to others
   *Treat others as would treat yourself
   *Abstain from stealing
   *Abstain from lying
   *Abstain from back-biting.

Is Divinity-Philosopher Orunmila a myth or a reality? Divinity-Philosopher Orunmila is a reality and not a hoodwinker. Orunmila is both a Divinity-Philosopher and a powerful and indispensable diviner or psychologist. During his life time, he was invariably theorizing about destiny or fate and the act of reasoning. One may not disown the fact that Frederick C. Beiser's book, *The Fate of Reason*, is an extension of Orunmila's love for destiny/fate and the act of reasoning. A downright cultivator of seminal ideas, without philosopher/diviner Orunmila, there will be no Book of Enlightenment, **IFA**-Ife Divination. And without the Book of Enlightenment, the Yoruba race could not have founded Ile-Ife and Creator-Philosopher Olodumare could have instructed another race to found Ile-Ife, said to be Olodumare's holy citadel on earth. Divinity-Philosopher/Diviner Orunmila is a big gun on the list of the inductees into the Divine Hall of the Yoruba pantheon.

Sango: Like his contemporaries, Sango was a well-known Divinity-Philosopher. He expounded about fire, especially lightning and thunders. He belonged to the first group of thinkers that settled in Ile-Ife. The discourse among the researchers and keepers of traditions goes on, endlessly, as there are two schools of argumentation in respect of his personage. The first school theorized that Sango hanged himself toward the end of his reign, whereas the second school knocked against the theory, postulating that philosopher Sango did not hang himself, but rose majestically to the heaven above.

Is Divinity-Philosopher Sango a myth or a reality? The entire world will say in unison that Divinity-Philosopher Sango is a reality and not a myth. A former king of the Yoruba people, philosopher Sango typifies lightning and thunder which we see every season. A prominent ancient philosopher during the proto-history, Sango is one of the early members to be inducted into the Divine Hall of the Yoruba pantheon.

Ogun: Ogun who succeeded in creating an indelible presence in the psyche of the world, represents weapons of single and mass destruction. He is the sole Divinity-Philosopher who theorized about war and peace. He expounded that there are good things in fighting as there are opportunities in tragedies. He is the only Divinity-Philosopher whose name appears in Yoruba calendar, as August—the eighth month of the year.

Putting Yoruba views and values in the right perspective that ought to have established their presence, it is not unlikely that Divinity-Philosopher Ogun is cognizant about the news and discussions going on about the 900-1400 AD terracotta artists. What is not clear though, is how he would establish the fact that the terracotta artists did form an Arts Guild that eventually involved into a Sculptural School of Philosophy. Quite a lot of things appear to be plausible during the proto-history of the world. But Divinity-Philosopher Ogun may be held responsible for an answer, for he is the sole philosopher whose love enables him to know how to start a journey on time and how to end it on time—successfully.

In order to know Divinity-Philosopher Ogun, we need to listen to how other ancient thinkers regard him or how they perceive him. The ancient thinkers regard him to be a brave warrior who could battle for days without looking back. The following will shed some light on how this author has poetically portrayed him:

> Ogun, thou ancient thinker
> Believer that there are good things in fighting
> As there are opportunities in tragedies
> Your head has devised the needed implements
> For the use of mankind
> Clear the road for me.
>
> Ogun, clear the road for me
> In my journeys day and night
> Whenever I deliver a glancing blow to my foe
> Knocking him down unconscious
> Clear the road for me.
>
> Whenever my foe rises,
> Wielding his double-edged machete
> Looking up at you
> Asking yet for another crushing blow
> Clear the road for me.
>
> Clear the road for me
> So that my own machete
> Could rain the rain of retaliation
> Upon his oblong head.
>
> Should there be any cause
> That I should be whisked away
> By the whirligig of life
> Tossing me up and down
> Clear the road for me.
>
> Recalling all the fights I fought for mankind
> Especially during the cultural civil wars
> When I nearly lost my cool—my head,
> Since I did not know which side to support

> However, I put the civil war to shame
> And reinstated philosophy of love
> Now finding an adobe to lay my head
> Clear the road for me.
> Ogun, clear the road for me
> As I find my adobe under
> The ruins of paradise
> Owned by the sculptural terracotta artists.
>
> Ogun, clear the road for me
> Should I find my way to the past paradise
> The Old Oyo Empire
> And the city of Ilorin
> Philosophizing about the past
> And present status quo
> Based on compromise and verisimilitude.

May we take it that Ogun is a myth or a reality? We must take it that Divinity-Philosopher Ogun is real and not a myth, for Ogun typifies steel and iron. He is the eighth month in the Yoruba calendar. Also, Divinity-Philosopher Ogun is the only Divinity-Philosopher who has the means to clear the road for road-users. He is a prominent inductee into the Divine Hall of the Yoruba pantheon.

Olokun: Olokun is the father of waters. He believes water is life, that water takes away the poison in the fire. His strong opinion is that he should be number one philosopher by virtue of his indispensability. Is Divinity-Philosopher Olokun a myth or a reality? All indications show that Divinity-Philosopher Olokun is not a myth but a reality. He typifies the oceans and seas and according to him, he has the watery power to sink the world in a jiffy and bend the world to his mercy. Olokun is a Divinity-Philosopher from the days of creation. He is a prominent name on the list of the inductees in the Divine Hall of the Yoruba pantheon.

Oya: Queen Oya is a popular philosopher who is arguably said to be the mother of divine Oshun. Wife of Olokun, she supports her spouse in all philosophical matters, pertaining to the purity and flow of waters, especially the oceans, the seas and the contents therein.

Is Divinity-Philosopher Oya a myth or a reality? Queen Oya is not a myth. She is as real as River Niger which she typifies. Divinity-

Philosopher Oya belongs to the ancient philosophers. Also, she belongs to the venerable ones who have been inducted into the Divine Hall of the Yoruba pantheon.

Oshun: Queen Oshun, was a young philosopher during the days of creation. In fact, her divine presence was not known until the landscape/geography of Yoruba land was marked out. But she is an experienced divinity in Yoruba religion. She succeeded in defining beauty and character, for she is an embodiment of beauty, character, productivity and honey-sweet waters. In her passion for life and loving-kindness, she lets us know that the pleasure of happiness with human beings and the feelings derived from happiness are ever present in our five senses—seeing, hearing, smelling, tasting and touching.

One could feel her beauty in the virgin zephyr. One could feel it among the aquatic places. One could feel it on the sand. Amongst the animals, birds, fishes, insects and flowering plants, her divine beauty endures forever. There is beauty in divine Oshun's footprints. But in all her beauty, what makes her the darling of all the ancient thinkers is her nonpareil character. She is a sight for the Gods, an aesthetic appeal. Her beauty and character is an illustration of duality that can force one to shriek out that there is beauty in the eyes of the beholder. Once upon a time, Creator-Philosopher Olodumare stripped her of her beauty, as a test. What was left intact is her character. Creator-Philosopher Olodumare, the giver of beauty was flushed with prideful joy. Since that day of testing her, Creator-Philosopher Olodumare has promised never to test her again regarding her exquisite beauty, for it is her character that begets her beauty and not the other way round.

Is Divinity-Philosopher Oshun a myth or a reality? The answer will be a monosyllabic yes. As long as there is River Oshun in Yoruba land, Divinity-Philosopher Oshun is a reality who cultivates eternal seeds of production and reproduction. Her treatise on Narrative Philosophy, in chapter thirteen, is another evidence that she is a reality and not a philosophical myth. Additionally, she belongs to those who have been inducted into the Divine Hall of the Yoruba pantheon.

Esu: Esu's philosophy symbolizes versatility or subtlety. In other words, and in order to be fair to his name, Esu is a trouble-shooter who believes in the aesthetics of contradictions. Versatile and subtle, he is a good debater, versed in pros and cons arguments.

Is Divinity-Philosopher Esu a myth or a reality? The answer is shrouded. However, his name is found in the list of the ancient philosophers. His name is also in the list, belonging to the Divine Hall of the Yoruba pantheon.

Yemoja: Yemoja's philosophy represents the ocean, the essence of the motherhood, and a protector of children, worldwide. She heals with the waves of energy from the ocean, washing over the healed. She is one of the pre-eminent divinity-philosophers on the list belonging to the Divine Hall of the Yoruba pantheon.

Is Divinity-Philosopher Yemoja a myth or a reality? The answer should be positive. Yemoja is one of the female Divinity-Philosophers known during the period when Ile-Ife was born. She is real as long as the oceans are real.

Soponna: Soponna's philosophy typifies destruction. Whether his philosophical mission is to fight for the righteous and punish the unrighteous is not clear. What is clear is that his scourge makes one chicken-hearted. However, many people in the land are wary of him, and have honoured him as a keeper of traditions and as a philosopher who has no respect for life and the antonym of life, as well as the belongings of the living. Is Divinity-Philosopher Soponna a myth or a reality? Many people including this author cannot give a definitive answer. But he belongs to the list of the ancient Divinity-Philosophers, as he belongs to the Divine Hall of the Yoruba pantheon.

Oshosi: Oshosi's philosophy has some elements of justice and hunting. He is a valorous, skilled and stealthy hunter who upholds the highest moral/ethical standards and always hitting his mark or target with his arrow (ofa). He is so good a hunter who could shoot down a butterfly in its erratic flight with one eye closed. He helps man maintain justice in spite of his love for hunting. His philosophy of uprightness teaches us to know that in Yoruba land the standards of the codes of morality are so high and precious that no one wants to go under the attack of bag-eyed behaviour. His uprightness qualifies him to be on the list of the ancient Divinity-Philosophers, making him belong to the Divine Hall of the Yoruba pantheon.

The fact that all the foremost divinities have their names begin with letter **O**, signifies yet another evidence that they are natural or metaphysical thinkers like Creator-Philosopher Olorun/Olodumare, the preeminent Creator-Philosopher whose name also starts with letter O. There are four exceptions above. The first is Sango, whose full name might be O'Sango, shortened to Sango for convenience. The second is Soponna, whose full name is likely to be O'Soponna, shortened to Soponna for the sake of convenience. The third is Yemoja whose full name is likely to be O'Yemoja, shortened to Yemoja, courtesy of convenience. The forth is Esu whose full name might be O'Esu, shortened to Esu for the sake of convenience. Shortening of names is a commonplace practice in Yoruba land. It is like a divine largesse from Creator-Philosopher Olodumare. In many parts of the land, O has a divine nexus with Creator-Philosopher Olodumare or Olorun who is the custodian of philosophy which in Yoruba language means *imo* or *ogbon*.

Can we rationally believe in the existence of our ancient thinkers who have never couched anything of their own? The answer should be in the affirmative. The answer, being in the affirmative suggests that we are duty-bound to believe in their existence as long as we believe in the past memories—written or oral. And as long as we believe that there is good and bad in the world we live in, as expounded by Divinity-Philosopher Oduduwa. Again, we have to believe in the existence of our ancient thinkers inasmuch as the Yoruba people believe in their past: insofar as the Yoruba cherish their past, as they cherish their present. They guide the land as ori guides the body. Due to the fact that the Yoruba people are downright pragmatists, they always seek to recall the past whorls of their ancient pedigrees, buried in their memory, exhumed as they pad along the memory lane. According to Divinity-Philosopher Oduduwa's theory of good and bad, the good cherishes the good seeds of consciousness vis-a-vis enlightenment, while the bad longs after the seeds of destruction.

It is important to note and to emphasize that all the Divinity-Philosophers possessed oral magnum opuses but not the written magnum opuses. Researching and remaking their written magnum opuses still remains and presents a Gordian knot if not a herculean task. But it is to our understanding that their minds were never distorted by material desires, as they lived and worked in the state of pure goodness.

Chapter 12

The Ontological Journey to the Atlantic Yoruba

Iwalewa—two in one: a portmanteau word. Whenever two meets, there must be a head (ori) that will tell or say the reason for the meeting. Otherwise, there will be no reason for meeting. Iwalewa is a portmanteau word: a product of duality. Its philosophical sublimity epitomizes felicity and stateliness, found in every creature and character of a person.

Toward the end of one of the nine journeys made by the children of the king Oduduwa, to founding lands, Iwa and Ewa met at the littoral settlement in Lagos, one of the littoral settlements closest to the Atlantic Yoruba Kingdom. Their fortuitous meeting occurred when Divinity Olokun was planning to establish the Atlantic Yoruba Kingdom.

The socio-philosophical account of how the expanse of waters that make up the Atlantic Yoruba would be beneficial to the world was not crystal clear. What is clear and far from being fragmentary is that both Iwa and Ewa could trace their long pedigrees to the holy city of Ile-Ife under the tutelage of philosopher Oduduwa. Ewa was the sole daughter of Divinity Oshun, while Iwa was the only son of Divinity Olokun. Olokun and Oshun were pleased to know that their children had fallen head over heels in love. There was no one to complain that they should not marry due to the common sense that they came from the same family tree. But the fact that the relationship was a distant one without a written record, the earth, the water and the air blessed their union.

After Divinity Olokun had established the Atlantic Kingdom, Prince Iwa and Princess Ewa got married and then founded the Kingdom of Ugbo. Moons later, they became the king and the queen, respectively. Soon, Queen Ewa gave birth to a baby girl, called Iwalewa, an exceptionally beautiful princess. The birth of Princess Iwalewa ushered in a lot of good things, as predicted by philosopher Oduduwa. Prosperity opened its doors to the kingdom of Ugbo. As a result of this prosperity, many people came from the littoral settlements of Lagos (mostly the Awori) to live on the littoral and wetland areas of the Atlantic Yoruba, stretching from the coastal parts of Benin City to the littoral communities of Port Novo. As the kingdom was expanding, the population of the people who were/are mainly piscatorial men and women was also growing. Cottage farming is their second occupation. Handicraft is their past time. The men are noted for their canoe building and the women are renowned for their weaving and terracotta pottery. These scions of Ile-Ife whose sub-ethnic classification or division is Ilaje, are one of the three sub-ethnic groups who escaped the scourge of the Yoruba civil wars. They are one of the few sub-ethnic groups of the Yoruba who do not carry or have to carry facial marks. The other two are the Ikale and the Ijo Apoi. Of course, the Awori do not carry facial marks, as far as our historical records of Lagos can bear.

A few years later, a mini-kingdom in the name of Mahin emerged. This was followed by Ipepe, a chieftaincy town-let. The former lies to the east, while the latter lies to the west of Ugbo, respectively. But Ipepe, in terms of fishing, is the most successful town-let in all these littoral settlements. Sooner than expected, its population became the largest due to the flock of people to the town-let every season, to learn the art and secret of fishing—fishing successfully.

In one of her tours of the littoral settlements, the crowned princess Iwalewa visited Ipepe Sculptural School where she met Omolara. It was a chance meeting because Omolara was supposed to travel to Atijere that day. Nonetheless, both of them were happy to have discovered each other as friends. The crowned princess was twenty at that time and Omolara was twelve, graduating in six to seven years. She would invariably take joy in reminding Omolara not to forget to make a mark, worthy of reference as Divinity-Philosopher Oduduwa once said, "My children, go forth and make a mark so that the next generation will have something to reminisce about, something to reference from one generation to another."

The following narrative is how Iwalewa, an indispensable attribute in Yoruba moral philosophy was sorely bruised, put on trial, and how it eventually established itself as second only to the head, in all matters pertaining to human etiquette, manner or character, following rectitude.

Omolara came to the Atlantic paradise under the vault of heaven at a time when most keepers of traditions and mothers in Ipepe had lost hope of seeing a child born to Mr. and Mrs. Koya. Mrs. Koya was already fifty and her husband was pulling seventy when Omolara, their sole daughter, was born. Three days after her birth, the whole littoral village of Ipepe junketed for seven calendar days. That was the first time in the history of the littoral Ipepe to see a fifty year-old woman giving birth to a baby. That was also the first time in the history of the littoral Ipepe to have a child delivered by the bank of Ipepe Lagoon, an extension of Lagos Lagoon.

To the villagers, Omolara was a mysterious child. Apart from her pulchritude and pleasant mien, she possessed full luscious lips and a waist that was ideal to embrace, any time, anywhere. In addition to these, her plaited hair tapered off to her bottom. And which according to the keepers of traditions, was forbidden to be cut, for the day her hair happened to be cut, would be the day she would die! Some people believed that she was an angel incarnate. As though her personality was not remarkable enough, she had at birth an ankh mark at the back of her neck and a mark of a star on her forehead. She also had earrings, a bangle on her left hand and a ring on her bellybutton.

At school, she was regarded Divinity-Philosopher Oshun's daughter. She had few friends, friends who had the daring to understand her peculiar appearance which she herself did not comprehend. She was the youngest female in this part of the world to practice vegetarianism, saying, "When you choose vegetarian foods, you'll find yourself light, relaxed and spiritually focused. The pursuit of happiness is easily found falling in love with vegetarian foods and vegetarian foods are embodied in the pursuit of happiness."

At the age of five, people started calling her a girl with a philosopher's head. The reason for that appellation is that she was considered wise and precocious, a whiz kid, perhaps, whose old head upon her young shoulders could answer many questions about the moral and narrative philosophy, about the whys and wherefores of life and death, as well as the whys and wherefores of the disappearance without trace of the Ile-Ife sculptural artists. Whenever people jocularly asked her where she was coming from, she would jocularly tell them that she was coming from her mother's womb. She would let them know that the womb is the first homey place a child knows.

She was six years of age when her parents and neighbours started to speculate what sort of life she wanted to lead. Every time she came back from school, she would carve exquisite masks and tell hair-raising stories. Among her listening audience were goats, sheep, parrots, cows, cats, chanticleers, woodpeckers and donkeys. Like her parents, friends and nodding acquaintances, they would sit around her, listening to her spell-bounding stories which no one had ever heard before in Ipepe. Also, the stars would twinkle and the entire firmament would be starlit and there would be haloes suspended in the air. It was as if the cultural Moremi or an angel had given her an exceptional head which no soul had ever possessed since the creation of Ipepe.

At first, her parents were somehow ashamed to go out with her. But as the time went on, they were used to the glances and the giggles in the market places, and the gossips, the pouting and the raising of eyebrows around the corners and the compounds. They even forgave a number of youngsters calling her Nightingale instead of her real name, Omolara.

At fourteen, five years before graduating from her Sculptural Arts School, she became pregnant. People were surprised because no one had ever seen a man with her before. Her parents were worried, so also her neighbours, especially princess Iwalewa. Anyway, she did not tell them anything. However, they had nothing to worry about, for Ipepe was a sacrosanct place where any baby born either in marriage or out of marriage was always accorded a full birthright and protected as the scion of Ile-Ife, the holy city, and whose umbilical cord would be in the likeness of that of philosopher Oduduwa, the founder of the holy city. In the case of Omolara, anything that could make her own situation unusual would be the revelation that she had been made pregnant by the Holy Ghost.

Months later, she gave birth to a bouncing baby boy. The child was named Jeki. He was a lovely child, adored by all. One day, three moons after her seventeenth birthday, a few hours before her parents came back from the fields; Omolara disappeared, leaving behind her three years old son with her grandmother, named Mama Taikayela.

Mr. and Mrs. Koya were astonished as they were dismayed on finding Jeki on the laps of Mama Taikayela, who lived in the same compound. Jeki ran to Mrs. Koya who asked Mama Taikayela,

"Where did Omolara go?"

"She went to Eko Atlantic City," answered Mama Taikayela with a worried moue.

"Goodness me! What on earth did she want in Eko Atlantic City?" asked Mr. Koya.

"I don't know. But remember that your daughter is a nonpareil storyteller and a gifted terracotta artist," replied Mama Taikayela.

"Omolara is a storyteller, mama," replied Jeki, smiling.

"A storyteller?" said Mr. and Mrs. Koya simultaneously.

"Yes, a storyteller," rejoined Jeki and Mama Taikayela in unison.

"Did she mention to you the name of your father?" asked Mrs. Koya with a frown.

"Yes, she told me that my father's name is Segun," answered Jeki with a nod.

There was nothing to be worried about. The kid had revealed all what his mother had told him. Mr. and Mrs. Koya knew Segun's parents. They knew Segun too. He was Omolara's contemporary in the Sculptural Arts School. However, there had never been any contemporaneous events that brought them together in the same compound.

One Sunday morning, Mr. and Mrs. Koya burst out caterwauling, simply because they thought that the Providence had never shown to them enough mercy and milk of human kindness. They did not stop to think of Omolara as a mysterious child, born late in their marriage life. She came to the world with many heavenly presents. Not only that, her long, plaited hair was like an enigma which no one dared to cut. And now she had gone to Eko Atlantic City, leaving behind her three years old son, without completing her Sculptural Arts School education. Indeed, her parents had no grounds to be proud of her. They had every rhyme and reason to be crestfallen. Their only pride, perhaps, was that they had an unusual daughter, at an unusual age, with unusual honey-sweet voice which gladdened the hearts of all creatures.

That Omolara had gone to the city was certain. It was as certain as the rainy season that succeeded the last dry season. It was as certain as an Abiku child who told their parents that they still have to shed more ritual tears ere it could acquiesce to staying with them, for good. Surely, it was as certain and unmistakable as the cooking aroma belching out of the kitchen of a loving wife, whetting the appetite of her beloved husband.

She was that mysterious sylph-like maiden who disliked living in a big city like Benin-City, Calabar, Enugu, Ibadan, Kaduna, Kano, Lagos, Ogbomosho or Port-Harcourt. These cities were too enormous for her. They were too intimidating. They were unsympathetic and un-natural. They had all lost all the sanctuaries and the aura, characteristic of the memories of our ancestors to the bosky niche of the countryside. She could not stand any situation, getting out of control. For quite a long time, she had the notion that while a city swallows its citizens, a village allows itself to be swallowed by its villagers. For this reason, she had chosen to live in a town called Darlingwood, lying between Lekki and Eko Atlantic City. Darlingwood is regarded a village due to its population of 10,000, but many people in Ipepe preferred to call it a city owing to its area of fifty square kilometres, and owing to the fact that it is the biggest literary movie paradise in Africa.

Five years had elapsed since she became a professional storyteller. She had taken part in Nigerian Story Contests on two occasions and she had won on both occasions—2011 and 2012, the first woman to win consecutively. She had toured many hamlets, villages, towns and cities around the country, as a Miss Nigeria Storyteller, healing the sick with her dulcet and spiritual voice. Her spiritual voice had also given hope to waifs and strays and the handicapped children. The honey-sweet voice in her stories had not only made her famous, it had also made her wealthy. Like most girls from the humble families, she was a generous giver. Her bank account had swollen. Many people in the country took her to be a millionaire. She sent money to her son and her parents regularly. But her mother, nursing a sorrowful heart, had vowed never to spend one kobo of her money. For her, it was not the money that mattered most to her but her coming home to her only begotten son, Jeki. Subsequently, the thought of her daughter had led to her not eating regularly. She had become emaciated so much that one could liken her to a stick figure.

Sadly enough, Omolara was only well-to-do, she was not happy. She was not happy because her manager, Dola, had been dishonest to her. It was not too long she discovered Dola had spent almost half of her savings. Dola, a podgy man of many years of managerial experience in movies had been unfaithful to her and now he was a mountebank, unworthy any longer to manage her. On more than five occasions, she had accused him of drinking too much. Sometimes he would walk like a sleep walker. A man who drinks too much dilution, misbehaves, is her personal opinion of any creature of a man that consumes too much dilution. She often used polite fiction to euphemize Dola's drunkenness by referring to dilution instead of alcohol.

The whispered skit about Dola was that he would never manage a woman with urbanized upbringing. Not only that, his clients had to come from the countryside where moral values, rites of initiation, ritual songs and dances were upheld. They also had to be pretty, ambitious and innocent as nymphets. The character of this podgy man who always wore a rainbow-coloured bandanna had never altered despite his many years of managerial experiences. He had been indicted and sued five times for hocus-pocus and cheating. And Omolara had heard about him almost as many times.

The following is the shocking revelation or confession of his tempestuous and fraudulent past: "I am from Dagora, a town between Jos and Ilorin. There in Dagora, I was trained as a professional hunter by my father who was also a professional hunter. I was a sharp shooter. I could shoot a cheetah running at an amazing speed. I could shoot even a butterfly during its erratic flight, with an eye closed. In short, I was a successful hunter who had no friends among animals and birds. Despite my success, the sweet temptation of coming to Lagos nearly twisted my neck. The news that Lagos State is a state flowing with milk and honey, plus the slogan that it is a city of excellence, dinned always in my ears every blessed day. Unable to bear it any longer, I yielded to the sweet temptation.

"In 1995, I moved to Lagos when its infrastructure was being developed. A week later, I joined the Lagoon Wrestling Club whose members were known for their bullying behaviors. One day, I lost my tooth while bullying a young man who was dallying with the affections of my girlfriend during a wrestling tournament. Although he was younger than I, his glancing blows had no sympathy for my tooth. He knocked it out of my mouth, giving my mouth a pretty-good sorry picture. I was impressed. The matter was settled before the smart Lagos police came to put their noses into our wrestling business.

"On hearing that the shrewd, resolute and sharp-shooting Lagos Metropolitan police were making extra money, I left the Lagoon Wrestling Club for the police force. Knowing that I was not making enough money as a policeman, I resigned nine months later and joined Sisal Roving Armed Robbers Club, robbing by force and making lots of money. Six moons later, one of my old friends recommended me to a clandestine club where the members made oodles of money by fraudulent means, such as forgery, chicanery and lying. The clandestine club is known as Subterranean 419 Club. The club was so rich and powerful that some of its members were based in Asia, Europe, North and South Americas. Within three months of my joining it, my asset was estimated at five million naira with some invisible pounds and dollars. My boss, Mask-a-Bee bought me a brand-new Mercedes Benz for being very artful in dealing with people. I was happy much as I was apprehensive, for I was aware that one day the smart Lagos policemen and women would nab me and put me out of the water like a fish. In addition to my material wealth and joy, I had three girlfriends, who were rich enough to join the Lagos Women Starlight Club, a very respectable club of first ladies and high grammarians. The Women Starlight Club is noted for giving scholarships to the needy children, especially the orphans.

"One harmattan evening, it was raining cats and dogs. As I was coming out of my subterranean hideout, I heard a rat-a-tat on my door. With a big adorable smile on my lips, I opened the door thinking that my visitor was Brazil-La-Ma-da, my youngest girlfriend. But to my astonishment, what did I see? I saw two police officers. They came in, handcuffed me and then whisked me away in their Toyota Corolla car. Then I started to whine like a cudgelled bully as my comeuppance commenced to weigh upon my conscience. Two days later, Judge Mercury sentenced me to twenty-four months of imprisonment.

"On my way out of the newly renovated prison, I promised heaven and earth to lead an honest life for the rest of my life. In order to make my bad deeds history: in order to be healed and forgiven diametrically from head to toe, I began to receive divine prayers from the Universal House of Enlightenment where members of the ancient believers, Christian believers, Muslim believers and other faiths worship, pray and interact in the name of one God, one Destiny, in order to enter the proverbial Kingdom of our Creator without taking with us our worldly possessions.

"In 2002, I was employed by the Breezy, Glamorous Life, one of the entertainment industries in Eko Atlantic city and after training hard for a period of nine months; I was promoted one of its managers. My job of recruiting sylph-like girls took me to all parts of Nigeria including some West African countries. I managed many talents, the foremost of whom is Omolara Koya whose storytelling touches warm-heartily like an angel and who dances like a firefly. Today, I am a born-again son of Enlightenment. Many thanks, I must sacrifice to the almighty Olodumare who gives me a new head to reason and to act, for without a good head man will continue to stumble and fall. Hallelujah, I am saved from a life of debaucheries."

Despite Dola's bad record with the shrewd Lagos Metropolitan cops, this armadillo of a man was the only man every female singer and actress desired to converse with. He had a dignified and dandified appearance and whenever he opened his mouth to talk, his heavy and adorable voice, amplified by his Adam's apple, whose up and down movements were like the movements of a seesaw, could gather all the dust in Oshodi plywood factory and make a rise out of it. Women love such a voice. It is a must-hear in order to have a good day.

One day, she woke up and commenced to cry like a child for what she could not control like an adult. Without taking her breakfast, she stepped out of her flat and entered the Rainbow Road that led to the arrondissement of Oshodi, one of the few districts in Lagos metropolis where *broken English* is hardly spoken. Grammatically correct English is the order of the day. That the nonpareil woman was caught between the two lingua francas could not be denied. However, *broken English* hardly flirted with her lips, especially in public. Other districts where *broken English* is hardly spoken are Darlingwood, Ikeja, Ikoyi, Surulere, Victoria Island and Eko Atlantic City, the New Lagos. Also, Oshodi is the only arrondissement left as an evidence of the cocoa boom of yester-years. There would never be another cocoa boom again in this century. If ever another cocoa village was going to be founded, that would be when another generation of cocoa farmers would be born, because there could never be a village without cocoa and vice versa. Moreover, there could never be a possibility for one to witness or experience any cocoa boom in the future without diligence and conscientiousness.

There was nothing novel and dramatic about the proverbial Rainbow Road save it acted as a cynosure and wonderment for whosoever trod upon it, especially the tourists who came from different parts of the world in order to feed their eyes on it. The Rainbow Road was said to be in existence prior to the foundation of Oshodi. But why was it called a Rainbow Road? It was called a Rainbow Road because the trees (especially the divi-divis), the creeping plants and the flowers along its sides bore the color of a rainbow.

That Omolara had heard about the magnificent Rainbow Road before could not be disputed. However, she had never trodden it before. Treading it now was devoid of curiosity, for it was not her intention to tread on a road whose origin her parents did not know. But today she has to tread it due to the exasperation she could not control; an anger that made her step out of her opulent flat for uncertainty that could be dangerous, painful and brutal. Even though she is a precocious young woman who is proud of her long pedigrees, she is nonetheless armed with the saying that life is a whirligig, and where everything created (palpable or impalpable) is found in the aesthetics of contradictions such as pleasure versus displeasure, good versus bad, happiness versus un-happiness, kindness versus cruelty, sorrow versus joy, et cetera, et cetera.

Dressed in muumuu and aso-oke chiffon, and looking very much like a fledging movie star-singer, she sat upon a pollarded afrormosia near her flat, breathed in and out, stood up gingerly and then started to walk. Having walked for twenty minutes, she saw a group of young boys and girls, singing and dancing in a merry-go-round. She joined them singing on asking them for their permission. They were happy and she was happy too. They all wondered how she got an exceptionally mellifluous voice. After a while, she left them. No sooner she left them than her happiness reverted to un-happiness. She stood still and burst into tears as she began to think, first, of her son, and second, of her parents. She knew it could have been a wonderful sight to see her only son singing and dancing like those kids. At this juncture, she felt a chill of remorse coursing her constitution. That kind of remorse would sit at the back of her mind until she could show repentance for what she had done.

While her heart was sorrowful and melancholic, she reached a man-made lake where a children's museum and the first aquarium were under construction. Everywhere was enchanting and splendid. She saw droves of haves and have-nots conversing and rejoicing as they credited their contrasts to the inscrutable Creator. Nearby was a hard hat area. Here she saw three lads coming from Eko Atlantic City, humming and praising Governor Fashionable for building a new Lagos for the *world* in general and for the *Africans* in particular. Soon, they started to argue over what, only God knows. Consequently, she saw two of the boys bullying the third boy. In no time at all, she intervened. Sitting down the quarrelsome lads, she let them know that bullying is hurtful to the bullied, and the bullies should be ashamed of hurting their fellow citizen. She asked them to make bullying history in order not to tarnish their names. "Make bullying history. Do unto others as you would others do unto you," she said, hiding a warning smile. They thanked her heartily and sisterly, and then entered the cosmos of their youthful exuberance and friendship again.

The Rainbow Road is a sight for sore eyes. It is a pedestrian zone where people could pad around and play from sun-up till sundown. It is built in parallel with the Red Line of Lagos Light Rail. It is a must-see, courtesy of Governor Fashionable. But one must add that the artificial lake adds to its beauty and scenery which Omolara was tremendously enjoying as she sat by the lake pondering what to do next with her broken life. Overwhelmed by sorrows and suffocated by sadness, an idea—a bad, foreign-fetched, and stupid idea came to her head. It was an ugly idea that was tempting her to commit suicide. As she was trembling violently and planning to yield her life to the antonym of life, a sand-haired youth appeared behind her, tapped her on her right shoulder and then gave her an envelope. Opening the envelope, she began to read a one-page ditty, thusly:

Walking in Beauty

From morn to even, you walk in grace
As the Day light yields its glory to the Night. I slept
Rejoicing in the Beauty and Blessing
Waking up to see and touch the blessed
Hiding from my sight and touch of Blessing
Yet I behold your Beauty in fullness.

As your body in flowers adorned

Jealous are the less fortunate
Standing your natural pulchritude
You may find none to hold
Nor any to feel and reflect upon
Save your double in a rainbow charming.

Your smiles like a rainbow, enchanting
Whenever invisible rainbow your visage caresses
Testifying to your prettiness
I may hold no brief for Nature
But Nature holds brief for me
Holding me witness to that which is invisible to you.

The invisible to me as your Beauty keeps me
Alive, awake: clothing and nurturing me
Enlightening me, gladdening my heart
Gosh, makes me sleep again
And your head pillowed upon my arm
Waking up in the bosom of your Beauty
To God's Blessing and Glory, I subscribe.

(Segun, alias Omo-Oba)

"Thank you," she said to the youth who vanished as quickly as he had come. As she was adjusting her chiffon, a smug smile caressed her lips and her pulchritude that had been under the weight of sepulture, rose from the dead again. Segun's ditty had uplifted her spirit. She would no longer take her dear life.

Knowing that Segun, a primary school teacher, would now be part of Jeki's life, she decided to look for him on getting to the arrondissement of Oshodi in the metropolis of Lagos. Segun was very happy to see her and she was very happy to see him too. Segun let her know that the youth who brought the ditty to her is his younger brother. Sooner than expected, she began to tell Segun how his ditty had changed her life.

"Your ditty had prevented me from committing suicide" she said, knitting her brows.

"How could that must have happened?"

"Lo and behold, I was empty, and indeed at the nadir of my hopes, when I realized that my manager, Dola had been dishonest to me by stealing my money from my bank accounts. But the thought that I have disappointed our son, Jeki is the thought that was wobbling my legs, bending my neck and pricking my conscience on a daily basis. Many nights, I could not sleep. Again, thank you for writing the enlivening and uplifting ditty that is still dinning in my ears, segueing from rhythm to melody and to harmony."

"I thank Olodumare to have directed me to write it, for I share the same guilt which our irresponsibility and stupidity has brought upon us. Both of us have deprived Jeki of his parental love. We must pray him to pardon us." He said, forcing a remorseful pout, holding Omolara by hand and essaying to be quixotic.

After spending five hours with Segun, the mysterious woman boarded the Red Line that took her to Eko Atlantic City and from there she boarded a bus bound for Ipepe via Darlingwood. It was a rush hour. The bus was full to capacity, but she managed to squeeze herself to suffocation by seating on a seat that was meant for two passengers.

Before she left her departure behind her, Segun told her in a remorseful voice that he would come the day after, giving her enough time to enjoy her privacy and to let her open up her heart of hearts to Jeki and her parents. As the hush of evening was creeping over the earth, when the chicks were roosting and the sun dipping behind the waves, she reached Ipepe village. She went straight to her parents' bungalow and met her parents demolishing their supper of pounded yams, fortified with yabbies. With tears in her eyes, she said, "I am a guilty conscience, mama, papa, for a guilty conscience needs no accuser," kneeling down lackadaisically before them.

"You are not only a guilty conscience; you are like a prodigal son who repented his actions. However, we are happy that you have come back to this compound, to where you belong. We are happy that you repent of your actions."

"It is my voice that caused my leaving this compound for the city, because to be successful nowadays, a storyteller or a singer has to go and live in a city."

"As the daughter of this village, you have to establish yourself first in the village before thinking of going to the city that swallows its citizens. If you don't have a firm basis in the village, how can you have a firm basis in the city? This is like a proverb which says— charity begins at home. I am not saying that one should not be determined in life, and aim high to reach, far from it. What I am saying, loud and clear, is that one should not overreach oneself. Moreover, it is one thing to be rich, yet it is another thing to be happy. There is no happiness anywhere without the prayers from the mouths of your parents."

"Now, I have learnt my lesson, and I shall always obey you so that my son, Jeki, can obey me. I will never leave this compound again for the city without your blessings and permission. However, I am grateful that I have made oodles of naira in a forte which was until now the domination of our male storytellers and singers."

She sat down and drank a cup of water from the table. Father and mother breathed in and out and released a munificent smile. At this juncture, Jeki walked in. It was the end of a school day. Kissing and carrying him in her arms with all the affection in the world, she sang her familiar Sunday song.

> I have a mother
> A paragon of beauty
> I have a father
> Marrying the paragon
> I have a son
> A blessing to the family of beauties.

This is the voice the whole village of Ipepe knows very well, a voice that soothes the heart of everyone that hears it. This is the voice which Ipepe had missed for three score moons, a voice which Mr. and Mrs. Koya's centenary gramophone could not replace. The old couple looked into each other's eyes. They both knew that the song was a nostalgic chord in the memory of their daughter.

As she stood up, opening her mouth to relate her experiences in the city, her experiences with her thievish manager, her experiences along the Rainbow Road, her experience with the bullying boys, her memory before the lake, her reminiscence of Segun's ditty; her mother shook her head left and right and said, "Omolara, if you have anything to relate, not today, not tomorrow. Our happiness today, it is, that you have been found, having been lost. If you have anything to relate, anything worthy of narrating during those five years of your absence from this compound wait until such a time when your father and I find it convenient, comfortable and necessary to listen to you. Is that alright?"

"It is alright with me, mother," she said, releasing a grateful smile.

"*Omolara,*" called Mr. Koya, "no matter how dulcet your voice is, you cannot imagine how worried your mother and I were during your absence. To have one only heiress and lose her to the amoebic and pulsating characteristics of a city life, is cathartic and heartbreaking. Look at your mother, look at her properly. She could hardly eat or drink since you left us. She has lost more than seven pounds. Now it is only your nonpareil voice that can drive away the pains in our bodies and the sorrows in our hearts. We all missed you badly. The neighbours missed you. The stars missed you. The animals and the birds missed you too. This compound had never been lively without you. However, I have to let you understand that if you know anything a little too less, it's perilous. If you know anything a little too much, it's dangerous too. This is the world we are living in—a world of joys and sorrows: a world of opposites. To have the finest and most enchanting voice in the land is not only envious but dangerous. Thanks to the keepers of traditions that you've been able to overcome the danger of being left in a forked road of life. Thank Olodumare that the road has never been your driver. All of this is the upshot of our ceaseless prayers for you.

"As you have previously said, you have been a guilty conscience for five fat years. To leave one's parents without a word for them can be compunctious. To leave one's child behind without a word for him, is compunctious. But as said earlier, we are very happy that you have repented of your actions. In this connection, no one, not even Segun shall hold anything against you any more."

"Father, I will learn to be dutiful and respectful, henceforth."

"You promise?"

"I promise, father," she rejoined and cachinnated hilariously like a jackpot hitter.

Chapter 12

That unforgettable night, Omolara called Segun and told him that she was trembling with a novel beginning, happiness and gratitude to see that Jeki and her parents are fine and dandy, adding that her bag-eyed behaviour has been forgiven. She summarized to him the conversations she had with them and Jeki, and her promise never, never to become a runaway woman again. Before noon, the following day, Segun and his parents surprised Omolara, Jeki, Mr. and Mrs. Koya with a flying but honourable visit.

Kneeling down like a man who knows the traditions of the land, Segun apologized for abandoning Jeki. He said he was afraid and too young to do the right thing. "Now I am a man and I shall conduct myself like a man," he said with panache.

Nine months later, when the rainy season was about to start, Segun and Omolara got married in a traditional temple, under the watchful eyes of the keepers of traditions. Many singers and movie-actresses attended the wedding. The dramatis personae of the Darlingwood International Carnival heard about it and came, in the name of love and unity without invitation. Dressed in blue theatrical costumes, showing the life-like characters of water-nymphs/mermaids, no one could deny the fact that they were the cynosures of the occasion. Wow. It was indeed a sight for sore eyes. Also in attendance was a bolt-from-the-blue surprise, Dola, the swindler. He had turned a new leaf after being jailed the seventh time for stealing money from his clients.

The epithalamium was recited by the crowned princess Iwalewa, thusly:

> If you lose your business
> You still have a head upon your shoulders
> If you lose your house
> You still have a head upon your shoulders
> If you lose your money
> You still have a head upon your shoulders
> But once you lose your character
> You definitely lose your head upon your shoulders
> And everything your head has borne for you.
> The earth
> The water
> The air
> Your head is compared to the earth that sustains your life
> The head is compared to the water that sustains your life

The head is compared to the air that sustains your life.
You cannot afford to lose your head
For losing your head is losing your character, your beauty and your life.
Remember Iwalewa is the fundamental cynosure. Hold on to it jealously.
May your Iwalewa grow from day to day. May it bring more happiness, peace and good health into your marriage life. Ase.

The happiest person that day is not Omolara nor is he Segun. The happiest person that day is Jeki. His happiness came to the brim on realizing that his parents have swallowed the ingredients of unconditional love that would enable them to love each other and live together as husband and wife (under the unbroken calabash of joys and sorrows) till the Sahara Desert replaces the Atlantic Ocean. Amen.

Chapter 13

The Theory of Narrative, Literary or Folk Philosophy

Section A

The Theory of Narrative/Literary/Folk Philosophy: It's the whole gamut of Yoruba worldviews—cardinal virtues, ironies, metaphors, parables, paradoxes, within the realm of Odu-Ifa and its branches or ramifications of 204, 800 stories, made available to professional and nonprofessional narrators in Yoruba scions in Africa and in Diaspora. The following are the narratives that fall within the theory of narrative, folk or literary philosophy.

According to the keepers of traditions who are versed in **IFA** Divination, there are 256 Odu Ifa. Each Odu contains 800 stories. Therefore 256 Odu will give us 204,800 stories, making Yoruba Book of Knowledge or the Book of Enlightenment arguably the largest in the world.

Traditionally, a good story is an answer to our problems (wahala). As a matter of fact, a good story from an honest mouth has the spiritual power to pour balm into one's anxious soul, including healing one's body. Philosophically, a good story increases one's wisdom and knowledge and leads one to a much larger realm of knowledge and wisdom.

Section B

A Continent without a River: One hazy Sunday morning, Kwame woke up from a dream he had alone had without his Alter ego. Sitting on a stool and facing his first cousin, Azuma, he related how Gottlieb, the German Chancellor held him by hand in the dream and said to him, *"If we can make it, you can make it too."*

Three days after this dream of encouragement, Kwame left Accra on a home made rickshaw and began a journey northwards without a chart or a herdsman. His soul rested solely upon the Divine Grace as his guide and guidance.

Shortly after his departure, it occurred to him that he had just woken up from his first dream to dream his second dream. He was bemused or rather mocked by shilly-shally. But he knew a great thing was in the star above for him, for dreaming a dream inside a dream is a mark of great things to happen.

On getting to Timbuktu, he met a group of Muslim men and women spreading their clothes on the path for him to tread upon. He could not believe what was happening before his very eyes. What he could only believe is that in some instances (if not in most cases) a prophet is never known in his/her homeland. Although he was somewhat embarrassed, he was joyous the way he was treated like a kinglet by those Muslim men and women who did not know his upbringing or his Christian background.

Speaking through an interpreter, one of the men with a whitish goatee beard prophesized and said to him that his star had risen and shone with iridescence from the throne of Grace and he would be made a great man in his country and his continent and throughout the four corners of the world.

As he was about to raise his eyebrows over the prophecy, ready to pooh-pooh it, the prophet added, "Man of pragmatism, you may not believe me because I am a Muslim and not a Christian prophet. But all the sand dunes in this Saharan paradise may disappear but my prophecy will not. It will come to pass whether you like it or not."

Slowly but steadily, Kwame padded to Nubian Kingdom and from Nubian Kingdom to Abyssinian where he was Selassie's guest of honor for three days. It was a memorable meeting, first of its kind, between the Horn and West and both of them enlivened it with optimism and ties of consanguinity.

On getting to Accra a week later, Kwame dreamed on the fifth of February 1957. It is a dream pregnant with interpretations but there was no interpreter. A month later, his country attained independence and he was made the prime minister of his newly independent country.

Days later, he began to remember what the Muslim prophet told him. Without wasting time, he sent an equerry to look for the prophet but the prophet was nowhere to be found in Timbuktu and all its precincts. Not even a trace of any of those Muslim men and women was seen. Again, he sent another equerry and the equerry came back without seeing the prophet or meeting any human being who knew the prophet.

He conversed with many West African leaders about his dreams of Africa and the Muslim prophecy. He was sure that a leader must lead his or her people into higher planes of enlightenment and reverent nobility. He believed that Africa has the natural resources to be one of the richest continents in the world.

In order to show his people that he was an action man, he decided to go by himself, in search of the Muslim prophet, making use of his rickshaw. On reaching Timbuktu, he was led by a northerly star that brought him to the bank of River Nile in Cairo where he sat upon a caparisoned hobbyhorse, supporting his cheeks with his palms and smiling munificently like a winner. His trip was pleasurable so much that he thought he was in his ministerial palace in Accra. And he seemed to have forgotten the idea of meeting the Muslim prophet. But there was nothing he could do now because he thought, and rightly so, what was happening to him was the will of Creator-Philosopher Olodumare.

Meeting him as he sat upon the caparisoned hobby-horse by the White Nile was Nasser. Breaking open a two-lobed kola-nut, Kwame gave a lobe to Nasser to chew and he chewed the other lobe. Soon after chewing the lobes, they hugged each other with a sincere spirit of friendship. The friendship was so genuine that it was likened to a friendship between identical twins, or a friendship formed during initiation rites, under the brightness of a full moonlit night.

A few minutes after their friendship had been sealed, they saw an opening in the middle of the White Nile. And emerging from the opening was a woman, a stately woman. Her name is known throughout the world because everyone born of woman needs her and loves her for what she is. This woman is beautiful in the eyes of those who are ugly and ugly in the eyes of those who are beautiful. The way I see her is that her beauty changes every twenty-four hours. I am a curious witness to this phenomenon of a woman.

Having introduced her name as Mi Rivera, she gave an oratorical speech that made the two friends thirsty and dying of desideratum.

Consequently, she went to the bank of the river and gave each one of them a gourd of water to drink.

Said Mi Rivera: "With this water inside your bodies, you will now continue to feel my presence even if I am dead and leave nothing behind me but the memory of seeing you without you being visible to other eyes". You will need me every day. I am that what I am— desideratum. You cannot do without me. If you attempt to do anything without me, you will die, die for nothing— without a mark or honor. So beware, my good friends."

Soon after drinking the water, an idea occurred to both of them. They slept, dreamt and woke up with the same idea that occurred to them immediately after drinking the water. They seemed to have been enlightened. Indeed, they were enlightened. They had found the Way of Enlightenment.

A few minutes later, Mi Rivera started to entertain Nasser and Kwame with singing and dancing. Her singing voice was dulcet and could only be compared to the story-telling voice of Scheherazade. She danced bewitchingly so much that one could easily compare her to Nefertiti. Sooner than expected, Nasser and Kwame joined her and both of them started to follow her lead. They were no matches for her. Mi Rivera was a miracle dancer. She was a woman with a blitz talisman in her dancing legs. She had the power to bewitch any creature into dancing with her. But the incompletion, alas, is that no one could dance as she danced. Knowing that her companions were no matches for her, she held them by hands and the three of them started to dance a dance of merry-go-round. They twirled, jounced, bounced, shimmied so much that they were victimized by dizziness.

As the dizziness overpowered them, an unexpected rain in form of drizzles began to touch their bodies like the touch of therapy. About thirty minutes later, this miracle dancer of a woman, disappeared, living his companions bewildered—and searching for a clue.

Two days later, she appeared in Addis-Ababa, in Selassie's palace. On giving Sellassie the living water to drink, the Emperor, popularly and controversially revered as the Lion of Judas, was instantly enlightened. The enlightened emperor knew something was happening, and would happen in Africa that very year, 1963.

On May 25, 1963, Kwame, Nasser, Mi Rivera and Selassie boarded Kwame's rickshaw and went from door to door collecting all the leaders of the newly independent African countries. Steering the rickshaw was Mi Rivera. After collecting a total of twenty leaders in a conveyance that was actually meant for four, Mi Rivera drove back to Addis Ababa and addressed all the leaders in a lapidary speech that shook the world and put tears in the eyes of one and all. Having given each one of them the living water to drink, she said, "With this water inside your bodies, you will now continue to feel my presence (and the presence of our great ancestors) even if I am dead and leave nothing behind save the memory of seeing you in your state of invisibility. You will need me every day, for I am that what I am—desideratum. You cannot do without me. If you attempt to do anything without me, you will die without an honor, without a palpable mark, without accomplishing your much-needed continental goal. So beware, my good friends.

"Remember our brothers and sisters in Europe have found their own feet in the republic of happiness: they have made the continent of Europe proud of them. If they can do it, you can also do it."

"Also remember that I am part of the River Nile, the longest river in the world. I am part of River Congo, the second longest river in Africa. I am part of River Niger, the third longest river in the continent. I am part of Lake Victoria, the largest tropical lake in the world. From all these bodies of waters, you have sipped into your bodies so that you may be useful and indispensable as these waters have been useful and indispensable to your people and the rest of the world from time immemorial." She drawled on the last eight words and then disappeared.

Suddenly, there appeared in the horizon a black and white screen. To this the leaders glued their eyes. Seconds later, they began to recite the following in a tearful voice, juxtaposing **Creative Thinking** with expediencies:

Ori (Head), the Sine Qua non of Yoruba Folk Philosophy

No one can perform
Without ori—head
Ori is the definition of the body
The substrate unto which
Other parts of the body

Are answerable
What I am writing
Originates from my head
My head that comprises
Four of my five senses
My head is my destiny-director
My head is my light, lighting my body
My head is my health, wherein lies my wealth
My head is my enlightenment
Source of knowledge, wisdom and understanding
My head is my love, my happiness
I dare not misuse it
I dare not lose it
For losing it is perilous
My head dictates to my writing
It's the dictates of common sense
In sciences and humanities
Fictional and/or nonfictional
My head/faculty is always at my disposal
Invariably leading me, enlighteningly to the realm
Of thinking, and to the act of reasoning
Adding meaning and fullness of life—to me
An upshot of **Creative Thinking**
My head, a source of **Creative Thinking**
Resulting from research ideas and literary experiences
And these ideas, are philosophically transformed
Into the new ways of thinking, reasoning and writing.

After thirty minutes of silence that came as an upshot of deliberation, during which time the twenty-three leaders were uplifted to the realm of enlightenment, it dawned on them that Mi Rivera was a god-send: an ancestor who had come with a message for them and for the rest of Africans in Africa and Africans in Diaspora.

About ten minutes later, the miracle woman appeared again. Looking at the leaders, she asked in a voice, as sweet as Moremi's voice. "Gentlemen, why are you here in Addis-Ababa?"

"We are here for a purpose," said all the leaders in one voice.

"What purpose is that?" asked the miracle Mi Rivera again.

"We are here to form an African organization to be known and called the **Organization of Africa Unity,"** said the African leaders in one clarion and confident voice.

Looking into the eyes of Kwame, Mi Rivera said his dream of one united Africa has been realized. Congratulating them, one by one, she admonished them not to let the water inside them dry if they wanted the organization to flourish like amaranth, which is her ancestral name.

Changing her silky voice to basso profondo, she said, "I have a story to tell. It is a story of my life. By telling you this story, you will be able to know me. I am neither a magician nor a prestidigitator as some of you must have thought. I hail from the Nubian Dynasty in Gazania, a fertile land, lying between the Nubian and the Kushite kingdoms. It is about a day's walk from the Blue Nile, noted for its mineral wealth and grains of paradise. I am the youngest from a family of three children. My mother loves me like her alter ego and she often calls me the apple of her sharp and jealous eye. The name of my oldest sister is Tata. My older sister goes by the name Jemina. My father's name is Keta while my mother's name is Lolo.

"One day, my two sisters took my father's felucca and went to fish on Blue Nile. About three hours later, my parents asked me to go and give them a bowl of pounded yam with okra soup, fortified with egunsi. As my boat drew closer to my sisters' felucca, they scowled at me and said, 'Here's Mi Rivera, our sister, the apple of our mother's eye. She is the love-child of our parents.'

"'Let's kill her and tell our parents that she drowned after her boat capsized," said Tata.

"'Let us not kill her but throw her into the water so that deity Olokun can bear her to the shore where one of the herdsmen will find her and force her into a polygamous marriage with hard labor," said Jemina.

"After giving them the delicious food, my sisters cocked a snook at me and then pushed me into the water. As I was drowning, and struggling for my life, a nereid captured me and was taking me to the atoll to the north of the river against the violently-moving currents. But before the nymph swam to its destination: before I lost my sense in hopelessness: before I lost the peace of my soul, deity Olokun, the seer and the commander-in-chief of all the seas, rivers and other watery elements, delivered me in the care of a mighty milk whale that gracefully brought me to the shore. On reaching the shore, I managed to crawl to the ripple mark. Here I lay whimpering, crying and sobbing, tired and disoriented. Before my very eyes were roses of ode—blossoming—giving me the feeling that I am still Mi Rivera, the daughter of a loving mother, whose husband is a man of valor to be found among the peace makers without peace and culture vultures without borders.

"Looking at the Blue Nile, it shimmered as the stars and the moon shone upon it. A feeling of ethereal aura descended upon me. Sooner than expected, I slept off, courtesy of a paradoxical sleep. As I was dreaming, I saw the figure of an ethereal angel touching my forehead, and said to me in a very meek voice, 'You will make heaven because you belong to the children in whom my heavenly father is pleased.'"

"On waking up from my seemingly paradoxical sleep, I saw two nomadic middle-aged men with their dromedaries standing over me, and looking rather ireful. I smiled affectly at them in order to remove the speck of anger on their visages and the agonizing joy of their nomadic life. They reacted to my pusillanimous but affected smiling by nodding. Consequently, they asked me to follow them and I followed them like a shadow—speechlessly. After three hours of trekking, we reached a fortified compound. Here they delivered me like an odalisque into the hands of a nabob, sitting on a deckchair at the entrance of his compound and regaling at a locally made cigar. He had some infectious aristocratic air that was interlaced with pomposity. Standing by his side was a graceful steed. As I entered into the compound, I was introduced to so many beautiful women whom I took to be the nabob's slave-wives or courtesans. His compound was magnificent and his slave-wives were lovely but I was feeling lonely and unhappy, and ill at ease.

"About five minutes later, the nabob walked into the courtyard and lay stark naked on a stretcher-like bed. In no time at all, six of his slave-wives/courtesans started pouring on him gourd-lets of palm-wine, coconut milk, camel milk, goat milk, honey and mock orange, and then began to massage his body from head to toe. The nabob began to snore, rather heavily, carrying on his lips a Mona Lisa type of smile. Soon, the stretcher-like bed broke down but the therapeutic massage continued unabated. The aristocratic snoring continued—unabated. He seemed not to be aware of his surrounding any longer. He seemed to have been dead as soon as the fingers of his slave-wives/courtesans began to eat into his skin. He seemed to have been carried high into the seventh heaven of carnal and punishable enjoyment.

"After staying in the nabob's awesome compound for one moon, I was transfigured into the vault of heaven. Consequently, I found myself among the benevolent angels, living in the Pearly Gates. My duty is to help everybody on the surface of the earth, when least expected. Additionally, I collect and narrate stories, proverbs legends, parables and fairy tales relating to Africana in Africa and Africana in Diaspora. Now I must love you and leave you."

Section C

The Crown Never Dies: If you want to rescue the crown from the fire, you will die but if you want to die in the fire you will be rescued. This is an old adage which is known in every kingdom where there is a head that wears the crown. Everyone knows this adage even if no one seems to pay much attention to it on a daily basis. Everyone also knows that the language of the kingdom is the language of divinity: for as the metonymy is the language of the crown, so also the language of the divinity is the language of the kingdom. Moreover, everyone knows that a story, from an honest mouth, has the spiritual power to heal. This is what I have been using to heal the world, respecting every word as valuable. My name is Mi Rivera.

As early as six in the morning when the chanticleer was doing his third and last ritualistic crowing of the day, there was a cry of fire! fire!! fire!!! in the town. Within a short period of time, the fire had developed into an inferno and from an inferno to a conflagration. Before the very eyes of the people of Inamania, the houses were burning, and were burning down to the ground by every thirty minutes. A scene of horror had descended upon Inamania. People just cried and sobbed and watched the houses being razed to the ground. There was nothing, apparently, they could do. They were simply helpless.

The last two edifices: the king's palace and the shrine were not spared the wrath of this devastating conflagration. They were attacked by the raging fire, ruthlessly and brutally like other houses. As the king's palace was burning, sending into the firmament a cracking noise, a sturdy man with a domed forehead stood up from the wailing crowd in Inamania's square. He bore a king's moustache. He walked like a homunculus and every step he took betrayed him to be either a weight lifter or a wrestler. He looked around the crowd, pulled at his moustache as though he was ready to attack the fire and put it out—to death.

"This must not happen in a town like Inamania where men are men—alive and kicking," said the sturdy man with a domed forehead, dignified by a king's moustache.

"What do you think you can do?" asked the priest, the healer and the head of the community shrine.

"I am going to do one thing which no one has ever done before."

"What is that one thing? Tell us."

"I am going to put out that irrational and merciless fire, now destroying our king's palace."

"Gentleman, hold your peace."

"Why should I hold my peace when a fire like this is destroying our lives in the community?"

"You should hold your peace because it has been revealed through divination in my shrine that a conflagration was coming to destroy everything we own in this community."

"Revealed through divination?" he asked, holding his right ear in the direction of the shrine-priest and flipped it several times as if he had not properly heard what the messenger of the deities had said. "If it is true that you had known before hand that a destructive fire like this is coming to destroy the only palace of our king, why is it that you fail to announce it so that a precaution is taken?"

"I tried all I could as the chief priest of our shrine but the god of fire refused to accept my plea. That's why it was not announced. The god of fire is aggrieved and this wrath of fire is our comeuppance."

"Is it a good thing if the crown should die in the fire before our very eyes?"

"It is not a good thing, hear me out. But what can man do when a god has spoken?"

"No one heard the god speaking anything. Let me ask you: do you think it will please the god to know that the king's crown, the symbol of immortality, power and obeisance, is perished by fire?"

"It will not please the god in any way. But if the god himself sets the fire to the crown, my answer may be the opposite of my last answer."

"The best thing is to ask the god to stop this fire, for no one knows how the god is aggrieved in the first place."

"If the king and his subjects eat the fat ram every now and then and they forget the god of fire as the consumer of what they consume that goes through the fire, the likelihood is that the commander-in-chief of that which burns without fuel may be offended."

"To be consumed by fire, is it the best way to punish the entire community?"
"I may say it's not the best way. But remember that whenever a fire burns, it burns without any regard to the finger that it burns. The only element fire is afraid of is the downpour or water."

"It is ridiculous to hear from the priest that fire has no respect for the king and his subjects but for the water. Is the community not founded by divination?"

"That the community is founded by divination, carries no doubt that swings like a pendulum. But remember that wherever water is found, it's found under the auspices/aegis of Olokun, the commander-in-chief of waters and watery places.

"Additionally, it is correct to say that fire has come to visit its people because after its departure, everything will be made anew."

"This is an unwelcome and utterly preposterous visit. No one needs this type of visitor in our midst—in this community."

"Never you forget that the fire is sent by its master and whenever a master sends his domestic on an errand, the domestic must deliver the message willy-nilly, whether the message is praiseworthy or derisive."

All of a sudden, a feminine and dulcet voice from the wailing crowd, owned by Mi Rivera, head of the Women's Cooperative Society, a woman noted for her transparency, roared, "Let Egopapa and the high priest stop their dialogue. Let them stop their needless balderdash. What are they blathering when the whole community is mourning the death of its belongings?" Her interposition was a surprise to the men's folk but her rejoinder was a welcome relief. Egopapa nodded and straightened her neck like an ever-ready soldier, while the high priest removed the mote that had danced into his left eye.

Consequently, a sheet lightning registered itself from the western to the eastern skies, followed by an ear-tearing thunder that drowned the wailing sounds of the hapless crowd. A dead silence from nowhere descended like a sledgehammer upon the community square. It was a short-lived silence that was quickly overcome by the whining sounds of the hapless crowd.

"What's the thunder doing in all this?" asked Egopapa, the sturdy man with a domed forehead?

"Thunder," said the high priest, moistening his lips, "is the god of fire's first cousin. Thunder and fire both possess the same dyed-in-the-wool attitude: the same temperament and the same philosophy. Like the god of fire, thunder is no respecter of any finger that is struck and bleeding. It strikes with precision, without warning and burns without fuel."

"I must go into action ere it is too late."

"What action are you talking about?" rejoined the priest, pulling his nose as if he wanted to add one inch to its length.

"I must plunge into the raging inferno in search of the king's crown. The king's crown is not supposed to be perished inside a shameless fire without a fight. I am ready to fight. I am fighting myself into the conflagration and bringing out the symbol of the kingdom and authority."

"Take no risk, Egopapa. I pray you not to toy with your precious life."

"Who else will do it if a man like me does not? Who else wants to prove that he is a man born and dandled on his mother's laps and carried on the back of his mother? The legends, songs, poetry, minstrelsies and parables of our community have always encouraged our men to be brave, and to learn how to take the bull by the horns and how to grasp the serpent by the tail."

It is ironically interesting to note that Egopapa who is always at loggerheads with king Dudu is now the person to plunge into the fire, searching for the king's crown at his own peril. Only two months ago, the king called him a traitor and a rebel for going as far as Mothlereth (the midway town between Inamania and Nazareth) to worship in the newly established church in the name of the new-born king. He is the first herdsman of Inamania to dream of seeing the shining star as the Messiah was born in Nazareth. Many times, he had preached with a handful converts, asking king Dudu of Inamania to yield his kingdom to the Messiah as soon as the Messiah is old enough to rule not only Inamania but the entire universe. Rumours also had it that king Dudu had threatened to banish him and other apostates to Mothlereth. Threatened but he could not banish him. The main reason is that Egopapa is a national hero. Twice had he won both the Wrestling and the Weightlifting Championships Belts. And it is not an overstatement to reveal that this hero of a man is more popular than king Dudu.

By now the fire razed to the ground the shrine. But its embers were still dangerously ablaze. The high priest showed no anger or knitted his brows for he knew what was coming.

Slowly but steadily, the conflagration was tearing apart the mud walls of the palace which were built to resist fire of any kind, of any anger. Egopapa was concerned only about the crown. He did not care much about the king's golden sword, golden stool or his waterproof slippers.

"I know from what I am hearing from your mouth, you're not only a valiant man but also a patriotic man who will not harm the crown let alone the head that wears it. I know the blood of your brave ancestors is actively running in your veins. Nevertheless, don't commit a suicide by burning yourself to death. This fire will consume you alive—mercilessly and hopelessly. So take my words and continue to enjoy the lovely company of your wife and children."

"Priest, may I ask you this? How many times does a man die?"

"A man dies but once. The revelation is this: if you want to rescue the crown, you will die inside the fire. But if you want to die inside the fire, you will be rescued. You are faced with two options, so think properly before you leap."

After say, two minutes of deliberation, Egopapa said something unintelligible and then danced around the wailing crowd like someone dancing his farewell dance to the world. Consequently, he shook hands with friends and acquaintances in the crowd. Looking heavenwards like a believer who was imploring God's protection, a smile of bravado emerged from his mouth. At this juncture, the wailing had died down to a mere sobbing and hiccoughing. *Egopapa is leaving the world behind him and gripping the hereafter,* some young men in the crowd whispered. Those who were very concerned wondered why he could not listen to the voice of the priest and give up committing suicide if only for his wife and children who were presently in Mothlereth. All of a sudden, he shrieked out, "I am going to die inside the fire in order to save the symbol of our kingdom. Goodbye brothers and sisters. A man with a beard must do what a man with a beard must do. I am a man with a beard. I am not a woman in the midst of children."

No sooner he said this than he ran toward the inferno and plunged into it. He was consumed as he was invisible from the eyes and a fresh smoke rose over his seemingly dead body.

Minutes later, Lily-mama, his wife and two young children walked into the wailing crowd. Mi Rivera quickly patted her and disclosed to her what her husband had done. On hearing that her husband had taken his life, she fell down and fainted. Her fainting added another measure of sadness to the people whose hearts were already saturated with wailing.

Since Lily-mama joined the crowd, fainted and resuscitated, the wailing had increased two-fold, as if her presence had added a sinew of energy to the anger and bitterness of the wailers. A hunter who had just come back from his hunting expedition said the loud and the sorrowful wailing, louder than tantivy, made him abandon his hunting expedition on discovering that many quarries were taking to their heels. He heard the wailing sound at a distance, more than two miles away from Inamania. He was scared and he had wanted to run into a cave if not because he was a seasoned hunter. His fear is that the town had been invaded by warmongers with their spears, arrows and venomous charms of mass destruction.

Again, the thunder growled. The feathered creatures, afraid, flew in different directions. Some were cooing and some were cawing. And some took to crowing and at the same time released their feces upon the people below—thankfully. Minutes later, the mackerel clouds had turned to grey and from grey to black. Seconds later, it started to rain. Many women, especially, and those with children quickly sought shelter under the trees whose leaves were extraordinarily large. But Lily-mama did not leave. She was among the very few women and a large number of men who ignored the rain and declined to move an inch. A few had umbrellas and those without, used their clothes as their umbrellas.

As the rain turned into a downpour and the sound of the thunder turned into a roar-like crescendo, a human being presumed to be a man appeared in the distance. His body was covered with ashes and he was carrying an aluminum bowl on his head. Despite his ashen body, his appearance was dignified but fearful, very fearful.

The grotesque appearance of this man had now turned the wailers into whisperers and murmurers. An intimidation had subdued the sound of sorrows and angers to the lowest ebb. The more this scarecrow of a man came closer to the square, the more fearful the crowd looked. The funny thing which was not less embarrassing is that the downpour, as heavy as it was, could not scour clean the ash-laden body of this stranger of a man.

About fifty yards to the square, everyone in the square had stood up—fidgeting feverishly, ready to flee. Recognizing that his own people were terrified of him and ready to flee, he screamed at the crest of his lungs, "Men and women of Inamania, don't flee from me. I am your man, Egopapa. I have died in order to save the crown of our kingdom, as prophesied. Please don't run away from me. I am bearing the crown with me."

"Show us the crown if you are bearing it with you," said the crowd in unison.

Dipping his hand inside his aluminium bowl, he brought out the crown and held it above his ashen head. In a split of a second, the concourse rushed to him and carried him shoulder-high and went from one part of the town to another, singing songs and ballads of heroic deeds.

About two hours later, the king and the members of the royal family emerged from their dank bunker, breathing with difficulty and looking half-dead than alive. But they are alive even if difficulty was evidently registered in their inhaling and exhaling. They are alive, thanks to the last-minute burst of fresh air into the bunker through the chink of the bunker that saved their lives. Addressing his subjects in the town's square, the king was so happy and so proud of his subjects knowing full well that there still is a man, a valiant man who could elect to die for the king's crown.

In his laconic words, the king enunciated, "Men and women of Inamania, sons and daughters of Inamania, we may have lost everything through this despicable fire. We may have starved for almost ten hours because of the fire which is no respecter of anybody: we may have been scorched by the sun for hours and beaten recklessly by the downpours, but you are all winners that never quit. You all possess one great attribute and that great attribute, coupled with your endurance is your support for me and the crown, the symbol of authority and divinity. Thank you all.

> "I may bestow on you all the honors of this land, but all your honors put together will never amount (either in a dream or reality) to one tenth of that gentleman who is today known as our rescuer, our champion and our hero, our Egopapa. For his bravery and for his unsurpassable patriotism, I hereby confirm on him the **Lamp of the Bringers of Light in Inamania.** As you know, this is the highest honor under the sun, anywhere on earth. Thank you all. Thank you, Egopapa, for risking your life, for inconveniencing your family, just for the sake of the crown that never dies."

In acknowledging his honor, Egopapa made no bones about the previous conflicts he had with the king. However, preaching the sermon of *forget and forgive*, he thanked the king and said that the existence of the crown is the existence of the king and vice versa.

Facing his wife and children, tears welled up in his eyes. His wife responded with a nod and a dimensional smile that she was lucky and happy to see him alive. Then the jubilation commenced.

On reaching the community burial ground where most of the past heroes are buried, Egopapa earnestly asked his shoulder-high-carriers to put him down. He told them he had something to do and would be back in a few minutes. During his absence, his wife and two children were carried shoulder-high in his stead, and the procession commenced with singing, drumming and dancing. The faces of the wailers which were once lugubrious were now ablaze with hilarity.

After thirty minutes, Egopapa appeared, a much taller man—on stilts—smiling and dancing like the hero he is. Accompanying him were two new and unknown men—also on stilts—and dressed like a scarecrow. On reaching the cenotaph between the ruined palace and the community shrine, he asked the people to die in silence. So everybody was dead in complete silence. Silence buried everything including the wind and the bees and the tsetse-flies that used to sting with abandoned impudence.

About ten minutes later, people started to emerge from the dead silence, one by one. Consequently, the hero harrumphed and said, "I am happy that you allowed me to take my fight to the fire. I am happy that I was able to die in order to rescue our king's only crown of authority and honor. This ashen body of mine will remain mine forever. It is a prize I have to pay for daring to die inside the fire (that burns without fuel) in order to rescue the king's invaluable. I thank the king for bestowing upon me the highest honor under the moon and the sun. Now that the god of fire has accepted our sacrifices by burning down our houses, let's start to rebuild them as soon as possible."

> "My advice to you all," said Modu, the Chief Priest, "is to start to rebuild our houses today. I mean today. If we invite our friends and acquaintances from Mothlereth and Nazareth, we will be able to have brand new roofs over our heads. And this could be possible in one or two days. We cannot allow our king to stay too long in that dank underground palace. The underground air is harmful and it may proceed to hurt his lungs and the lungs of his royal blood. The earlier we start, the better, taken into consideration that he is already an octogenarian."

With the help of the people from Mothlereth and Nazareth, Inamania was rebuilt in three days and three nights, bustling with life again. All the houses are more beautiful than they previously were. With some reason which goes with the culture of the land, the king's palace is the cosiest (the flagship), followed by Egopapa's. The Chief Priest's house is the least beautiful. The builders made it known to one and all in the kingdom that they had taken such an action as his own punishment for hearing the voice of the deity and yet refused to tell his people.

Section D

May a Snake Be Under Your Bedroom Bed: Once-upon a time, there was a good-for-something man in a peculiar village called Dodamomo. This man whose name was Kama was a snake-keeper, (a reptilian) as well as a snake-charmer. His wife, by name Mi Rivera, was also a snake-charmer. They both had over 400 snakes—big and small—poisonous and non-poisonous. Their profession of snake-charming always brought a record number of visitors to the village every calendar month. The people in Dodamomo loved them like a miracle but they hated their reptiles like a bete-noir.

The population of Dodamomo was approximately 350. The majority of them were farmers and palm wine tapsters. A small number of the men were hunters who could shoot daddy-long-legs in their erratic flights.

Dodamomo had one big menace. That menace was tearing apart the village and reducing its population rather embarrassingly. The menace that was tearing the villagers apart was the large presence of rats and mice in all the houses in the village, except one. The funny thing about these elfin nuisances was that they were found only in the night after the chicks had gone to roost and the silence of the night had fallen upon the village. Due to the fact that the menace was out of control, almost all the villagers resorted to sleeping outside on the backyards and front-yards of their houses.

One steaming evening, Kama decided to have a meeting with all the villagers, consequent upon the problem they were going through. The villagers decided to hold the meeting in the courtyard of Bobo, the Chief of Dodamomo. After Chief Bobo had opened the meeting by referring to the villagers as the most hard-working people in all the villages and towns below the Equator, he also referred to the menace that was being caused by the presence of the rats and mice in Dodamomo.

Standing up like a man celebrating his fortieth birthday, Kama said, "Chief Bobo, I call this meeting today because I know something has been troubling our people for so long in this village. And that troubling thing is the presence of rats and mice. I make no bones about my preparedness to solve this perennial menace."

"How would you solve the menace when you yourself keep four hundred dreadful snakes under your bedroom bed?" said Kike, a cocoa farmer who spoke like a memsahib and walked like a squaw.

"This is why this meeting is important. I may have a lot of snakes under my bedroom bed but my house is devoid of the menacing rats and mice," said the snake-keeper-and-charmer.

"You don't have rats and mice in your house?" asked Kike at the top of her voice.

"Yes, I don't have rats and mice in my house," answered Kama in a voice, stronger and much more assertive than the previous one.

At this juncture, more than half the population of the women in the meeting stood up, and then stared at the snake-keeper as a hoodwinker and as a liar who should not be in the presence of the people whose honesty is their most salient characteristics.

"Brother Kama, are you telling us a cock-and-bull story, or what?" asked Kike again, pouting and adjusting her head-dress.

"This is not a cork and bull story," said Mi Rivera, Kama's wife who sat unnoticed in the gathering. "My husband is an honorable gentleman. He means what he has said and he has said what he means. That we have a remedy for your perennial problem is incontrovertible."

"How do you want me and the entire people of Dodamomo to believe that your house is the only household in the village without rats and mice?" asked Kike, facing Kama, waiting for an answer.

"As my wife had pointed out, that we can solve your perennial problem is indisputable. Seeing is believing. Trying will convince one and all."

"You want us to come to your house and be attacked by your venomous reptiles, including the cockatrice? Is that not what Brother Kama and his wife are trying to say?" said Kike in a smile blended with sarcasm.

"No. No. That is not what my husband and I are trying to say," answered Mi Rivera in a mellifluous voice. "As I said earlier, my husband, Kama is an honorable gentleman. He is not a noble savage. We love Dodamomo and we think Dodamomo loves us too. And we are here because of that love and wisdom which can share together in the name of peace."

At this juncture, there was a strong wind, forcing the women to hold on to their multicolored gorgeous head-dresses. The same strong wind forced the flowering plants in the courtyard to pay an obeisance to the elemental fury of the wind.

Immediately after the wild wind reduced its elemental fury and started behaving normal, Chief Bobo chortled and said, "Enough of this question and answer situation. The people of Dodamomo are hard-working people. I believe in their philosophy of hardworking. I believe love will not abide with us or sit in our sitting-rooms until it becomes an open-air sesame of happiness. Let's take Kama for his words and let's allow him to put an end to our bugaboo once and for all." He gave three royal nods and he harrumphed in a jumping voice like an epicurean who had just relished a delicious meal of a boomslang.

"The solution to the menace is simple," said Kama nodding and thanking Chief Bobo. "What I need to do is to bring a snake to each house and leave it for three nights. After three nights the rats and snakes will disappear because the snakes must have eaten them up. Snakes are no friends of rats or mice. This is how my house is devoid of them." He pulled out of his pocket his gangrened left hand which was attacked some years back by an amphisbaena, one of his surprisingly friendly reptiles.

As early as seven o'clock that evening, Kama and his wife, Mi Rivera were going from house to house leaving a snake under the bedroom bed of each household. Seven days later, the villagers trooped out rejoicing and thanking Kama and his wife, Mi Rivera, for putting an end to their problem. The reptiles had eaten up the rats and mice in all the households. Since then snakes have become the sacred symbols of Dodamomo, loved by every one in the village, which many tourists and visitors now call Snake Village. And the raillery on the lips of the people is, "May a Snake Be Under Your Bedroom Bed."

Surprisingly, Chief Bobo did not give Kama anything that could be regarded as a guerdon for what he had done. But he asked the snake charmer and his wife to always dine with him during the first phase of the moon.

Another thing which makes Dodamomo a peculiar village among other villages, south of the Equator is that it has no burial ground. That the village is clean and healthy can not be disputed. That it is a village of friendly people is as true as Kama and his snakes. But no one knows where its dead are buried. Many of the villagers surrounding it, including the tourists go to the extent of believing that the people of Dodamomo are immortals who had eaten the forbidden Elysian amaranth of immortality, having traced their undocumented genes to the biblical Methuselah. This seems to be a secret no one wants to talk about—day or night, or make an egregious blunder about. Not even Chief Bobo wants to make a slip of the tongue about it. It is a *village gaff* which nobody wants to blow. Because of this secret in the air, wafting over the village, most of the tourists refer to it as a place of the living and dead.

Compounded with this nonexistence of a people's burial ground is the news of an ancestral marketplace, where only the abiku children could buy and sell. And in the centre of this marketplace is a terracotta museum where a sick person goes in from the backyard door and comes out from the front-door, hale and hearty! Many foreigners do not believe there is a healing power inside a museum. They pooh-pooh it as a relic of superstition. The only things they believe—seeing and touching—are the snakes and the snakes' owner.

Section E

The Road-Sweeper and the Benedict: It was the New Year-Eve of 1989. My brother Kole, a Benedict, still relishing the success of his seven days old marriage to a mannequin, and I were mooning away some early afternoon hours, together with Mi Rivera, the mannequin. The fog was still a tarpaulin—a thin layer, below the firmament by the time we reached the center of Lagos, now promising itself the status of becoming a mega city. The prepossessing commercial metropolis was enchanting and pulsating as ever. We could still feel the fog's filmy veils on our visages like a filmy mosquito-net, serving as the sole refuge whenever one is waylaid and chased by an army of blood-sucking mosquitoes.

Most of the streets and boulevards around the center of the city were festively decorated. This is the only time of the year when the Christians, Muslims and traditional believers embrace one hope, the hope of seeing a better New Year full of harmony, happiness and prosperity.

All of a sudden, on crossing a bridge over a brook whose water made a drumming sound, Kole said we should enter a nearby Catholic Church and pray. So we entered and prayed. Leaving the Catholic Church, we entered an Evangelical Church and prayed. Leaving the Evangelical Church, we broke into the compound of a mosque and prayed. It nearly irritated me that we had to worship from one *"holy place"* to another. However I declined to question the nimble mind of this Benedict. I know, traditionally, that it is neither my moral nor my spiritual obligation to question my elder, for fear of insulting his seniority and wounding his jealously guided pride. Also, I feared of receiving a sideswipe that could send me reeling on the ground.

On coming out of the mosque's compound, from the rear, we saw a road sweeper, complaining and swearing. "They don't work and yet they are rich. I swear, I will break their necks one day, when least expected. Where do you pluck your money from?" pointing to the three of us in general and to Mi Rivera, the mannequin, in particular.

"I will show you," replied Mi Rivera in a mellifluous, lady-like voice.

"Yes, I know, from the politicians," he said, knitting his brows. Why are you women very rich in this country? You have everything except the sun and the moon. What next? One day will be one day: I will pour a chilly water inside your bowl of gari and turn upside down your calabash of kola nuts. Then I will own that magic tree that produces your nairas, your pounds and dollars." He moved closer, raised his broom high in the sky as though he wanted to wedge into two Mi Rivera's head. The mannequin staggered backwards—frighteningly—in her hobble skirt. The hobbledehoy laughed jeeringly and ghoulishly.

Holding Mi Rivera in one hand, Kole roared, "If you dare strike her, you will regret it till the end of time. I will pummel you until kobo goes into your mouth and finds its passage through your anus. In other words, I will pummel you so much that a Christmas sense will go into your head, making it impossible for your kind to recognize you in the New Year."

"Who are you by the way?"

"I am Kole, alias Kookaburra, if you don't know me. You had better do your work or else go home and rest your sozzled head."

"I am not sozzled, half-cast, half-native, half-overseas. I know your story, Mr. Colored."
"Who is colored? Who is Mr. Colored?" asked my brother with an angry roar in his sweet bridegroom-like voice. He moved some steps towards him as if he wanted to nail his head with a punch. I held him back, and prayed him to leave the hobbledehoy with his drunkenness so that we could enjoy ourselves now that the fog had almost receded.

"Will you shut up your mouth, rent boy? Or do you want me to give you a clout that will be your everlasting memento?" He pouted and cocked a snook at me.

Puckering up my lips and looking at him disrespectfully, I told him that six hands are better than two. I felt like punching his lips so that he could feel the strength of my teenage hands. No I won't do that. Seven years ago, at the age of eight, I punched in my school, removing a tooth from the mouth of my age-group classmate. My father spanked me, pulled my ear to the point of tearing it, and sternly warned me not to punch anyone even if the *punched* was the trouble-maker. Up till today, the *punched* has a gap (a miniature window) in the upper set of his teeth. Teasingly, my father said to me that in years to come, my punches could be likened to Jay-Jay's, the national boxer whose one punch always knocked down and knocked out his opponents. But now at fifteen, and if ever I become a boxer in the future, I told my father that I would prefer to box like Morila-Bush who talks like a royal minstrel, glides like an eagle and stings like a bumble bee.

Suddenly, a man in red, about thirty dry seasons like our attacker, appeared from nowhere and said, "Hey man, you're here to work and if you can't work, go to your wonted home—behind bars."

"You are also one of the cormorants in this country. You chop, chop and chop, and forget other people are living," riposted the road sweeper.

Thanking the man in red, we walked away. I discovered that the road sweeper's left ear carried a big hole, quite bigger than what could permit for an ear-ring, not even a Masai culture vulture would ever allow that for an ear decoration. Whether one had pierced his ear with a knife, an assegai or a gun during a robbery, my feeling was that he was a cretin, a weirdo perhaps, of questionable character. My second opinion was that he must have been a street Arab ere he was rescued.

After five hours of mooning away the afternoon, we came back to my brother's residence. Each one of us heaved a sigh of relief, thanking Olodumare for answering our prayers, the reason why our encounter with a drunken road sweeper had not been bloody.

On asking my brother if he could have given the attacker a glancing blow if the latter had hit Mi Rivera, my brother said "yes" and he would then call the police to carry away the nuisance for being a killjoy.

As each one of us was sipping a glass of mango juice, I noticed that my brother looked worried. He pouted like a pout and continued to hiss like a mamba, the way he used to do whenever he was tortured by shilly-shally. Robbing his cheeks affectionately, his mannequin wife asked if there was anything he would like to drink on top of the mango juice. Scratching his left ear, he asked for a cup of melon juice which was given to him in less than two minutes. After he had emptied the content in a gulp, he began to shake his head left and right. Consequently, he made it known to his pusillanimous wife that to be called a *"colored person"* did not only sadden him but also dehumanize him. Of all the misnomers, of all the suffixes, prefixes and derogatory remarks associated with miscegenation and its offspring, the only one he abhorred most is to be called a *"colored man."*

Still feeling beaten and ill at ease, Mi Rivera decided to tell her husband a story about a lovely woman whose stories did not only have the spiritual power to entertain and heal, but also to put a troubled mind at ease. After listening to the story, my brother's sadness was instantly replaced by felicity. We laughed and laughed—joyously and triumphantly. We did not stop laughing until a neighbor came to share with us a portion of our happiness. The only thing that saved the attacker, the dirty-tongued road sweeper was a feeling of unconditional love, the kernel of a progressive community, inherent in gentlemanliness, often (but not always) found in the republic of happiness.

Section F

Happiness Comes Home—the Sanctities of My Home: I promise the world from the outset that I will be carrying my stories from the back of beyond to all the nooks and crannies of the world without wearing my heart upon my sleeve. And this, I have done through the grace of Olodumare. The world has known my stories. The world has grown healthier and happier through the sanctified stories. I am so happy that I do not violate the sanctity of my oath.

Now I am home—back to where I belong. Through thick and thin, I have been able to take care of the world. Now the time has come to take care of my hometown, Stumble and Rise. You will giggle that it is a funny name but it is my home—my treasure-house, and home is always home for every thoroughbred.

This is an interlude. I will start my career again as a troubadour and raconteur. For the meantime, let me regale with my grains of paradise in my pied-a-terre and lean back with relief and platitudinous pleasure and felicity.

Section G

The Garden of Love: "Let every index finger point to the Garden of Love." This is the news on the lips of Mi Rivera, the town-crier as she went from town to town and from village to village, telling one and all that there is one place where one could be blessed with either ephemeral or permanent love. After one week of disseminating the news, a concourse of people filed out on their way to the Garden of Love. The scene was like a pilgrimage to the holy land. Everyone was talking about a permanent love. Only a few people did not bother whether their love is permanent or ephemeral. So the concourse was partitioned into two files. The frontal file belonged to the anthophilous men and women yearning for a permanent love, while the file following it belonged to the men and women looking for an ephemeral love.

On reaching the Garden of Love, Mi Rivera brought the two files of people to a piazza where goddess Ife sat resplendently on a stone throne of honor. The time was around 4 in the early evening. In Ife's left hand was an apple. In her right hand was a bunch of red berries. After a long silence that was broken by a sylph's love song: a song, so dulcet that everyone in the piazza was crying tearfully and asking for more, goddess Ife gave Mi Rivera the bunch of the red berries and the svelte Mi Rivera distributed the pieces among the people who had chosen to be serious and had fallen head over heels in love with the permanent love. While giving the food to them, she told them that it was their hors d'oeuvres.

Consequently, the epitome of love cut the apple into tiny pieces and gave them to Mi Rivera and the story-collector distributed the pieces (which she referred to as their hors d'oeuvres) among those who had chosen the path of ephemeral love. Adjusting her headgear and patting Mi Rivera on the back, she said, "I am so delighted to see all of you in the Garden of Love today. This is the soil, otherwise called the Garden or House where love was born, as you all know. Olodumare is love and to be part of Olodumare's love, you must learn how to love yourselves in order to love others. That may sound like magic but I tell you there is no magic wand in the world of lovers. And I have none to give you for my love is natural, permanent and unconditional like the love of nature," she laughed winsomely and continued. "If you are going to be healthy, responsible and be an epitome of love to those coming after you, you need a permanent, unconditional and natural love."

"Those who have come here, believing in permanent love, have taken a bold step. It remains just two steps to realize that love and the act of loving is inevitable in this day and age. You need two steps more. And I think you can do this with the creative love-energy you are now receiving from me. I want you to be part of the Bringers of Light."

"Those who are here with ephemeral love, have a lot of work to do. You are at the bottom of the ladder. You are at the bottom of the act of loving. The breeze fanning my tongue and my ears nearly knocked me down as the kola-nut in my mouth nearly made me retch on hearing that you are ephemeral lovers. Ephemeral love cannot carry you anywhere. It burns temporarily and dies temporarily—with nothing to write home about it. So what you need to do is to start to love yourselves, believing that Olodumare loves you so much that he gives you a place called the House/Garden of Love. On getting home, my daughter, Mi Rivera will inoculate your bodies, hearts, souls and minds will stories that will help you acquire the three ingredients of love I am talking about. I want you to become the Bringers of Light. Good evening. I recommend Divinity-Philosopher Olorun/Olodumare to be your guide and guardian. May the creative love-energies from the Bringers of Light give you the best under the vault of heaven."

Section H

Calming a Violent Wife: The following gloaming, when the chicks had retired to their roosts, Mi Rivera started moving from house-hold to house-hold telling love stories and the act of loving. The first family she met was tumultuous and it appeared things were getting out of hands for the husband. So what Mi Rivera did was to ask the family man to tell her what he was going through before curing the problem with the power of love. Here is the man's anecdote.

> "Before I got married, there were days I looked for sunny days without the sun. There were days I looked for water without rainfall. There were days I yearned for friendship without friends. Helplessness nearly mocked me as I stood between loneliness and shilly-shally. In most cases, I was pent up with the sound of silence."

"Lo and behold, my stories have beguiled children from all the four corners of the world. They are being beguiled so much that many of them forgot to wake up for their breakfast of pap and akara. My stories had kept the Elders singing the chants and reciting the axioms of their philosophies as well as their epigrams and ditties into the wee hours. Many times, I found happiness twinkle in my eyes."

"One day I went to the shrine where the priest was reported to have heard the voice of the Prime Creator whenever he went there to pray alone. There was a soothing zephyr stealing through the chinks and knot-holes of the shrine. Although I did not know its source, however, as it caressed my body from head to toe, it guaranteed an assurance of healing me physically and spiritually.

No sooner I knelt down like a grasshopper than I heard the voice of Olodumare saying, 'Be patient with your wife. Patience is a virtue. All you need to do is to pray."

"My name is Oja, a corruption of Ojare. For many years people know me as Ojare until I disclosed myself to Mi Rivera and the rest of the world that I am not Ojare—a tortoise but Oja, a human being of flesh and blood. I am no skeleton dragged out of the shadows to dance a bone-dance in the middle of the leading strings. Those who do not believe my humanness are not attacking me but my shadow."

"The name of my wife is Mama Yam. She is called Mama Yam because she knows how to prepare yam, otherwise known as the pounded yam. A lot of people around the world have tasted her pounded yam. Many have fallen in love with the pounded yam so much that the food has become their beloved breakfasts. A few who were not wary enough while eating the delicacy had bitten their tongues and lips to bleeding. Must I offer an apology for those who had accidents for relishing my wife's delicious meal? I can do this out of decency and courtesy."

"Five years into our marriage, I began to notice that Mama Yam was becoming an aggressive woman. Her words which were hitherto sweet and romantic were becoming sour, snappy and cloudy. There were days when she would be afraid of the roars of the lion. There were days when she would be afraid of the roars of the thunder. There were nights when she would be moping because there was no moon on the sky. There were some evenings when she would be moping because the sun was setting without its gorgeousness. Gosh, I was concerned about her disorganized or disintegrated personality. Consequently, I started to pray, first by myself and later I adjured her to join me. She did. We prayed two times in a day—while going to bed and while waking up in the morning.

"Two months later, her aggression dissipated. Her anger had been mollified! We were both flushed with joy. We thanked Olodumare for answering our prayers. Weeks later, I noticed that Mama Yam had developed another problem which was nothing but a slap- stick, a kind of playful violence. Let me explain what is meant by a playful violence or fun arising from violence. A slap-stick is when a violent person indulges in violence by not knowing that he/she is violent. For example: If a person playfully and smilingly hits you with a piece of stick: you feel the pain: you complain and ask him/her to stop hitting you but instead of stopping, he/she is still doing the same thing, playfully and smilingly/laughingly, this is a slap-stick—a playful violence. This occurs very often during plays among friends and acquaintances—in twos or more—and between husbands and wives.

"Apart from fasting and praying, what I used to do to mollify/calm her and box her violence was to give her a therapeutic massage. This, among other things included a music therapy—playing of sekere, banjo, didgeridoo and talking drum. Sometimes it would last for forty-five minutes and sometimes when I could hardly control my manhood, it would last for twenty-five minutes and some invisible seconds. After the massage, she would sleep like a baby and snore like a queen. This message is ninety percent effective, for other families who were lucky to receive it from me attested to it. (I must confess that I took to my heels one day when for some reason, her violence became uncontrollable. I did not come back until the wee hours).

"Today, there is neither a trace of violence nor a crawl of aggression in her blood stream. She is fine and she knows that she is doing fine. For my success and for the source of that success, I must always point to the Prime Creator, and reverence him and thank him for showing to me how to cure his creature without swallowing a tablet."

As soon as Ojare finished his anecdote, Mi Rivera gave him a millipede-like dibble as a symbol of patience. Then she began to tell both of them how her stories had cured a king with a running nose. The running of the nose was so bad, so unusual and so embarrassing that the king neither eat nor kiss his queen for a score and five days.

That day alone, Mi Rivera turned the hearts of many ephemeral lovers into the hearts of the permanent lovers. There were tears of joy and songs in the air before the storyteller vanished into a beautiful and sanctified dale for her much-needed rest-cure, and sound sleep which invariably presupposes a mind at rest.

Section I

Pent Up by the Sound of Bovine Stupidity: Kai was a well-known palm-wine tapster in Adire. Adire is a small town built on the top of a hill overlooking a lake. In the middle of this lake is a palm which has grown into maturity whose sap is being sought after.

Kai, now in his fifties, let the people in Adire know that the palm is the only palm in Adire whose milky sap has not gone down the gorges of the people of Adire. As the most seasoned tapster, he must be the only one to climb the palm to the top and tap its succulent milky sap. He must do this before he drinks the cup of death.

Many, many years ago, say about two thousand years ago, say about the time the Son of man was born, the only means to reach the palm is a large mudfish on whose back the tapster would stand. But after the industrial revolution, the large mudfish has miraculously vanished, leaving the young and old tapsters surprised and searching for a clue that's never found till today. But the tapsters and some of the people of Adire believe the large mudfish must have left for a deeper body of water as much of the lake is being reclaimed for the building of factories, demanded by industrialization.

One hot morning after the wisps of the clouds had disappeared from the surface of the sky, Kai sat down on a bamboo stool in the front of his hut, supporting his cheeks with his palms, pondering over what to do to tap the palm. His face bore wrinkles of sadness.

No sooner he sat down than Mi Rivera appeared to him. The story collector asked him why he was melancholic. He told Mi Rivera that he was hearing a sound from the palm asking him to come and tap its milky sap. Mi Rivera cachinnated and told him that it was his alter ego that had been pent up by the sound of stupidity. She lets him know that what affects his alter ego affects him and vice versa.

The following day, he found a boat when least expected on the lake and rowed it to where the palm was. He tapped the sap and brought it to the people of Adire to relish. He too, regaled on the milky sap. He had tasted the best milk when he was a baby, now an Elder, he will taste and drink the best milky sap before he leaves and joins the rank and file of his ancestors. The Adire people were happy that he was able to make his dream come true. There was a short-lived celebration and needless to say that he was exceedingly flushed with joy. After this, he asked the Prime Creator to let him pay his debt to nature. The Prime Creator refused to let him die. Instead, the Author of Life and Death gave him twenty-five more years to spend on the surface of the earth.

Section J

The Changeling from the Shantytown: She came not one time, not two times but three times. Each time she appears, she will bedeck her hair-do with a rainbow-colored chiffon made of sisal. Mi Rivera was afraid, predicating a notion that she was an abiku child who invariably disguised herself like a changeling. Kokodia is the only town in the Saharan Oasis without an abiku child being born or the rumor that one will mistakenly be born one day in the future.

Due to the fact that no one knows her name except that she is a woman dressed like a woman, and walking like a woman, people including Mi Rivera call her a "Changeling from the Shanty-town." And because there are many shantytowns in the country, Mi Rivera started going from shanty-town to shanty-town searching for a woman with a rainbow-colored chiffon made of sisal. While many shanty-dwellers believed that the rainbow-colored chiffon was a run-of-the-mill, Mi Rivera had conceived a notion that anything that looks like a rainbow must be a paragon of beauty.

Section K

I Saw a Future Before Me: "To one and all, I must confess this. I can no longer hold it beneath my tongue or swallow it like a fondant," said Mi Rivera as she crossed a precarious bridge made of catgut. For some unexplained reason, the bridge is built upon a treasure-trove. The shine of the moon was like the shine of the sun on a cloudless sky. Everywhere was aglow with light, and the four-legged creatures aglow with pleasure—whisking their tails continuously. Everywhere and indeed everything was bright, so bright that one could read the veins of the leaves on the surrounding trees. The salubrious weather was enough to change the world into a temporary paradise.

On crossing the bridge, Mi Rivera said she could tell how the future would be in the next twenty years from now. Thus "I saw the future before me" becomes the talk of the town. This is part of her serendipitous destiny. Weeks later, Mi Rivera was promoted a diviner, a soothsayer and a prophetess in Lucky-land which only a story-collector could tell its future.

There is no one promoted a diviner in Lucky-land without a ritual celebration. So seven days after Mi Rivera was promoted a diviner, the town-crier padded to all the towns and villages in the lower territory of the Atlantic, inviting the people to Mi Rivera's inauguration.

During the inauguration, Chief Zoro of Lucky-land thanked Mi Rivera for her magnanimous contribution to the cultural landscape of Lucky-land in particular and for injecting spiritual awakening and enlightenment into the social ramifications of all the towns and villages in the lower territory of the Atlantic, in general.

Mi Rivera was very happy beyond bounds. In her acceptance speech, she said, "Every creature is a miracle. As I am a miracle the way I was born and the way I am acting, so also you are a miracle the way you were born and the way you are acting." She closed her mouth with the sound of *chi* as though she was pronouncing the twenty-second letter of the Greek alphabet.

Section L

Justice Prevails: Once upon a time, there were two kingdoms in what is today known as Africa. These two kingdoms are Abiye and Abiku. The Abiku Kingdom which was very powerful was to be found north of the Equator, while the Abiye Kingdom was to be found south of the Equator. The Abiku Kingdom had a strong and fearful army of 10,000 able-bodied men and animals, trained to fight like the gladiators.

Due to its military might, many people loved to go and stay in Abiku Kingdom. They would mill to the kingdom in tens and twenties. The Abiku Kingdom had become the breadbasket. The Abiku Kingdom was a place to make money, big money within a short period of time. But it was not a place to live and enjoy the peace of mind. The king of Abiku Kingdom who was popularly known as King Zigzag, proud and selfish, pegged out their claim to many lands belonging to the Abiye Kingdom, under king Abimola. King Abimola complained without a change of heart from King Zigzag. Thus, he suffered in silence.

For some reason, which could only be explicated by changelings, people started to mill to Abiye Kingdom. Many of them believed that wealth without peace of mind is like a sleep without a sweet dream. King Zigzag was jealous because of this. He blamed King Abimola and threatened to punish him until he could no longer enjoy his favorite pepper soup, enriched with sweet potatoes and goat meat. But King Abimola was not afraid of his threats. He made it known to King Zigzag that he had no control over the people milling to his kingdom.

Months later, King Zigzag invaded Abiye Kingdom with weapons of mass destruction. Abiye Kingdom had only light weapons such as knives, catapults, cutlasses, sledge hammers, arrows and assegais. The invasion lasted only three hours. But to the surprise of the citizens of both North and South Equator, the Abiye Kingdom, beat back the invaders. Many of them, as well as their weapons of mass destruction were captured. From that day, King Zigzag commenced to pay King Abimola a yearly fine of one hundred goats, sheep, cows, camels, horses, donkeys and buffaloes. From that period, predicated with respect, King Zigzag had learned by heart the sayings: *"Let the sleeping dog lie,"* and *"Justice will always prevail, sooner or later."*

A few weeks later, Mi Rivera, the raconteur and the story-collector, met with King Abimola. She was happy on learning that *"a small hand"* had defeated *"a big hand."*

Section M

Don't Be Judgmental: There was a kind-hearted peg-leg in the town of Wisdom, about fifty miles from Ile-Ife. Every morning, as early as the third cockcrow, the peg-leg would go around Wisdom distributing kola-nuts to every family in the town. This man's name is Jina Wada. It was a labor of love, very hard to do without some ingredients of unconditional love. Because his love for his people was unconditional, Jina Wada never felt tired of doing what he loved to do. And the people of Wisdom never felt tired of praying that he would never die in harness.

One day, hardly had he covered a distance of three miles when he miss-stepped and fell headlong inside a relatively dry pond, surrounded by low-growing groves of horseradishes, in the middle of which was a gnamma. The pond which had a little amount of water inside it, was infested by cockroaches.

Two hours had elapsed since he had been waiting for help without one. All of a sudden, a preacher-man carrying a book of hours with letter C on his gown was passing by. He begged him in the name of Olodumare to pull him out of the cockroach-infested pond. The preacher-man was ready to help him. For some reason, the preacher-man asked him if he belonged to letter C, the peg-leg smiled and said that he belonged to the Divinatory Book of Enlightenment.

"Are you ready to be converted?"

"Why should I be converted?"

"If you are converted, your soul will go directly to Olodumare, for my faith is the seed and cotyledon of everlasting life."

"I am not prepared to be converted, and become an apostate or neophyte, for the Divinatory Book of Enlightenment can lead me to the everlasting salvation. All I pray you to do is to pull me out of this pond of death."

"Sorry man, if you cannot change your belief, let me go on preaching. I have a job to do."

Ten minutes after the preacher man left, came another preacher man, carrying a book of minutes and wearing a gown with letter I in its front. As the peg-leg saw him in a distance, he began to cry for compassion. "Have compassion on me, preacher-man and help me out of my predicament," begged the peg-leg with tears rolling down his cheeks.

The preacher-man was overpowered by pity and he was prepared to help the unfortunate man by all means. For some reason which could only be explained by the Providence, the preacher-man asked the man if he belonged to letter I. The peg-leg said he belonged to the Divinatory Book of Enlightenment.

"The Divinatory Book of Enlightenment is a thing of the distant past. It is a pet aversion as it is a run of the mill," said the preacher-man, smiling rather derisively.
"The Divinatory Book of Enlightenment is what my grandfather passed unto my father and my father has passed it unto me. To renounce or pooh-pooh it will be like disrespecting the culture of our land."

"It does not cost you anything to become a new man who will be qualified to visit the Holy Land."

"Thank you for your generous offer. I prefer to die in this Holy Land of my cultural pride where my ancestors have lived to be kings and queens for hundreds of years. This land is holy enough, preacher and I beg you to quickly help me, for the cockroaches inside this pond are menacing my life."

"Sorry man, keep your Divinatory Book of Enlightenment and let me keep mine. My duty is to preach, convert and help the blind man like you. Goodbye."

Two hours after the preacher's departure, and a few minutes before the chicks began to hurry and scurry to their roosts, Jina Wada saw Mi Rivera with her two assistants on their way to attend Palm-wine Festival in a nearby village, called Ado. Jina Wada was elated. He rubbed his hands in the air and prayed for favor from Almighty

Creator. "May these women have compassion on me, O Olorun," he said in a submissive voice shaken with fear, anger and doubt.

"Mi Rivera, please get me out of this hole before I pay my debt to nature."

"Goodness' me, Jina Wada, what are you doing inside a pond at this time of the day."

"I slipped and fell inside it."

"How long is this?"

"Since the last crow, I can't recollect precisely."

"And since then, no passerby saw you?"

"I did not clap my eyes on any one but some people apparently saw me."

Mi Rivera harrumphed and put her index finger across her luscious lips as though there was a classified snippet of information to be kept. But inside her heart of hearts, she knew Jina Wada saw some people who must have refused to help him out of the pond of cockroaches. As an experienced teller and collector of stories, she knows there is something hidden inside, "I saw no one but some people apparently saw me."

Without wasting time, she pulled out the unlucky peg-leg with the help of her assistants. On getting out of the pond, he was exceedingly happy, even if he discovered that all his toes had been chilblained. He hugged and kissed each one of them with a sound louder than the sound of thank you.

The incident became the sad news in the town of Wisdom and its surrounding villages and Mi Rivera, in her characteristic show of latitudinarianism, peace, love and unity promised all the practitioners of the native faith as well as the practitioners of the imported faiths that she would find out who the preachers were before she would proceed to put a pox on them.

Section N

The Mendicant That Dined With the President: She had been a mendicant since she was thirty-one years old: the very age she lost her right hand in a terrible fire accident that killed her husband. Every night she would be found at the entrance leading to the Eko Atlantic City, the city of skyscrapers and wave-makers, asking for alms. This is the second stage of her profession.

Now let's go back to the first stage of her profession. A few months after she lost her right hand, she was trained to make scarves—knitting four to five scarves in a calendar month. She made some good money, enough to pay her rents. But when least expected, she became restless due to frequent outages in her Portakabin, constructed for her by Corolla Levi, one of the one hundred and fifty rabbis living in Eko Atlantic City. (These rabbis are some of the fine non-Nigerians who are cultivating the flowering vitality of the heterogeneity which the mega city administrators have sworn to promote, with might and main, to the acme of meaningfulness.) She could no longer wake up in the night to do her work. She started to lose her customers and money. As helplessness was buffeting her, she decided to become a professional beggar, choosing Eko Atlantic City, knowing full well that it is the quaintest part of the mega city where money is on the lips of every resident.

In 2010, as early as the last cockcrow, Kara woke up, dressed like a Nollywood star and boarded the express train from Lagos to Abuja. That was the first time she would ever go to Abuja. Stumbling and falling, she remembers that for any creation to have a meaningful existence, it must undergo some hardship. Unable to find her way so easily, she slept inside a jalopy outside the walled city, close to a popular shantytown, surrounded by stunted breadfruits, the sole place allotted to squatters, mendicants and peddlers in the Federal Capital Territory.

Waking up the following day with a yawn and a stretch and bidding the roof over her head a cathartic farewell, a therapeutic rainfall greeted her and she began to sing the following lilt:

Hello Tai-ma
Hello Tai-pa
E ba mi ki mama mi (Say me well to my mama)
E ba mi ki baba mi (Say me well to my papa)
Tell both that starvation

Nay loneliness has put me
Out of joint, out of kilter.

Sooner than expected, she saw a cabman and flagged him down. On telling the taxi-man that she was attending the birthday party in honor of the first political citizen of the country, the cabman regarded her with dignity and it didn't take him much time to resolve to carry her to her destination, free of charge.

"Madam, may I ask you a question?"

"I no be madam o, I be Lady."

The taxi-driver paused in meditation and then said benignly, "Lady, your retort makes me think of the king of Afro Beat."

"I know the musical icon, the daring king of Afro Beat, you have in your thought. He was the maestro who said that girls and women in their youthful exuberance preferred to be called ladies in lieu of madams or Missis."

Both the passenger and the taxi driver laughed heartily as though they had known each other for years. This kind of friendly atmosphere and exchange of humors are a commonplace among the Abuja public drivers in which the taxi drivers are said to be the best statistically.

Still feeling good, Kara said, "Now that you know me as a lady and not madam, go a head with your question."

"Is there any cultural value in names?"

"Yes, of course. Without a cultural value in a name, you can easily be called Mr. Nobody or Mr. Lagbaja.

"Must a name carry a meaning?"

"Yes. Otherwise you will be unpatriotic to your cultural root and values. Culturally, a name is like a fruit that comes out of a flowering plant/tree of a family with a root."

"Must our kith and kin in Diaspora carry names depicting their past and present cultural values?"

"They can carry either of the two as long as there are meanings attached to them, for every creature has a name by which Olorun calls it."

The taxi-man did not notice anything but he knew that his passenger's index finger is longer than her ring-finger, the cruelty of the fire that burns without regard to anybody, young or old, rich or poor.

About fifty yards before she reached the gate, she got off the taxi gratefully and thankfully, praying the road not be the cabman's driver. Then she started to walk toward the cozy palace of the President. The gate, a table-legged structure, was a cynosure for her. As she was feeding her eyes on the table-legged gate, she discovered three signboards. The one to her left reads, "Any lore that widens people's horizons and presents food for thought is the beginning of philosophy." To her right, the signboard reads, "An imaginary literature is the foundation of pleasure." Over the arched gate, the signboard reads, "A sound sleep presupposes a mind at rest." She followed the overhead signboard because she knew pretty well that her mind is at rest after the deep sleep she had enjoyed inside the jalopy.

The unusual tunnel to the navel of the party is treacherous. Thus she was being accompanied by two points-men, acting like sworn security men, and grinning like hodmen. About seventy yards to the navel of the party, she heard a sweet voice. Inside that dulcet voice was a sweet sound that was sweet enough to smell, to taste, to touch, to feel and to hear. Although she thought she was under the spell of hallucination, she knew from the bottom of her heart that her five senses would be experiencing the most palatable meal of her life.

Eventually, she reached the Presidential Palace at Aso Rock, the fountainhead of the party where the President was celebrating his sixtieth Birthday. Smiling winsomely to everyone like a jackpot-hitter and curtsying like a pusillanimous gentlewoman, she dignified herself as one of the invited guests to the party. The party was not brutally lavish but was attended by a heterogeneous group of political, economical, social and cultural climbers and creepers. During the dinner, she sat down facing the President on the same table where she could view the Abuja's bluish sky and the silhouetted palmettos, as the heavenly bodies were jealously watching over her, through the stylish transparent roof of the building. She declined to eat and drink like a dignified guest but she took several pictures with Mr. And Mrs. President. When the President eventually read her story in the media, his hair stood on end, and he felt a chill running down his spinal cord. Consequently, he collapsed into a comatose. On waking up after thirty seconds, he was asked why he chose to collapse into a comatose. His answer is that Kara had made his day—giving him the best memory of all his birthdays put together. Looking at his concerned wife and his bodyguard, he said that had he not married, he could have elected to marry the mendicant for better and for worse. Twenty-four hours later, he sent her a check for one thousand American dollars. In addition to the check, the President gave her the women's Courage-Pride Award, the most feminine award in the world.

Before the end of that month, Mi Rivera sent her a check for 50,000 Naira for the Blessing of her Helplessness. It is not clear whether she is still a mendicant, for the Federal Government has presently restored electricity to all the nooks and crannies of the mega city.

Section O

The Queen's Hair Dresser: She had started her career as a student hairdresser. She would go from house to house soliciting for customers and making money to pay her school fees. This was a time she was a sophomore at Obafemi Awolowo University, an institution whose campus is said to be the most elegant but short of being the most attractive in the world. A history student who failed all her papers in European History before transferring to the Department of African History where she passed all her tests with distinction. Also, she failed most of her papers in European literatures before she found the light at the end of the tunnel, on choosing African Literatures as her elective. Consequently, she saw the rainbow of enlightenment as she washed her face with the first rainfall of the year. Since that time, she has diametrically fallen head over heels in love with African History and Literatures.

One flower-smelling Friday morning, she decided to visit the Museum of Literati for the first time. In the museum, she was impressed to see many writers she had never heard of before and during her immersion in European Literatures. The museum is partitioned into eight sections. The first section, which is the largest, contains the oral narrators—palace minstrels, heroic singers, hunter balladeers, praise singers and sycophants. The second section contains metaphysical storytellers. The third section contains folklore—legends, myths, superstitions, proverbial tales, philosophical aphorisms and moral tales. The fourth section shines upon the historical and sociological writers. The fifth section illuminates the political writers. The sixth section embraces the political, sociological and cultural poets. The seventh section houses playwrights and mime artists. The eighth section, which is the most eclectic of them, contains writers whose threads can be found among the aforementioned sections. They include creative writers, narrative/literary philosophers, magic realists and cultural/folk philosophers. Some of those to be found in section eight are the Diaspora writers who are promoting the writing and publishing of the first Nigerian English Dictionary to contain patois such as *abiku, adire, agbada, akara, ase, asewo, atare, bukaria, eba, fanimora, gari, ife, ijala, moyin-moyin, oba, Olodumare, Olorun, orogbo, wahala* and many others,

The next museum she visited that morning is the Historical Museum. This museum, she finds very interesting in that it contains all the facts and figures of the oral traditions, the pioneering fortitude of the ancestors, the keepers of traditions and the written traditions of the present age. Here, for the first time, she learnt how Queen Moremi sacrificed her only begotten son to save the entire nation of her people. Here also, she learnt about the 16th century Queen Amina, whose bravery and annexation of many territories extended the borders of Zaria, growing in importance and becoming the center of the North-South Saharan trade and East-West Sudan trade. The Queen is said to be the first female to seat upon the back of a steed. Since then, the two heroic Queens have been Lade's inspirers.

One harmattan day, when visibility was so poor that many birds were knocking their heads against beams, posts and pillars, Lade managed to reach the house of one of her clients, Joke. While braiding her hair, Joke disclosed to her that Queen Patience-Mode of Ketu wanted her to braid her hair. She paid little or no attention to what Joke was saying, for she knows that Queen Patience-Mode is a very, very hard human being to please.

Said Lade, "What are you talking? What a joke is this?"

"It is true, Lade. It is not a joke. Queen Patience-Mode needs you," said Joke.

"No hairdresser has ever pleased Queen Patience-Mode when it comes to braiding her hair. You know this."

"I know she is hard to please. But give it a try. You are a professional hairdresser. Aren't you?"

"This is what I am. But do I need a Queen to underrate my work? I am not going. This is my last word."

An hour later, Lade finished her braiding and went home, imploring God to let Queen Patience-Mode forget about her.

Two weeks later, Queen Patience-Mode sent one of her attendants to fetch Lade. She had run for some time but she has no place to hide. On getting to the Queen's palace, the Queen said she wanted her to braid her hair so that she could be pleased with her style.

In no time at all, she started to do what she loves to do most, praying to Olodumare to give her the knowledge to perform her profession to the satisfaction of a hard-to-please Queen. After three hours of braiding, she finished and gave an admixture of a smile and a sigh. Consequently, the Queen stood up and went to the bathroom. On coming out of the bathroom, her face was aglow with delight. She called Lade to her and patted her three times on the back, telling her that she had stylishly done what others before her had not been able to do—braiding the rear and making the front pompadour.

Said Queen Patience-Mode, "Lade, you've made my day. Prior to my being a monarch, my hair had invariably been a phenomenal thing to me. Since my coronation, it has rebelled against my pleasure. It never pleased me and I never stopped telling every hairdresser who came to give me a pleasure of blessing."

"I am very pleased to be the source of your felicity. If it pleases Her Majesty, I may want to mention this happy episode, born-again-happiness of yours in my literary memoir which I have just commenced to pen," rejoined Lade.

"With pleasure that's giving me a joyful heart, go ahead," said the monarch, smiling and showing her pretty gapped tooth.

A year after she had successfully completed her studies, Lade was invited by Queen Patience-Mode to a sumptuous dinner, during her fifth coronation as the first Queen of Ketu. Other invitees include the bevy of highly accomplished hairdressers. After the dinner was over, she announced to the world that Lade would henceforth become her personal hairdresser.

Section P

Clean It Or Lien It: The plot near the one and only Roundabout at Ajegunle has been earmarked for a two-story building for ten years. No one has seen the owner, yet neighbors always confirm that someone is invariably seen in the night (during a moonlit night) posing as the owner of the plot. The officers of the Ministry of Housing and Urban Development were worried. They are worried because they have to find out this nondescript nocturnal man in the night when they are supposed to be sleeping.

Three moons of trying to cross the man's path had come and gone. The fourth moon was in its gibbous state when they met him as he was emerging from his lair. He is a big shot, wearing agbada and more than five chains of diamonds around his ostrich-like neck. His name is Kokomore. Without wasting time, a nocturnal court was set up to try this queer man whose dwelling place is a lair.

"Mr. Kokomore, why can't you clean your plot or at least lien it if you are too preoccupied in your underground dwelling?" asked Judge Doherty.

"This is a good question, Judge Doherty. When I bought this plot ten years ago, my plan is to build my house on it two years later. But I postponed my plan because the Ministry of Housing and Urban Development did not keep its promise of keeping Ajegunle clean."

"But you need to play your civic virtues as a decent man."

"Your Honor, I know this but according to the contract signed with the Ministry of Housing and Urban Development, they are supposed to lead the way. They promised me that as long as Ajegunle is clean, my plot of land must be clean, day and night. And I believed them. I trusted them, not knowing that they would ever break their letters and swallow their words. Today, my plot is not clean because Ajegunle is the filthiest district of all the thirty-six districts in the mega city of Eko-Akete, the House of Wisdom."

"Is this why you abandon your civil obedience and choose to become a troglodyte?" asked Judge Doherty, hiding a civilized smile.

"Yes."

"And what stopped you from liening it for a while?"

"Because there is no reason to lien it when I owe no one whose debt must be protected."

"And why do you always appear during a moonlit night?"

"Your Honor, it is because I want to remain incognito to my neighbors."

"Should Ajegunle become a clean district tomorrow, will you then clean your plot and build your house?"

"Absolutely. I will leap for joy. And that day will probably be one of my happiest days in this populous district."

"What life it is to be a troglodyte?"

"Your Honor, life as a troglodyte is tough. It is excruciating. Only a tough weirdo like me can endure what I have endured for the last ten fat calendar years." He smiled like a gentleman and rolled both sleeves of his agbada upon his shoulders."

"Mr. Kokomore, I am exceedingly happy for you. I am happy that things have changed for better since you elected to become a professional troglodyte. The current Lagos Administration has promised heaven and earth to clean and make Lagos one of the quaintest and cleanest Metropolis in the world. Go around the city and see things for yourself. Ajengule is the only district of the thirty-six districts still remaining and with my order, and the weight of my gabble in conjunction with the proactive dedication of the present administration, Ajengule will assume a novel look in the next six months. Are you excited and ready to be part of this new look?"

I am excited and ready from head to toe."

"Thank you very much. The case is dissolved."

Two years after building his house, Kokomore remains the pride and prim of the people of Ajegunle. By now his name has become a household word. One early Sunday morning, when the streets of Lagos were under the spell of quietness as though a ghostly war had been fought, Kokomore was going to Sure-Love, one of the most fashionable districts in Lagos (known as the Darling-wood among the literati) to attend the naming ceremony of his cousin, Tito. As he was going, he started to discard onto the streets the litter from his Lexus car. All of a sudden, a patrol officer appeared to him and gave him a ticket, notifying him to pay N1, 000 or to appear in the court and tell the presiding judge why he should not pay. He chose the latter. A week later, he appeared in the court with his wife, Tombola. Sitting on the throne of judgment is Judge Doherty, the very judge who acquitted him from his first brush with the law.

"This is a familiar face," said Judge Doherty, as Kokomore entered the dock. "Am I right?"

Said Kokomore, "My Honor, you are correct?"

"Why are you here?" asked Judge Doherty, feigning inadequacy of the matter.

"I am here because I want the judge to exonerate me from my fine, for this is my first time of throwing litter on the streets," said the accused, cupping his smiling lips.

"The Lagos government has zero tolerance when it comes to keeping the city clean. Do you know that?"

"I know, sir."

"Then pay your fine. Your wife may need you sooner than you expect."

"My feeling is that there are citizens appointed to keep the city clean even if one throws litter all around."

"I view your feeling as somehow preposterous. Listen to me: if your house is set on fire, won't you do your part before the fire fighters arrive?"

"I will, for sure."

"Everyone has to do his or her part in this country. It is your failing to do your part that brought you here today. It makes no sense contesting a case when you know you are wrong. When are you going to pay the N1, 000?"

"Next week."

Judge Doherty hit his table three times with his gabble, rose to his feet and said that the case is closed.

Section Q

Iyatunde and Babatunde: In 1999, Sera was the second oldest woman in Comatose. She was 108 and her senior in age was 114 years old.

Sera was a smart and energetic woman. She was a good dancer who had fallen in love with Juju music, produced by I.K. Dairo, the maestro. She also liked to dance to the sound of didgeridoo. (She had learned to play didgeridoo, presented to her by her koradji friend.) But her favorite instrument is xylophone which she started to play ever since she was four. Eight years ago, she won Kuku Trophy in a nationally televised Centenarian Dance, organized by the Society for the Elders-Never-Die.

In 2000 when she was 109, her children, grand children and great grand children wanted her to pay her debt to nature. She implored them to allow her to live and enjoy her life till the age of 120 years but they declined. They let her know that 120 years would be like immortality on the surface of the earth.

Three months later, Sera slept and never woke up, taking with her Jose, her doting husband who was 115 years old. Her children were sad that she could not tell them her last story of wisdom and experience before her departure.

Two years later, one of her grand children gave birth to twins—a boy and a girl. Sooner than expected, there was a party of well-wishers. As the well wishers were rejoicing and readying to say that the two babies should bear their natural names, Tai and Ken, an oracular voice descended upon them and let them know that in addition to the babies' natural names, they should be called Iyatunde and Babatunde, respectfully. Singing and leaping for joy is Mi Rivera, telling one and all in her song that Sera and Jose had reincarnated from what she called the holy land, Ile-Ife.

When the news wafted to the threshold of the first cultural citizen of the Yoruba land, the king of the mythical cradle of mankind, he was discomfited. He advised the children of Sera and Jose to stop being the victims of credibility gap. Additionally, he scoffed and scathingly rebuked them for behaving as though they were the un-circumcised scions from a diluted culture.

Section R

The Man Called Mathematics: Since he left Ijebu-Ode Grammar School, no one knows him as Bode any longer. He has assumed Mathematics as his first name. He is confident and proud of his new wear of identity. His friends and acquaintances were worried in his absence, but in his presence, they had no reason to believe that he had discarded his original name.

One day, blessed with a salubrious weather, Mathematics, appearing sozzled, Pollyannaish and, looking fine and dandy—dressed up *to kill*, a lei of Morning Glories around his neck, Mathematics climbed to the rooftop of the magnificent Independence Building in Lagos, the unbecoming megalopolis, hailed with ear-pleasing accusations of becoming the first Mega City in Africa and then started gesticulating his hands like a traffic warden/pointsman. In less than three minutes, two heavily armed police officers in pinstriped suits—a man and a woman arrived in a city helicopter, landing at the Racecourse heliport, surrounded and beautified by heliotropes.

In no time at all, they began beckoning to Mathematics to come down peacefully. But he did not heed their instruction. The man continued with his mimicry of traffic control, his hands pointing right and left. Sometimes he would pirouette. Sometimes he would move his body as if he was a break-dancer. Sometimes he would wiggle, jiggle and shake his body like a marionette. Gosh, he was enjoying every bit of his actions, for there was a glow of happiness on his countenance that resembled very much that of an owlet. The police officers tried to persuade him again. This time they began to blow their whistles whose pleasing ear-tearing sound could be heard in the thirty-six districts of the mega-city. The blowing of the whistles continued for almost five minutes, praying Mathematics to descend and earn his safe passage to sanity and sanctity. He declined the message in the blowing of the whistles. What he did next was eccentric enough as he commenced to cock a snook at the gorgeous sunset as though he had a decade-old score to settle with the heavenly body.

> All of a sudden, this wonder of a man began the following roundelay:
> Thank you, O God
> Thank you, O Governor
> *We are: we are grateful*
> For turning the ungovernable metropolis
> Into a governable metropolis: a phenomenon.

On hearing the roundelay, the two minions of the law were pleasantly amazed. Now, it is only now they realized that the man is neither an eccentric nor a cretin, behaving like a lunatic.

On descending, he quickly let the law enforcement officers know that his name is Mathematics and that he had climbed to the top of the roof of the house in order to demonstrate to the world that mathematics is the mother of all the subjects. (By this time, a huge concourse of people had arrived and formed an orderly ring in which the man and the police officers had found themselves.) Also, there was a flock of white condors gliding majestically below the wisps of white clouds as if they had come to celebrate the departure of this kudu of a man.

> "Mathematics, mother of all subjects?" replied the officers in one clarion voice.

> "Yes, I mean what I say. What I say is what I mean."

> "How can you explain or prove to the world, Mr. Mathematics?" asked the female police officer.

"How many of two, officer?"

"We are two," said the male police officer.

"You are two in number, right?"
"Yes we are two in number," answered the two officers, one after the other.

"How do you know that you are two in number?"

"By counting each one of us. I am a number and my colleague is also a number," answered the female law enforcement officer.

"Is it correct to say that each one of you is a digit?"

"Yes, it will be correct?" replied the male officer.

"Will it be correct to say that one plus one is two, and two minus one equals one?"

"It is correct as far as mathematics goes," said the two cops unanimously.

"If you will agree with me that one times one, plus 2 equals three: you will want to agree with me that additions, subtractions and multiplications are used every minute throughout the world. Do you then believe that you use mathematics in your private and public life every day?"

"We do?" answered the two officers, hiding smiles that forced them to take a right turn.

"Then you are part of my name, Mathe—matics. As said earlier, Mathematics is the mother of all the subjects on the surface of the earth, for there is nothing you can see, touch, smell, feel, hear or even eat without the presence of addition or subtraction, both of which belong to the foundation of the sense of Mathematics. In any profession, Mathematics is always the primary ruler. Arithmetic, algebra and geometry are parts of mathematics. As long as you deal with numbers, quantities, measurements and shapes, no one will spank you if you elect to carry Mathematics as your universal name. Imagine the occupation of farming (the first humble and indispensable occupation in the world), there is no way you can prosper on your farm without Mathematics, because there will always be the need to know the number of your farming implements, the number of ridges made, the number of seeds and the number of the hands needed to plant the seeds and to harvest the crops.

"Take the case of our market women, for example. They are the practical examples of how mathematics is being used with little or no reference. The knowledge of the market women when it comes to mathematics is amazing. Their knowledge of mathematics has always opened my lungs and washed my eyes. If you think you can cheat them because you are a college graduate, you will hear them say, "Akowe, (bookman) we may not have read ten books but Olodumare has taught us how to take care of our business." All over the country, mathematical knowledge is also being displayed by women working in bukarias (the indigenous restaurants.) The waitresses in these restaurants can tell the number of meatballs in your plates even after you have devoured/gorged the meal and washed it down your throat with a freshly tapped palm wine.

"Collectively or individually, mathematics is the shaker and mover (the player) of our everyday life. Nowadays, children at the age of three or earlier, can show their little knowledge of mathematics by counting their fingers. They can tell the difference between one color and another. Colors rather than digits are a sense of mathematics.

"It is a rational thing to always assume that there is a number in our everyday life whenever we do business with Mathematics. It does not matter whether that number is minus zero or plus zero. Is anyone of you familiar with additive identity and additive inverse?"

"I won't have an answer for you until I add Mathematics to my police training," answered the female cop and smiling philosophically. "However, it will be interesting to know what you mean by additive identity and additive inverse."

"By way of Mathematics, an additive identity means an element (as zero in the set of real numbers) of a mathematical set that leaves every element of the set unchanged when added to it. For example, 12+1=13+0=13. Zero is an additive identity. Why? Because when zero (0) was added to 13, it leaves the number 13 unchanged. If that is settled, let me say something on additive inverse. An additive inverse is a number that when added to a given number gives zero. For example, 0+0=0. Zero is an additive inverse. Why? Because zero, when added to zero, gives zero as the result."

"Thank you for your mathematical entertainment," said the two cops in unison.

"You are welcome."

As the police officers were leaving, they warned him that he had gone too far in making his point. They wagged their truncheons at him, indicating to him that if he ever climbed any public building again, he would have his hands handcuffed behind his back and taken to jail. (Before the wee hours of that day, it was confirmed that Mi Rivera was the one who personified the female police officer.)

Beaming like a winner, and grinning like a Pollyanna, he promised to invariably carry himself like a gentleman. Pointing his index finger toward the earth, he implored the road not to be the officers' driver. Consequently, he profusely thanked the bobbies for their patience, cooperation and understanding and for always acting like the friends of the public, for the public and by the public.

Looking askance at the faces of the happy-go-lucky crowd, and moistening his lips like a public speaker, he said with some air of panache, "If any one of you thinks mathematics is not the mother of all the subjects in the world, let him/her raise up his/her hand and challenge me to an open-air debate on mathematical sense. If he/she wins, and I lose, I will leave the debate with my head bowed low and my tail between my legs."

Section S

The Holy Land: This has just come in. I do not want it to be a part of this collection of stories knit together like a novella by Mi Rivera, the nonpareil story collector and protagonist-narrator. But Mi Rivera insisted that it should stand like a discourse between the benighted and un-benighted.

It was March 21, 2009, my twenty-first birthday that two crazy people, a man and a woman started arguing, swearing, punching the air and molesting the peace of the community. Their argument soon changed into diatribe. Their eyeballs had turned reddish. The skins of their leather-like lips had started peeling off due to lack of saliva, and they had commenced to fall victim to dizziness, when I recognized Mi Rivera. Wonders shall never end!

"Mi Rivera," I bawled out. "What's up? *What is aching you?* Why are you punishing your soul in such a swelteringly hot afternoon?"

"Kismet, you're home? We could have come to your house had I known that you will be at home at this time of the day. Anyway, Yoyo is the one to be blamed. Yoyo is the cause and curse of our diatribe."

At this juncture, both of them were about to faint as a result of dehydration, as they were swaying left and right like a palm tree in a stormy weather. I rushed out quickly and assisted both of them to my house. I was so scared that they would die as un-benighted scions of the land. The mention of a sledgehammer in their accursed diatribe also intensified my fear.

After demolishing a huge calabash-bowl of kedgeree and washed it down with chilled coconut juice, I adjured them to replay their acrimonious dialogue as friendly as possible. The following is the thread of their acrimonious duologue.

Said Yoyo, "Mi Rivera, why are you always referring to Ile-Ife as a holy land?"

Said Mi Rivera, "It is because Ile-Ife is one of the holiest places on the planet."

Said Yoyo, "Stop your insinuation. For a place to be regarded a holy place, it must have had a history of sanctity of not less than two thousand years."

Said Mi Rivera, "Is that your yardstick?"

Answered Yoyo, "Yes that is my yardstick."

"Verily, verily I say unto you, Ile-Ife has a history of sanctity for over two thousand years."

"Apart from being a city of cultural sanctimony, will you say that it has any art work of value that is known all over the world?"

"They are many. For example, there are royal masks. There are philosophical masks worn by sages and people with nimble minds. Also, Ile-Ife is one of the few cities in the world where you find extraordinary terracotta vases, busts, heads and full-size human beings. According to our culture and religion research-scholars, every country has one place at least which it can refer to as a holy land."

"Turning a mythical imagination into a reality is what you do for living. Turning misconception into conception is your cup of lemon tea."

"I know you are a lover of imported culture. This land and the sky over it are too polluted for you. The next thing the holy land will do is to ship you behind the waves where the tiger sharks will be able to dally with your balls."

"Tiger sharks dallying with my balls? Gosh, this is not funny. You are intoxicated, my friend. You have consumed so much from the Pacific waters."

"Aren't you intoxicated by drinking too much from the Atlantic waters?"

"Mi Rivera, all you have seen or read is a gimmick. Nothing more: nothing less. Wake up from your slumber. A holy land is where you hear the voice of Nature. Do you think a holy land is like a Chinatown which you can find in any commercial and capital cities around the world? I say wake up from your slumber."

"You had better not insult my intelligence, Yoyo. Our cultural and religion experts know the difference between a Chinatown and a holy land."

"I am not insulting your intelligence, Mi Rivera."

"Yes you are, thou unbeliever."

"Don't call me unbeliever, for I am not an obsequious person like…"

"Somebody has to clout your over-size head for you."

"Clout it. I say clout my head with your fist and with your sledge-hammer and let me die like an unbeliever."

I told both disputants to continue with their long-established friendship and not to allow the question of Ile-Ife being a holy land break apart their friendship. Both of them smiled and nodded. Consequently, they added that the solution to their acrimonious argument might be found on the lips of the Elders and keepers of traditions.

Section T

My Hero—Forever: Walking into the podium of the exotic stamping ground, the Pearly Gardens and holding by hand a handsome man with a confused countenance is Mi Rivera. It was the first Saturday in the month of August 1999, the period of the year which is always bee-busy with the ordinary and professional people from all walks of life—poets, singers, dramatists, painters with their palettes, drawers with their easels, oral narrators, sculptors, carvers, ethicists, philosophers, models, puppeteers, ayo players, chess players, knitters, mobile tailors, snake charmers, shoe-shiners, kite-flyers, day-dreamers, leisure-seekers, birdwatchers, fire-eaters and many others who think they must do something to overcome the impending ennui, peace and ill-at-ease. More than half of these people spend fifty percent of their productive lives bivouacking inside the stamping ground.

Others, at the four corners of the sprawling Pearly Gates, with tears in their eyes are the moon watchers who worked during the day because the moonlight is the sole light they could see. There are sun watchers who toiled during the night because it is the only light they could see. Shedding tears is their happy consolation.

The exotic stamping ground is a great place to be, for anyone who happens to settle in the happiness of its vicinity will be shocked to see that his/her attention is diametrically called to the chiaroscuro of the paintings.

"My hero-friend, Ojale, has something to confess to the world. Please listen to him," said Mi Rivera with an admixture of panache and a spread of happiness on her face. Her cockney cum American accent betrayed her as a woman whose tongue is a pendulum between United Kingdom and United States.

"I was born to be a man of valor, honesty, probity and responsibility but on becoming the Minister of Promise-Breakers, and joined a bag-eyed company, I started breaking every letter and every word in my promises. A bag-eyed behavior became my cup of lemon-tea. I embezzled money earmarked for the improvement of the national electric power. I embezzled money voted for the agriculture, works and housing, tourism, transportation, and I was greedily involved in selling used/second-hand generators to the public. Within two years, I have accumulated bags of money, some, under my pillows. I was globe-trotting like a seasonal bird of passage and enjoying myself with abandoned insouciance. But many nights, Gosh, I could not sleep because my conscience was waging wars against me, reminding me that what I have done is unpatriotic, despicable and preposterous.

"As my insomnia was becoming so acute and killing me, I was rushing from pillar to post—seeking a miraculous healing. All the modern and indigenous prophets told me that my salvation is in my hands. Consequently, I started to reflect upon what would be my legacy after paying my debt to nature in spite of all these monies in my piggy banks and under my pillows. I discover that there is no legacy for an embezzler like me. I cried and sobbed for days. All over my compound, I heard susurrations telling me I should do the right thing so that I could enter one of the Pearly Gates when I leave behind my wealth. Months later, I started building shopping malls around the country. Today, I have forty malls, one in each state, one in the Federal Capital and three in the Commercial Capital. These forty malls currently employ 2,000 citizens and sixty-nine immigrants. From my hearts of hearts, I think I must add some milk of human prosperity to many blue and white-collar workers. "

"Ladies and gentlemen," called Mi Rivera, "when Ojale first told me his story of embezzlements, I could not believe my ears, neither were my eyes in the position to see the reality. But on swearing in the name of Olodumare, I believe him, as my eyes became a pool of the Atlantic, and Mama-water began to dry them with her nipples." She paused momentarily, smiling smugly and looking like an impartial football referee. Then she continued, "If there is anyone in this extraordinary stamping ground, the Pearly Gardens, today that will kick against this born-again fellow citizen of being a national hero, let him or her say so or else forever contain his/her peace inside an invisible, sky-high and explosion-ready gourd."

Silence fell upon the Pearly Gardens, reminiscent of the silence that used to fall upon a compound that loses its proactive Elder. No one harrumphed. No one scratched. No one moved. But the facial expressions of the people said everything in the name of felicity, agreement and approval. *"Ojale is a born-again good man. He's from a zero to a hero,"* everyone seemed to be saying and rejoicing.

All of a sudden, two sturdy men rushed to the podium and carried Ojale on their shoulders, singing, "Ojale is our hero—forever. Ojale is our hero—forever. Let's make him have a niche in the Temple of Fame, nay shame. Let's martyrize him and tie his balls with the catgut and hang them with dignity inside the martyry. Others embezzlers will follow suit."

"So I think, pray and hope," said Mi Rivera in a voice, more hopeful than that of the born-again honest citizen.

Section U

Why and How the Elephant has Huge Ears: One day in the month of August, shortly after the water creatures under the leadership of Mr. Dolly, the Whale, had had their festive annual meeting, Mr. Roar, the Lion had a meeting with all the animals in the Animal Kingdom.

In this meeting, which covered an area, big as Lake Victoria, the carnivorous and graminivorous beasts sat separately but they maintained a spirit of unity, love and respect for each other.

As usual, King Lion and Queen Lioness sat side by side on the throne, flanked by hippopotamus, elephant, zebra and reindeer. The sole observer, invited from the human kingdom is Mi Rivera who sat down in the glory of a penumbra, taking notes like a shorthand typist.

All of a sudden, Jumbo, the Elephant began to warn orangutan not to trespass on his territory any longer. The orangutan replied by saying that only the king and his queen had the authority to tell him where to go and where to stay. The Elephant was not happy with orangutan's reply and then started to wag his index finger at him. He began to insult orangutan by cocking a snook at him but orangutan did not utter a single word. The king and all those at the throne of the high table adjured him to calm down but he would not listen. He was stamping, trumpeting and grunting. He declined to listen to the order of the meeting. (From all accounts, written or unwritten, there was/is no suppurating evidence that orangutan has ever trespassed upon Jumbo's preserves. Jumbo was simply picking on him. His problem is that he was not happy with a small-bodied creature like the lion to be coroneted the king of the beasts and the warlord of all the carnivorous and gramnivorous quadrupeds.)

The king became upset when the meeting was disruptive, for he was unable to let them know the purpose of the meeting that is to stop man from killing them, and to resist being the victims of Diaspora. Consequently, he asked those at the throne to punish Jumbo. Those at the throne prayed the Creator to enlarge Jumbo's ears. In a twinkle of an eye, Jumbo's ears had grown so large and so ugly in such a way that all the animals in the meeting were embarrassed and sorrowful. On seeing how huge and how ugly his ears are, Jumbo began to grunt, as well as trumpet for mercy. But the king of the beasts told him that it is too late for the Creator to change his new appearance, for the Creator-Philosopher Olodumare has always said that it is good to listen to one's leader or master.

Section V

How Alade Tarnished his Family Name: "This story has just come in. It is contemporaneous with the supra. Because there is only one room for it, I have decided to include it. Its inclusion is belated due to the fact that I could not find it until this hour, having searched for it for twenty-five fat years. Only two hours ago I was directed by the Creator to go to my father's graveyard where I found it. Gosh, happy, I am," said Mi Rivera, the troubadour and raconteur, adjusting and balancing her several fashionable string-bags on her shoulders like the Lagos, Accra, Johannesburg, Nairobi and Addis-Ababa models and pacesetters.

Alade began his stubbornness at the age of twelve when he joined a bad company against the wish of his parents. But his parents did not stop telling him that he would fail and woefully too, if he did not listen to them.

At the age of 15, he rebelled against the standing orders of his parents, keeping late hours and acting like an adult. He often told his parents that if he failed in life, they had also failed as his parents, mocked inability to train him properly. In addition to his rebellious attitude, he shot and killed one by one all the homing doves in the town of More Love.

At the age of 18, and of age, Aladdin became so radically uncontrollable, visiting many parts of the world at the expense of his wealthy parents. One night, his parents, Mr. and Mrs. Kudu Lapede, were crying and sobbing because of their only son, Alade who was unruly, and ready to follow the path of destruction. "How can our only son turn against us when we give him everything in life? How can our only boy follow a life of debaucheries?" they wondered and squeaked, tearfully.

At the age of twenty-five, two years after graduating from the University of Moral Education, Alade was arrested by the More Love's police as he was shooting and killing (in mass destruction) the homing doves which had been brought anew to the town. Tried and found guilty, he was sentenced to five years of imprisonment with hard labour and everyday mass instruction of obedience.

In his first letter to his parents, which he wrote in the middle of the night with the light of a candle, Alade said that he had wronged his parents beyond the heaven of forgiveness. The second paragraph of his letter asked his parents to forgive him and accept him like a servant, for he is not fit to be their son any longer, adding that it is good for one to listen to one's parents.

Section W

A Man-Made Earthquake: Speaking at the Boss Stadium to the families of those who have lost their loved ones and the wounded survivors during the last conflict that claimed hundred of lives, Mi Rivera said, "Dear collateral friends, I cannot but tell you today that my eyes are heavy with tears, and my heart heavy with sorrow and with blood pressure on hearing what happened a few months ago in my adopted beautiful city of Boss.

"Shame on the causes of these deadly conflicts. Why must two faiths (in the presence of the Creator) be maiming and killing each other when Ogun has stopped asking for the blood of lemming let alone ram, in the name of sacrifice? Shame! Shame!
"We have the blessings of rainfall and sunshine (albeit taken for granted), while other parts of the world may face, alas, the calamities such as snowstorms, brushfires, tornadoes, hurricanes and wraths from the blue waters. We are not grateful to the Creator, because we are not grateful, we begin to buy a peace-loving trouble known as a man-made earthquake, killing ourselves in the name of faith, nil God or Allah.

"In the past, the faith-bearers came with pens and swords to forcibly convert my grandparents. Today, the descendants of those faith-bearers resort to killing the grandchildren of our grandparents in the name of a foreign faith that nearly strangled my own indigenous faith. Shame!

"There are many things which are mysterious or miraculous such as births, deaths that occur every hour throughout the world, the whys and wherefores of which we do not know or which we cannot explain, because deeper into what man knows is a lot of what he does not know.

"We know much about history, geography, mathematics, physics, chemistry, biology, zoology, literature, politics, economics, sociology, anthropology, medicine, cartography, et cetera, et cetera, but one thing which we do not know anything about, which we think we know much about, is what is destroying us every season. We have visible and invisible quagmires and quicksand lying before every step we take but the Grace of Olodumare saves us. But it seems we are not grateful. If we are grateful, must we then create the deadly man-made earthquake? Fie on the casus belli. How long shall we allow other countries to be our leaders (in sciences and arts) when we have the Grace and the Blessings of the Creator to be the leaders ourselves? Ladies and gentlemen, let's put an end to this nonsense. Let's be lovable to our neighbours—brothers and sisters.

"We must remember that the successes of our sports ambassadors always depend on the good behaviour and sound psyche of the citizens of their country. Thank you all."

After distributing a truckload of gari and wheat to the victims of the barbaric conflict (the man-made earthquake), the raconteur left as quickly as she had come.

Section X

The Demise of the Corporal Punishment: If there is any story worth side-splitting, eye and ear tearing, this one may be close to such a story.

On emerging from his dromedary-like catacomb in 2000, for the first time since the dawn of man, the first thing Mr. Tortoise did is to build a Cultural School of Philosophy in Belvedere, a small town between Lagos and Ibadan. In less than three months, he had accepted and registered 55 students (aged 16 to 20) from each of the fifty-five African countries. The fifty-sixtieth student, Armadillo is his cousin. (This is the first time Tortoise, hitherto known as Ijapa, the folk hero and the fabled protagonist of antiquity of African folktales, would show to the world that he is a human being of flesh and blood.)

The mission of the Cultural School of Philosophy is to intimate the students with love and beauty of philosophy from the teenage age so that they can ruminate upon the past, analyze the present and prepare for the future, as a prerequisite to finding the Way of Enlightenment. Additionally, the school will enable the youngsters to grow in age, in love, in wisdom and knowledge, opening their faculties and allowing them to comprehend that any lore that widens people's horizons and presents food for thought is the beginning of philosophy.

Armadillo is a good student who had much time to play but less time to do his homework. Tortoise, a disciplinarian, was not pleased with a student who could not score ninety percent in philosophy of life and death. Every time Armadillo got less than ninety percent, Tortoise would cudgel him like a dullard. Tortoise, like many teachers knew that corporal punishment was more effective than words of mouth, for he believed that he would never spare his rod to spoil the child.

That Armadillo was a stubborn student cannot be disputed. That he is not the only student who was cudgeled for not scoring over ninety percent is as true as the minor and major terms. Stubborn or no stubborn, Armadillo did not like to be disciplined with a cudgel that sometimes made him cringe and cry like a latchkey child. One has to forgive him for saying that he did not like Mr. Tortoise whose front chest pockets always carry the following: "In the physical world, Safety is Knowing. In the spiritual realm, Salvation is Praying." He had told Tortoise many times that his intellectual ability could not carry him beyond eighty percent on the average. He had accused his uncle many times for asking him to learn many things at the same time, explaining to him that it is not possible to learn what no one knows.

One Monday morning before Tortoise came to the class, Armadillo knelt down and began to pray thusly: "God, Good God, of all creatures, it is only man you have created in your image and after your inscrutable likeness. Surely, there are other creatures—animals, birds, fishes and insects. They can move from place to place like man but they are not created in your image and after your likeness. It is no gainsaying that man is the greatest of all these creatures. Next to man in greatness are birds. Why is it that a bird is the greatest after man? The reason is that only birds can swim, walk, run, dive and fly. Great as man is, O loving Father, man cannot fly, which means birds are even greater than man. In this wise, and before heaven and earth, I want a bird to punish for me my uncle, Mr. Tortoise. Too much knowledge has wedged his brain into two and impaired his vision. Please Father, answer this prayer speedily as a way to pay him back, for my back is aching, my palms are blistered and my buttocks are sore. Remember me, O God, your little stubborn Armadillo. Amen. Yet, another prayer, knowing full well that my uncle is a tricky weirdo/eccentric, may my uncle never go to the extent of importing the weirdo philosophy of same-sex marriage to the shore of this country, dotted with numerous potholes of holiness. Amen. Amen."

Two months later, as Mr. Tortoise was going to school, there was a flock of redstarts, sparrows, gulls, and terns in the sky, gliding and diving as if there was a festival of feathered creatures in the offing.

Suddenly, the sky was inundated with flocks of big birds of every description. Below these large numbers of birds, was a small flock of pelicans—about fifty in number. Just about halfway to the school compound, the pelicans began to pelt Tortoise with their defecations. In no time at all, his head and shoulders had assumed a white coat of armor, as the defecations turned into a kind of milky guano.

Rushing back home, in a state of bewilderment and nervousness, he plunged into a slow-flowing brook, infested with gavials. But none of the reptiles attacked his balls, lucky teacher! About a score and ten minutes later, the slow-moving stream scoured him clean.

As he was coming out of the runnel, the clouds began to gather. And there was a strong wind tickling the mango and the orange trees, brandishing and plucking their fruits. Soon, the lightning commenced to stab across the cloudy sky. Consequently, it started to pour. It was a heavy pour and many feathered creatures crashed to the ground as a result.

When Armadillo and his classmates heard what had happened to their frugivorous preceptor, they exuberantly cachinnated and said in one clarion voice that Armadillo's prayer had been answered. Since that day, Mr. Tortoise never again attempted to cudgel Armadillo or any one of his classmates. This is how corporal punishment in schools and colleges in Africa was killed and interred. Sooner than expected, an edict was proclaimed and Mi Rivera was never too quick to sign it into law in the presence of fabulists and folklorists, while the students and their parents were cathartically watching, each one bearing a face twisted by disbelief and a mouth beautified by a pout.

Adjusting her peignoir, and rising to her feet, Mi Rivera said in her usual silky and sweet voice, *"I am blessed, grateful and glad to have listened to, and collected all these exceptionally hair-raising stories (informing, enlightening, educating, entertaining, inspiring, and inoculating my body with the ingredients of life) from the keepers of traditions, for a society without a record of its traditions is like a ship* without a ruder. My second mission will not commence until the 22nd century. O dabo o. Alafia."

Fait Accompli

Fait Accompli: "Be patriotic to your Motherland." It is the title of the nine uncommon folktales which Mi Rivera borrowed from Aloe Kikimu, narrative philosopher and the keeper of traditions, Museum of the Ancients and Folklore. Each folktale has "fait accompli" as its cliff-hanger. Symbiotically, "fait accompli" leads to nine philosophical anecdotes, each entitled Life, Love, Help, Belief, Faith, Probity, Honesty, Determination and Hope. They reflect true and honest stories from the mouths of honest raconteurs, narrated for a dying soul. By the time the ninth story was narrated to the end, (and this is the quintessence of the denouement) the dying soul had woken up from his deathbed, diametrically healed, smiling thankfully like a woman who has given birth to a bouncing baby without a midwife.

Said philosopher Truth, "On my shoulders is a huge thunderbolt of felicity and thrills of joy evidencing that the purpose of this collection has been met—the book will heal spiritually and corporeally any soul that reads it (with faith and honesty) from the beginning to the end."

"Fait accompli," announced Mi Rivera with tears of accomplishment. "I announced this with a dual vow of happiness while kowtowing and genuflecting." When least expected, she held Truth by hand and said, "Hear me O Creator-Philosopher Olodumare, vouchsafe that my words, as my unspoken words tickle and din in the ears of my hearers.

Chapter 14

Vicissitudes of Yoruba Philosophy

Yoruba philosophy is so vicissitudous that one may want to compare it to two paradoxical statements made by nine moonlit night travellers from the east to the west during the Yoruba renaissance (circa 16th to 19th centuries) when any announcement must go to or come from the palace, before made public. The king was troubled that the nine travellers could make seemingly contradictory statements in one night and at the same time. But after reflecting for nine days, the king found the two statements to be true. But before we go to the self-contradictory statements which will be found at the end of this chapter, let's examine why Yoruba philosophy is inundated with vicissitudes. It is full of vicissitudes because it changes from oral to written and from written to oral from time to time in the eyes of every Yoruba philosopher. And these vicissitudes go with questions such as how, when, why, what and who.

Let's consider the *how* question: Many Yoruba philosophers do not want *how* to be their driver. Yet they will not stop asking themselves *how* they would begin to write about Yoruba philosophy. Some of them will say thusly, "How can I turn to expound on Yoruba philosophy when I did not study it in school? How do I write on a field which has no adequate references? How do I write on a subject that is wrapped in a kind of verism and religion? How do I write on a subject which is mainly narrative with little or no room for analysis? How can I convince my colleagues that proto-history Yoruba is real and its philosophy worth learning? If I should write on philosophy at all, as a philosopher, I would prefer to write on the philosophy of Africa, for it is guaranteed that I will have enough material by writing on the philosophy of the whole continent of Africa with fifty-six countries."

Let's consider the *when* question: Those who consider themselves a friend of *when* do not forgive the Yoruba philosophy for being vicissitudous. They want to ask *when* Yoruba philosophy becomes anything but anachronism.

Let's ponder over the *who* question: The knowledgeable ones who do not want to write or talk about Yoruba philosophy sometimes wonder *who* will buy their published books on Yoruba philosophy. They want to know *who* will distribute their books to all parts of the world.

Let's ponder over the *why* question: Many who love to philosophize on oral and written Yoruba philosophy always want to know *why* Yoruba philosophy must be an attractive subject of academic pursuit. Yet others believe that its romantic dispensation might be too complex to comprehend, and that is *why* they are reluctant to dabble into it.

Let's deliberate upon the *what* question: The established and the aspiring Yoruba philosophers always ask *what* will happen if Yoruba philosophy is marginalized. Yet some will say, "*What* am I going to theorize and explicate about an old culture with so mythical worldviews? *What* import will Yoruba philosophy be to non-Africans? *What* happens to my book-manuscripts if I don't find houses to publish them?" Additionally, many want to know *what* the European philosophers think about Yoruba philosophy as a mere drop in the ocean of world philosophy.

The above are the uncommon vicissitudes of Yoruba philosophy. While some non-Yoruba philosophers fear that Yoruba philosophy will parachute them from parterre to the vault of heaven due to the fact that all the Yoruba ancient philosophers come from Creator-philosopher Olodumare, others say that it is wedged between absolutism and determinism, adding that they cannot ascribe to its logical determinism. According to them, there is no room for expressive determinism, plus the fact that there are many paradigm shifts.

The two self-contradictory statements made by the nine night travellers, as hinted in paragraph one above are these. First, during the moonlit nights, there are less mosquitoes but we swat more mosquitoes during moonless nights. Second, people with small heads can grow as much hair on their heads as people with big heads.

Chapter 15

The Sociology of Yoruba Philosophy

How are we going to define sociology in relation with folk philosophy, knowing full well that it is more difficult to define a word than to give an illustration of its uses? If sociology deals with the functioning of human society, therefore sociology has some element of humanity that is akin to folk philosophy which is part of that human society. Already, we know what folk philosophy stands for in a human society. The vividness of the folk philosophy is a crystal-clear picture at the backs of our heads as long as we do not forget that the folk or cultural philosophy epitomizes love and wisdom, as contained in the Book of Enlightenment. And if we consider this too short a definition, we may jump to it and verbalize that a folk philosophy is a narrative philosophy, explicating and pointing to the knowledge of the causes and nature of things, affecting the corporeal and the spiritual universe and its wellness. Moving from the valley to the plane, we can certainly say that both the folk philosophy and sociology are nodding acquaintances. They both deal with individuals or groups of individuals in a human society.

The Effects of Country Sociology on Yoruba Philosophy: The way the people in the country carry themselves sociologically is simple and full of natural innocence, always considering to the fullest the natural and the cardinal virtues. They love with innocence and marry in innocence. They strike a ritualistic deal with the earth. They listen to the voice of nature with due respect. They are spiritually friendly. Without the voice of nature, they are reluctant to do anything else. Their act of thinking is based on, and directed by the functioning of human society.

The Effects of Urban Sociology on Yoruba Philosophy: The effects of urban sociology on Yoruba philosophy are no doubt the opposites of what we see in the country or bucolic sociology. The urban people have little or no time. They believe not very much in nature. Most of them are not as patient as their country counterparts. They are victims of paroxysm of impatience and fast life. What they have in common is ori—the head, the philosophy. Their world views are often influenced by the vortex of political, economic and social activities in the urban sector.

Let's consider two narratives, as an accretion. One day, Ijapa the folk philosopher told his spouse to go around the community, asking girls why they were slow at climbing Timo, the only mount in the community. He let his wife know that he would be asking the boys why they could not balance gourds of water on their heads like girls.

Sooner than expected, Maribor, Ijapa's wife had started her interviews in earnest. She had interviewed the first, the second, the third, the fourth, the fifth, the sixth and the seventh girls, all telling her the same reason why girls could not climb the Timo mount with the same pace as boys.

While she was interviewing the girls, her husband was busy interviewing the boys and asking them why they could not balance gourds of water upon their heads like girls. He had interviewed nine boys altogether. And all of them entertained him with the same reason.

First, we will consider the reason given by the girls. The reason given by the girls is that Nature and the human society has endowed the parts of their bodies with feminine grace and tenderness that calls for no reason to hurry like the boys while climbing the mount.

Second, Ijapa stood up like a well-up classroom teacher and told his wife why the boys cannot balance gourds of water on their heads like girls. "Listen dear Maribor," said Ijapa. "I have interviewed nine bright boys, altogether. To my surprise as to my happiness, some of them wanted to study folk philosophy and sociology. Now, let me tell you the reason. The reason is that the heads of the boys are not as smooth as the heads of the girls. Additionally, I pocketed the fact that the girls are more at ease than the boys."

After he had given the reason, he let the world know that Maribor, his wife is a trained sociologist. And he need not introduce himself as a folklorist, better known as a folk philosopher who carries both the human and amphibian identities.

Chapter 16

The Symbolism of Oshogbo School of Arts Movement

We may want to know what symbolism actually means. Symbolism means the act of representing a place, an environment, one's profession, and one's thought: one's condition with symbols that vividly and perceptively depict such a condition, etcetera, and etcetera.

There are four kinds of symbolism that are pertinent to the Oshogbo Arts Movement or the Oshogbo School of Arts Movement: They are the following:

On Religion: A religious symbolist is a person who favours the use of religious symbols in religious services.

On Literature: A literary symbolist is a writer who seeks to express or evoke emotions, ideas, etc by stressing the symbolic value of language, to which is ascribed a capacity for communicating otherwise inexpressible visions of reality.

On Philosophy: A philosophical symbolist is a person who employs symbols that call for deep reflection in his or her work.

On Arts: An art symbolist is an artist who seeks to symbolize or seeks to suggest ideas or emotions by the objects represented, the colours used, etcetera, etcetera.

Now let's talk about the Oshogbo School of Arts Movement. The Oshogbo School of Arts Movement came into being when the Yoruba people and indeed the entire people of Africa were wondering how philosophy would be able to divorce itself from religion. As noted in chapter one, it is clear that after philosophy had ushered in religion, religion became the face of the world, telling the children of the world that it would lead them to an eternal life or salvation after they must have been set free from fear of death. So, religion had put a tight rope around the neck of philosophers, until now. The Yoruba and their African brothers and sisters could not conjecture how philosophers would save them or drive away their fear of death without religion. So religion was winning and winning the battle for attention and trading the fastest way to climb the ladder of salvation, while philosophy was brushed aside to the stygian corner, adjacent the backburner.

As pragmatist Susanne Wenger and Ulli Beier arrived in Yorubaland in the 1950s, the novel act of reasoning, otherwise known as philosophy, started to widen the horizons of the young artists in Yoruba land. Professor Beier and Artist Susanne Wenger, who did not believe in religion as the born-again Yoruba do, began to show interest in many facets of Yoruba cultural values, especially its rich naturalistic artefacts, some of which had been neglected for hundreds of years, as good-for-nothing works of art. The two European connoisseurs of Yoruba artefacts began to encourage these emerging artists. Susanne Wenger and Ulli Beier were quite aware of the diligent terracotta artist-philosophers of the 9th to 14th centuries, believing that if the proto-history artist could be productive, the 20th artists could as well be productive.

The rationality of the Oshogbo School of Arts Movement commenced at the University of Ibadan in the late 1950s, and by 1969 (the year I saw Twin Seven-Seven perform in German Cultural Centre in Lagos), it had begun to define itself as the most unique School of Arts Movement in the world. Sooner than expected, its artistic impact began to influence Efuntola Adefunmi who founded Oyotunji African Kingdom in 1970 and became its first king, the first African-American king in modern America. Also, it was a great honour to the artists when Professor Ulli Beier, the writer and connoisseur of the Yoruba artefacts created an artistic centre at the University of Bayreuth and named it the Iwalewa House in 1981. But why is it the most unique School of Arts Movement in the world? It is said to be the most unique School of Arts Movement in the world because the symbolist artists in the school, in the persons of Chief Jimoh Buraimoh, Prince Twins Seven-Seven, Yinka Adeyemi, Ademola Oyelami, Isaac Akindele, Kola Adeyemi, Bayo Ogundele, Tunde Ogunlade, Raimoh Olugunna, Phillip Olufemi Babarinlo, Rufus Ogundele and many others were able to use their heads (ori) to the utmost, and build on the ingenuity, love and wisdom of the terracotta sculptural artists of the 9th to 14th centuries, who diligently worked in guilds known as the Sculptural Schools of Arts.

The two most influential of these symbolist artists are the late Prince Twins Seven-Seven (1944-2011) and Chief Jimoh Braimoh. While Prince Twins Seven-Seven was a painter, sculptor and a musician, Chief Jimoh Braimoh is principally an oil painter. Most of their art works depict Yoruba naturalism which is an integral part of the cultural/folk philosophy of the land, past and present.

Chapter 17

The Political Philosophy of Chief Awo (1909-1987)

Let's consider the effects of Chief Obafemi Awolowo's (popularly known as Chief Awo), philosophy on Yoruba literary, folk or cultural philosophy. Chief Awo's philosophy on Yoruba cultural philosophy is the most discernible and the most transparent up till today. While he was studying in London, he founded Egbe Omo Oduduwa (Yoruba School of Thought, and Realism, designed to raise consciousness of the Yoruba people), which on coming to Nigeria, eventually became Action Group, the name of his political party. He succeeded in creating a moral atmosphere for a moral society to thrive, impacting a moral majority to which idealism belongs and from which realism emerges. He was the leader of the Yoruba people, and his philosophy, while he was the premier of the Western Nigerian government from 1952-1959, brought peace, good governance and abundance to Western Nigeria in particular and to the rest of Nigeria in general. He developed the Western Nigerian Civil Service to such a transcendental level that the Western Nigerian Civil Service was said to be one of the most reliable in the world. Thus his philosophy was often referred to as pragmatic and effectively starlighted as Awoism.

Again, let's take liberties with the Yoruba philosophy from which we learn and comprehend the postulation that forbids one to allow the grass to grow under one's feet. Chief Awo was aware of this. He was aware that it is philosophy, the thought of man and the reasoning of the mind that actually leads the faculty to the creation and the practice of religion. Also, he was cognizant of the theory that stipulates that Yoruba philosophy is a tripartite book of enlightenment, a folk/cultural philosophy, explicating and pointing to the knowledge of the causes and the nature of things, affecting the corporeal and the spiritual universe. Based on the well-disposed assertions above, Chief (Asiwaju) Obafemi Awolowo believed in the discipline of the body and mind before any effective progress could be made. A realist, he subscribed to the belief that acquiring knowledge, wisdom or any achievement requires restraint, self-sufficiency and self-sacrifice. The notion that head (ori) is the substrate of the body is inherent in Yoruba thought, both among the *thinking thinkers* at the acme and the unread masses below, at the bottom of the ladder. It is present today, as it was present hundreds of years ago, and it is necessary to appreciate it so as to comprehend the mythology, anthropology, psychology and sociology underlying the princely rivalries which had convulsed Yoruba land under its various city-states.

The revolutionary philosophy had an up-to-date view of the world, enlightened by his travelling, reading and reflection. He was aware of the nonmaterial drives or forces such as love, empathy, art, aesthetics, kindness and patriotism. His political savvies, his business acumen, his romantic dispensation, his visionary theories, and his burning desire to be number one in whatever he did, all this put together, was not an act of serendipity. Surely, there were more representative paradigms in his vocabulary than hypotheses. How this could have been otherwise? The *"irascible and concupiscible appetites,"* as Saint Thomas Aquinas called them are a part of the creation and ever present that no savant can easily stay aloof from them. Indeed, he was wiser during his confinement. This remains incontrovertible. His ethical values were a practical convenience, an honourable benchmark and a highly characteristic aspect of his personality, because he did not derive his strength, his cardinal virtues, his vision and his wisdom from an unethical source. The unremitting hubbub/vortex of politics which he had so far witnessed, his disappointment in the hands of his cronies could have been so hard for a man of his temperament and calibre to endure if he had no such protection.

As seen in his numerous publications, he was one of the few scions of the land who could sustain a closely knit conversation/discourse for one or more hours at a stretch without bringing into it something of a religious doctrine.

Like most visionaries, he visualized before, during and after his imprisonment that nationalism alone was seen as insufficient answer to the ills confronted by mankind. Thus, he fought hardest to clothe those who were cloth-less and even roofless, whose philosophy is that because they were born in nudity, they must enjoy their lives in nudity and pay the debt of nature in nudity. He had found the means to educate his people. He had made farming number one if only man and nationalism would succeed. All the above he had done. By his spoken and written philosophy, we can envision that he was a sublime nationalist to the depths of his constitution, cognizant of the saying, "Life is a book that has no end in life," and one has to learn it as one learns a foreign language or a multiplication table. Subsistence farming, he believed, is a natural gift which every human being must practice. And it is difficult to think of disputing the rationale that it is not a moral gift.

Chief Awo's individualistic philosophy also dwells upon the past, rather nostalgically, upon the unwritten movement or period of vigorous artistic and intellectual activity (known in Yoruba land as Yoruba renaissance) during which most of the naturalistic works of art in Yoruba land were produced. "Each time one looks at the life-size Ife terracotta arts, one yearns for the second-coming of these terracotta artists, as one yearns for the second-coming of the Son of man," said Chief Reuben O. Ogunyemi. Who believed that Ile-Ife is the centre of antiquity, city of aesthetics, curiosities and a sight for the sore eyes.

Chapter 18

The Sublimity of Fagunwa's Philosophy (1903-1963)

The Metaphysical Corpora of D.O. Fagunwa (1903-1963): The greatest metaphysical philosopher from 1930 to this day is probably D.O. Fagunwa. He employed a great deal of metaphysical imagination in all his teachings and five novels—Ogboju-Ode Ninu Igbo Irunmale, Igbo Olodumare, Ireke Onibudo, Irinkerodo Ninu Igbo Elegbeje and Aditu Olodumare. They are also in part, a repertoire of his rhetoric and moral philosophy. He was a master describer whose descriptions always lured his reader to his metaphysical cosmos.

That D.O. Fagunwa was a manful hunter that was well up in Yoruba cardinal virtues cannot be disputed. That he was one of the manful hunters in the world is as true as the holy city of Ile-Ife. He was a real folk/cultural philosopher whose faculty (ori) led him to a unique hunting expedition that was later regarded his manifest destiny. He was indeed a bringer of light to Yoruba folk/cultural philosophy. His metaphysical world is beyond the compass of understanding. Each one of his books is like a heaven or a world, deep beneath the earth. His corpora (some emblazoned with romantic dispensations) fully displayed the aesthetics of contradictions, for he would be surrounded by splendours and luxuries of life, in some cases, whereas in other instances, he would be faced with calamities and the ruins of paradise. But his passion for the aesthetics of contradictions always made him a winner.

In page 39 of Ogboju-Ode Ninu Igbo Irunmale, we can feel him even if it is not possible to see how he evocatively called upon his beloved mother from the dead to rescue him when he found himself in the quagmire of sorrow, loneliness and hopelessness. *("A! My mother, my mother, my mother, how come I do not hear from you this particular time of the day?").* Did his mother appear from the dead? Yes, his mother did appear from the dead, as the earth yawned open. His mother's words of loving-kindness enlivened him and uplifted him to the paradise under the vault of heaven. The appearance of his beloved mother thus confirms Yoruba's notion that there is life after death. Here we commence to feel and in deed see the sublimity of Fagunwa's folk cum narrative philosophy. Without going to the valley to find the truth, the work of D. O. Fagunwa has helped one to re-assert that Nature and its dependants unequivocally point to the metaphysical concept central to Yoruba philosophy, religion and literature. The power of metaphysical imagination in Fagunwa's corpora evidences how much Oduduwa, the father of Yoruba's narrative philosophy had concerned himself largely with the theory of the universe in terms of cosmogony and cosmology. Perceptively, evidently and vividly, Fagunwa had derived his power of metaphysical imagination from philosopher Oduduwa's exposition of the universe—visible and invisible—as referenced to in chapter eleven.

How can we define or summarize Fagunwa's folk/cultural philosophy? It is very hard to give a conspectus of his corpora. One thing that is sure which we must not predicate without the subject is that his corpora have unfolded his passion for ontological journeys to a metaphysical hunter's cosmos where figments of imaginations were embraced as the real world of flesh and blood. These metaphysical imaginations depicted lots and lots of serendipities, many hues of magic realism, lots of aesthetics of contradictions and many whys and wherefores of life and death that seemed to be a food for thought, as we reflect upon the magic away, magic carpet and magic stone (including folk song, folk dance, folk love, folk lore, folk medicine, folk memory, folk wrestling, folk life and folk etymology) which are a commonplace in his five novels containing blood and thunder.

The following may stand as the last but not the least. D. O. Fagunwa was not only a folklorist but also a great symbolist whose picturesque writing is the richness of life's tapestry.

Chapter 19

The Royalties and the Yoruba Thought

Social and Political Philosophy: Social and political philosophy investigates and examines issues of justice in the society in order to inform and enlighten the society. It examines the social, economic and political attitudes or behaviours of our leaders in their leadership positions. Here, I have employed **Natural and Cardinal Virtues** as explicated under *The Royalties and the Yoruba Thought*. The royal house is the custodian of natural and cardinal virtues, otherwise known as the attributes. In Yoruba land, and as contained in chapter twenty-six, there are seven natural virtues while there are nine cardinal virtues. The seven natural virtues are love, temperance, prudence, valour, honour, fortitude and justice. Increased by two attributes, the nine cardinal virtues are love, honour, honesty, temperance, morality, justice, valour, prudence and fortitude. The royalties are duty-bound to always manifest all these attributes of natural and cardinal virtues. Additionally, the power to theorize, the power to perceive, the power to mediate, the power to divine, the power to coronet, the power to prophesize, the power to moralize or to ethicize and the power to philosophize has been vested in the domain of the king. They are king-philosophers. Philosopher-kings guide the kingdoms as Reason guides the human souls. The de jure king knows this. The subjects know this unlimited authority from Creator-Philosopher Olodumare or Olorun whose representative on the surface of the earth is the king, and his crown being an attribute of the kingship. The king's subjects comprehend this truth of fact that the metonymy is the language of the crown as the language of the divinity is the language of the kingdom. Some of the king's subjects, if not all, entertain their imagination that the king ostensibly lives in a sequestered environment.

In some of the royal territories of the Yoruba land, the royalties are the royal heads that hold sway over the people and their farming lands. In some cases, the royalties claim ownership to heroic deeds and some hair-raising folk narratives. No one has the audacity to challenge the king and the members of his royal house. Every subject must pay homage to him and his family members. The king-makers are parts of the sustenance of the royal house. They are the king's decision-makers or philosophers whose opinions are indispensable. They are invariably engaged in serious brainstorming. In some instances, their voices are as consequential as the king's voice, because the king appreciates their act of reasoning and the love and wisdom, derived from the sacred Book of Enlightenment.

But, I say but, there is one man who always challenges at will, the king. He respects the king. He reverences the king. He vows to die for the king. But his respect, reverence and vow to die for the king do not stop him from challenging the king to any royal battle. The name of this brave protagonist-philosopher is Ijapa, the endomorph of a being whose life is split between ridiculous and sublime. We must not but add that protagonist-philosopher Ijapa is adept in all arts of cunnings and dissimulation.

There are two folk narratives in which he showed the king of Alape that he is smarter than him without being coronated the king of the town, Alape. The first narrative: One day he went round the town telling one and all that he could become a king at any time. Soon, the news reached the palace and his accusers asked him to tell his story or to swallow it. Instead of letting his accusers know that his story was a refined wit or an Attic salt, he was trying to prove his masochism. Instead of swallowing his story to avoid comeuppance or expiation he decided to tell it. The king was enraged and Ijapa was asked to leave the town as an unpatriotic citizen.

He agreed to leave the town but he said he had some news for the king. He prayed one of the king's equerries to supply a pot of boiling water. In no time at all, the equerry had brought a pot of boiling water and put it down before the king and his royal kith and kin, the keepers of traditions and some members of the public.

With a sorrowful heart, Ijapa said, "The matter has come to the crunch and the chips are falling. Well, I know I have gone too far. I have used my emotion to drive the bad part of my head to think for me. At the same time, I know what I have said is as true as our Majesty. Because I have said the truth and I will prefer to die in truth rather than leave this beautiful town for the unknown for the rest of my life. If this hot water kills me, please bury me amongst the brave men and women who had left before me in this town. But if it happens that I survive, I may ask the king to rescind his order and allow me to continue to live as one of his loyal subjects."

"Well said, Ijapa," rejoined one of the kingmakers. If you die that will be the end of an unpatriotic philosopher who is supposed to know that the king is the head of every thinking head in this town. Dying is better for you, for you will never come back to throw insults upon our king."

A few seconds later, Ijapa poured the boiling water in a calabash bowl and readied himself to gulp the terribly hot liquid. He went from one person in the audience to the other telling them that he was ready to drink and die without being buried like a hero but like a traitor and like a man who had pointed his left index finger to his father's house of honor and dignity. He knitted his brows, hissed like a mamba and said, "I have been rude to the king but I cannot accept to go to another town and be humiliated like a vagabond, a pauper or riff-raff. My final decision is to die here like a valiant man of love and wisdom.

The unanswered question is whether I have made too many follies that I should assume that there is no salvation for me. The little honor I may have, I will carry it with me to the grave and then to my Creator. This is my philosophy."

"Let Mr. Philosopher drink and die like a buffoon. He is a quisling who will never be allowed to hold a riding-whip, let alone ride a horse. This is your desert, Mr. Philosopher," roared a keeper of traditions from the audience.

"I will die like a man. Surely, not like a buffoon," replied Ijapa with a smile suggestive of mockery. I choose this penalty myself because I don't want to be thrown inside a conflagration like Kite who was caught stealing the king's chick. I know I am a recalcitrant fellow but I have done enough to be recognized and invited to become one of the kingmakers.

"Every man commits a malarkey. With love and wisdom, my record shows that I have entertained my people all the days of my life. I have brightened the illusions of my people's ambitions. While enlightening your hearts, and my heart, I have learned that man who makes mistakes is the man who learns to be wiser after his mistakes."

Consequently, he put the calabash bowl to his mouth and started to drink. The boiling liquid had cooled down at this juncture, so he drank the water to the last drop in the bowl and bowed respectably to the king.

The king shook his head, waved his flywhisk, smiled royally and then said the protagonist and philosopher Ijapa should continue to live as a loyal citizen in the town of Alape. Ijapa, in accordance with Yoruba's reference to ori, as the substrate of the body, had properly made use of his head, ori.

The second narrative is about two yam farmers, Rosa and Tera, respectfully. Rosa always produced big and long yams, whereas Tera always produced small and big yams. Their friendship qualified them as sisters. The de jure king and the members of his royal house loved to order the small yams which according to them were tastier than the big yams. One day in the first month of the dry season, a couple of weeks after the yam festival, Tera went to Rosa's barn and surreptitiously carried four baskets of Rosa's big yams, replacing them with four baskets of her small yams. On discovering the theft, the buxom Rosa confronted the buxom Tera who denied stealing Rosa's four baskets of yams. Thus the two of them started fighting and insulting each other over four baskets of big yams. When Rosa knew that Tera would not give back to her the four baskets of yams, she went to the king. In the presence of the king, Tera vociferated that she had nothing to do with the stealing of the four baskets of Rosa's yams. The king was gripped by shilly-shally. Consequently, Ijapa whispered something in the king's ear. Seconds later, the king came up with a decision. That decision was to burn all the yams. Thus he asked Ijapa to burn the eight baskets of yams and give their ashes to each one of the quarrelling buxom farmers. Tera jumped up and clapped her hands, saying that the king's judgement was the right thing for both of them. But Rosa begged the king not to let the yams be burnt into ashes, as that made no sense. With tears in her eyes, she prayed the king to give the eight baskets of the yams to the needy in the town instead of burning them into ashes. After a moment of reflection, the king realized that the four baskets of big yams belonged to Rosa and not Tera. In showing her gratitude, beautiful Rosa gave the king and the members of his royal family two baskets of her big yams. The people of Alape praised the king for his wise head and nimble mind, and he was not reluctant to take credit for the two folk narratives, the love and wisdom of his head.

In most narratives of the land, told directly or indirectly, the king hardly takes credit for anything unpropitious. The king always takes credit for everything propitious because the palace is the bedrock of morality. The way the king speaks, the way he eats, looks, greets, answers questions and the way he attires himself must show a suppurating evidence of morality. In short, whatever the king does exhibits either ethical or moral philosophy which is an integral part of folk or cultural philosophy.

Additionally, the king is supposed to be versed in most of the consequential syllogisms, proverbs, parables, legends, allegories, hunters' chanting and expeditions, including heroic deeds. His ethical position makes him the flagship of his people. More often than not, he acts like a rudder and whenever a flaw is found in his character, the ship may be heading towards a moral vacuum or disaster or a cataclysmic nadir.

Chapter 20

The Import of Ijapa's Philosophy

"I open my heart to the pulsation of life, adjuring my destiny to lead me to my full potential that will be enlightenment to the community and the entire universe." This is the sign on both the front and the back doors of Ijapa. Occasionally, people would converge on the parterre of his house trying to hear words of wisdom and knowledge from the mouth of the wise.

No fabulist can replace Ijapa as the folk hero and the fabled protagonist of antiquity in Yoruba folktales and folk philosophy. As pointed out earlier in chapter nineteen, above, the personality known as Ijapa is adept in all arts of cunnings and dissimulation. For generations, he has been represented as a tortoise, and has been called a trickster without equal. Children love him and he loves children to the point of no return. Today, the culture-conscious Yoruba people cannot believe or forced to believe, or accept in totality that a four-legged tortoise, known for his whims and caprices, is the darling protagonist of a culture, endued with Ifa-Ife, the sacred Book of Enlightenment, under the auspices of divinity-philosopher Orunmila.

Before we go further, let me unfold my personal dream experiences and contacts with Mr. Ijapa. They are the following: As I began to cudgel my brains about the writing of *Introduction to Yoruba Philosophy, Religion and Literature*, Ijapa appeared to me like a changeling. He stood on my way like a conjurer who had the entire world under his conjure. On penetrating his rude obstruction, he said to me, "The door shall be open to every soul that knocks."

The second time when I saw him, he appeared like a revenant to me: It was on completing *The Political Philosophy of Wole Soyinka and Other Narratives*. He said to me in a basso profundo, *"Whosoever seeks shall find."*

The third time, he appeared to me like an omniscient narrator, wearing a dashiki whose front carried an emblem of a terracotta vase, while its back bore a philosophical mask of the king of the holy city, Ile-Ife. It was during the writing of *The Enchantress of Triple A*. He chortled and said, "If you don't ask, how can you find what you are looking for?" I told him that I always asked myself why I have not been able to put a smile on the lips of every creature.

While leaving me in peace, he let me know that there is no shadow without an object. He smiled merrily and enjoined me to implore and caution the Africans in Africa and Africans in Diaspora not to let the grass grow under their feet in the 21st century.

The historical genesis of Ijapa who is both a metaphorical allegorist and cultural/folk philosophical is not certain till this moment. But it is, seemingly certain that he does not belong to the league of the divinities, led by philosopher Oduduwa to create Ile-Ife. Because Ijapa is sly, unpredictable and crafty, we may confine him to the clan Igbo belligerents who on many occasions menaced the Ife people ere they were put to rout, courtesy of Queen Moremi, who with her exceptional love and valour sacrificed her only begotten son for the cause. (It is likely that Ijapa was the commander of the belligerent Igbo people). But the questions on the lips of every researcher are: "Where was Ogun, the warlord or the Commander-in-Chief of all the Yoruba wars, real and unreal? Was he on a different warring mission?"

Here are two schools of thought on Ijapa today which will continue to shed light on the personality of Ijapa, the most-talked about fabulist and cultural philosopher of our time. The first school of thought which is defined by the common sense of the present tense is that Ijapa, a tortoise, will forever remain the folk hero and the fabled protagonist of antiquity of Yoruba folktales. The second school of thought subscribes to the theory that the culture-conscious Yoruba people cannot honour, or forced to honour or honour in totality, while their heads still perch resplendently upon their shoulders, that a four-legged amphibian is the darling hero-protagonist of a culture imbued with Ifa-Ife, the Olodumare-given Book of Enlightenment—book of love and wisdom, revised and frequently up-dated by Divinity-Philosopher Orunmila.

Additionally, and as an accretion to the unexplained, but nay belated, the Yoruba people are clinging firmly to the fact that as long as Yorubaland is a society of people from the same head, upon a taproot, it stands to reason therefore to regard every Yoruba scion (including Ijapa) as a prince or a princess, who can refer to the ancients of the land as a people who had contributed to, and made use of their good heads—as philosophers.

My research does make me believe that Ijapa is the greatest unsung narrative philosopher that Yoruba people have ever known. Like the divine philosophers, who are the Bringers of Light to Yoruba culture, Ijapa has partaken in the seeds of enlightenment. Thus he belongs to the avant-garde culture vultures or the keepers of traditions who have been inducted into the Yoruba Divine Hall of Folklorists. He is also a great user of ethical proverbs whose passion for the aesthetics of contradictions is to entertain his listeners, day and night, with maxims or aphorisms. A versatile creature of a man, Ijapa's mien is awash with ambivalence. Perceptively, his eclectic worldview is second to none.

Ijapa is real as a human being whose birthright and birthplace but remains implausible to conjecture. He loves Yoruba land so much that he can take his life for the people, as he himself tries to demonstrate in chapter nineteen. The man, versed in natural and cardinal virtues, is prepared to tell his own history but he is invariably difficult to reach. However, he is ready to display his triple personality in Yoruba culture—literary philosophy, religion and literature. That his indelible mark has remained in the psyche of the land is incontrovertible.

Once salubrious day, Ijapa appointed himself a judge in the presence of the following triplets—Earth, Water and Air. Watching the triplets in the distance was Fire. But he was asked to keep his peace until philosopher Ijapa asked him to open his mouth. What he wanted to prove was to show how important he was in the society in which visible and invisible things or elements live side by side.

> Said Water, "Sometimes I feel like covering the earth with my water."
> Said Earth, (Terra firma), "You don't want to do that anyway. Do you?"
> Said Water, "If I should do that, I am not committing any crime, for that was how you were before Creator-Philosopher Olodumare came to change me."
> Said Air, "You two, you should not ignore me because everything—animate or inanimate needs me. No creature can live without me."

All of a sudden, Fire shrieked out, "Gentlemen, my name is Fire. I can be good. I can be bad. Whenever I am good, I cook your food. And if I should choose to be bad, I will burn you all to ashes without warning. In short, what I want to prove to you three is that I am the boss."

"I should be the boss because all the creatures need water," rejoined Water.

"One moment," prayed Air. "I think I have every dignity to be called the boss because no one can live without breathing me in and out."

"Let's go to the beginning, to the drawing board, and let the act of reasoning be our way of enlightenment," said Earth. "Without me, Earth, all of you, including our judge, will have no basis or sustenance. In other words, the earth sustains water, air and fire."

After five minutes of reflection, Judge Ijapa, declared Earth to be the boss over Water, Air and Fire.

From what evidently and conspicuously stands above and from what we will read later about Ijapa, we cannot deny the fact that the whims and caprices of Ijapa are numerous. They make Ijapa cogitate that he will continue shimming and jouncing on the tight rope (like a funambulist) of success, showing to the scions of Ile-Ife that he will remain and continue to remain the flagship with a passé-par-tout, needed in all forms of narrations.

Let's examine the following narrative with a view to analyze it, if necessary. Ijapa and his wife, Jemila were travelling to Feramola town to see minstrel Telo, his brother-in-law who was just rescued from drowning. Jemila was carrying a pregnancy of six months. Thus this trip was very important for both of them, especially Ijapa who was thought to be impotent. He would prove to his brother-in-law that Jemila was pregnant, and the rumours that he was impotent would be put to rest, once and for all.

It was a nice day of cool zephyr, the grass was wet with tickling fine dew and the atmosphere was cerulean when husband and wife woke up from their bed. A couple of hours later, they started the trip as early as the sunrise, understanding that the road was hilly and treacherous. There were many winding pathways and lots of puddles too, covered with water lilies and water hyacinth. The first hill was easy for both of them to climb over. The second was easy, so was the third, the fourth, the fifth, the sixth, the seventh and the eighth. When they reached the ninth obstruction, it was not a hill but a log of wood, lying across the road. Only Ijapa was able to climb over to the other side. While Jemila was trying to climb over, Ijapa was waiting and encouraging her.

> "Be careful, my dear, you know you are pregnant," said Ijapa heartily to his wife.
> *difficult to* "Yes I know. But this log of wood is proving conquer," said Jemila, looking jaded and frustrated.
>
> "Move to the smaller part of the bole to your right and give it a trial. Apparently, this is the sole elfin nuisance before we reach your brother's house."
>
> "I have tried the smaller part of the bole already, my dear. It does not work for me. I don't just know what to do."
>
> "If your head can reason out how we successfully climbed over the eight hills, I am cocksure, you will be able to climb over this log of wood. Just be wary of your pregnancy. We to go, quickening our paces, for the shadows are beginning to lengthen."

At around four o'clock, Jemila was still trying to overcome her impediment. Her husband was scratching his head and fidgeting, and looking very worried. He did not know what to do to help his beloved wife.

At about an hour later, a young-looking sculptor was passing by and saw how Jemila was sweatily trying to climb the log of wood to the other side. He looked at Jemila concernedly and said that her husband could have gone to a dolmen-near settlement of the sculptural artists, across the street and could have borrowed an axe or a machete to cut the log of wood. "Whenever a tree falls down across the road, blocking the road, it is a man who sacrifices his body, while making use of his head to find a solution," said the sculptor, putting his lips together, as though he wanted to pout.

On overhearing the conversation between the sculptor and his wife, Ijapa felt piqued and defeated like a husband who yielded the killing of a python to his wife. I have been put in a box by a stranger who thinks I have nothing to bequeath to my expectant wife, he murmured to himself.

Sooner than expected, the young sculptor began to chop the log of wood into pieces, and with the help of Ijapa, the road was cleared of its elfin nuisance.

By the time husband and wife reached Feramola town where his brother-in-law was living, the chicks had begun to roost and a speculating storm had begun to gather threat and peril. Soon, Telo in his minstrelsy voice, began to question Ijapa why it had taken him and his sister the whole day to reach Feramola town, in a distance which normally took six hours to cover. Ijapa had no defence. He simply told Telo that he was happy that he did not die drowning. Looking apologetically like a late-comer, he let Telo know that he was so happy that his wife was pregnant. "The curse of impotence is now removed from my head, as the curse of bareness is being removed from my spouse's head," he winked successively and cachinnated like a man whose wife had delivered twin children in the midst of the night.

Whenever ori—head is not properly used, or whenever there arises an egregious blunder or a bag-eyed behaviour, there is always someone to point out. The import of Ijapa on Yoruba philosophy may be visible on a daily basis, but that does not signify that Ijapa, as philosophical as his mind is, is perfect and free from the stupidity.

Chapter 21

Yoruba Philosophy of Happiness

I was delivered in a felucca-like boat of love. My body was lotion-massaged with the coconut oil and surfeited with fructiferous passion. My piscatorial parents told me that the only thing they would be obliged to give me is love, and safety of good health, that all other things I would have to discover them by myself as I would be growing—day by day—with happiness, using my faculty (ori) and nobody else's. Because it was during the years of my childhood/innocence, I fell head over heels in love with happiness so much that I thought human beings are immortals. That heart of immortality was broken when my grandmother paid her debt to nature in the years of my innocence. Owing to their success and happiness in their piscatorial industry, they gave me a name that epitomizes *born-to-be-rich*. One thing I remember asking them is; "What is the date of my birth?"

> "There is no record of the date of your birth," they answered in unison. They looked at each other and continued by saying, "Your birth date is the love, contentment and, happiness that must be your daily pursuit, and your treasure of a life time. We will keep you healthy but Olodumare will give you that enduring good health, safety and longevity we can never give you."

When they died, one after the other, I lost the power and magic of their parental oneness. However, I resolved to whole-heartedly pursue a full-fledged happiness, thanking heaven and earth for being born in a century of complete civilization in which there will be only rumours of wars but never, never a shooting war. The following paragraphs on Yoruba philosophy of happiness are the summaries of my research interviews carried out between 2004 and 2010, together with what I experienced ever since I have been growing and living with the organic happiness as my alter ego. Every one of us was born with a smile of happiness on his/her lips. Every one of us started growing up with smiles of contentment. Why then should our smiles of happiness turn into the ruins of happiness in this highly civilized world we are, in this 21st century? In order to answer this question and in order to find out why happiness is like a grain of paradise that never withers, why happiness is a lifetime treasure—a spring water that never dries, and the need to be happy, and why people may be or may not be happy is the principal reason why I resolved to carry out the interviews.

Some of my interviewees are vegetarians and their philosophy of abstaining from eating meat has uplifted them spiritually and physically. Even those who are the aspiring vegetarians comprehend and attest to the fact that they are more active every time they have dishes of vegetables as their repasts. All of them entertain the idea, explicitly or implicitly, that becoming a vegan is a recipe to quick attainment of happiness. They do not shy away from vociferating that too much of eating animal food has crocked up the world.

From my own perspective, I am happier since 2000 when I turned my life from eating meat to consuming vegetables and plant-based diets. Additionally, my dyed-in-the-wool anger seems to have packed and vanished from every day of my life.

Just in from the archives of my perceptive memory: Before my happy but often argumentative parents demised, they warned me not to permit my anger to supersede my happiness, adding that a little bit, just a little bit of my mirth/happiness will be taken away whenever I am angry and my face is twisted and my mouth a caricature of an ugly pout.

> "If you turn yourself into a home learner," they advised, "you will be wiser when you are ready to take your princess as your second-half best friend, for life."

In 1902, Willa Cather wrote, "One cannot divine nor forecast the conditions that will make happiness, one only stumbles upon them by chance, in a lucky hour, at the world's end somewhere, and holds fast to the days, as fortune or fame."

During the day, there was a sun of happiness in my eyes. During the moonlit night, there was a moon of happiness in my face. Once, my teacher asked me, "Why is it that you're always laughing and looking happy?" My reply, "This is my propensity, my Creator's creation. I think I have an abundance of happiness inside of me."

Yoruba Philosophy of Happiness: Yoruba Philosophy of happiness appears like a bridge over a river whose mermaid is ululating for exquisiteness in spite of her unparallel pulchritude. Happy people are cognizant of their personal philosophies. The major premise is that all philosophers are happy. The minor premise is that you are a philosopher. Therefore you must be happy. That is all what the philosophers can tell you because they themselves are searching for the absolute happiness in the secret recesses of their hearts as they are searching for the meaning of life and its ugly-headed antonym.

Again, philosophers are trying their level best, but they are still in a puzzle about the world and its invisible Creator-Philosopher, in spite of their sporadic second sight.

As in chapter twenty-four, The Way to Enlightenment that may lead to the enlightenment of the soul is the ultimate goal of most spiritual philosophers. As any knowledge acquired is an open door to wisdom, so also any lore that widens people's horizons and presents food for thought is the beginning of philosophy. On our way to enlightenment, there will be many paradigm shifts as the search for an everlasting happiness continues.

Life is a whirligig. And Yoruba philosophy of happiness is found or evidently apparent in the whirligig of time, inasmuch as man is answerable to his five senses—sight, hearing, smell, taste and touch, as he grows every day to make a mark in the world. What makes the Yoruba people the happiest on earth is that they believe in Creator-philosopher Olodumare whose Book of Enlightenment has been a beacon of light and direction from time immemorial. Yet another phenomenon that makes Yoruba people happy is the bearing of children, most importantly the twin children. This is like a blessing from God above, for every family in Yorubaland has twin children, young or old, living or dead. But the proto-history has shown that the genesis of the Yoruba philosophy of happiness was the period when the cultural icon, Queen Moremi saved the holy city of Ile-Ife from being captured and occupied by the rebels living in a community called Igbo.

Yoruba Philosophy of Happiness and Greetings: As our research shows, people who love to greet people are very happy, sociable, amiable, affable, understandable, tolerant and compromising.

In many cultures around the world, in which tradition is but an integral part of culture, greeting is a sine qua non. That happiness and greetings are universal well wishes, is incontrovertible. But let's cite that of the Yoruba people only. Amongst the Yoruba people, greetings are like blessings, especially right-handed and pure-minded greetings. As a matter of fact, they are blessings in disguise. Greetings are regarded as uplifting. They are regarded as enlivening the mind and the soul, allaying fears, doubts and replacing them with confidence and wellness. Thus, it is safe to say that greetings are synonymous with happiness, for a sad/unhappy person rarely opens his/her mouth to greet. (What is interesting and indeed special about the Yoruba philosophy of happiness, as associated with Yoruba greetings is that any situation in which one finds oneself, there is a greeting of happiness that suits that situation). Yoruba claim that every greeting characterizes friendship and friendship characterizes greeting which is an integral part of iwalewa.

Once, there was a woman named Tata, whose parents wanted her to marry a gentleman in a town called Zulu. One early morning, a man from Wade-town set out to ask the hands of Tata in marriage. He was tired and hungry by the time he reached Zulu. So he asked for food without greeting the Elders in the compound. After finishing eating, he heaved a sigh of relief, greeted the Elders and then proceeded to rest his limbs. While doing this, another suitor from Wade-town, looking exhausted and hungry, walked in, greeted all the people in the compound and then informed them that his mission was to marry Tata.

The first suitor, on hearing that, jumped to his feet, ululating that he should be the right man to marry Tata because he got there first. But Tata's parents and the Elders let him know that he was not a gentleman enough, explaining to him that all he wanted was food and that he had had without even greeting anyone in the compound. Thus happiness eluded the first suitor while the second suitor went home with a double portion of happiness.

Yoruba Philosophy of Happiness and Naming: Yoruba philosophy of happiness and naming are similar to philosophy of happiness and naming in other parts of our cultural world. Without placing quandary upon reality, naming depicts the circumstances leading to the birth of a child. Bearing children automatically leads to many thrills of joy/happiness for the parents and for the neighbourhood. This is why the happy parents give names with happy meanings to their children.

Many families like to give good names to their children, for they believe that as names are epitomes of happiness, so also they portray divine luck, fortune, heroic deeds, royal lineages, the long pedigrees or power to overcome diabolic machinations. Good and meaningful names are pleasant to the ears and they are supposed to be a treasure of a lifetime.

Since my born days on the surface of the earth, I have never met any human being whose name carries no meaning. Even when a person's name is Water, it still has a meaning. Water, the most important liquid on earth has a meaning. It is indispensable. If a would-be mother likes to drink lots of water prior to the birth of her child, it is likely that her child is named Water when it is born.

In some old cultures, children have natural names. Such names are Tai and Kehinde, which are given to twins in Yoruba culture. The keepers of traditions believe that such names are heaven-given and they must be given to the children, willy-nilly. In sum, a name is the most valuable and meaningful identity that distinguishes one creature from the other. It is a point of contact and reflection in the head of every creature of human being in the land.

Yoruba Philosophy of Happiness and Beauty: Pardon me if I should take organic beauty as a neuter word in this respect. It is for the convenience of both males and females.

"Here we go again," said a renowned Lagos beautician who goes by the name Clara Bode. "Every human being is beautiful. One may start to feel the pangs of ugliness if one loses one's self worth or self-esteem. That's all I can say as the Queen of Beauties who always advises women not to forget their God-given beauties, their natural identities," concluded Clara Bode and laughed as though she is a royal Queen surrounded by her stately maids. At 52, she is still looking as if she has just marked her 26th birthday.

That beauty makes every man or every woman happy cannot be discounted. That beauty is the most pleasant word in the ears of a woman, is as true as the eyes that behold the beauty. Every day, thousands of nairas are spent on beauty, the abstract, and the beautiful things. For many, beauty is synonymous with happiness. Monarchs have traveled across borders in search of beauties. Hundreds of men and women have given up their citizenships because of beauty. There are tons of jealousies and numerous quarrels every day, because of beauties. Wars had been fought, thrones had been vacated, gourd-eyed ostentations had been displayed because two men had vied to marry what they considered the most beautiful creature of a woman on the surface of the earth, beneath the vault of heaven.

All these longings for a beautiful face are a thing of recent. But in the days of our ancestors, a beautiful face or the pulchritude is second to the iwa, the character of a woman or a man. In those days of yore, a man looked first for the character of a woman before looking for her beauty. The Yoruba philosophy of happiness as it concerns itself with beauty sums up the commonplace saying that if you want to marry and be happy, marry iwa, the character and not the beauty that may fade away with the passage of time: not the beauty whose words will vex a saint. The contents of character are more valuable than the contents of beauty, even if both make man and woman happy. Beauty pleases the sight (eyes) but good character gladdens both the sight and the heart of happiness. The philosophy of happiness and beauty lets us perceive the fact that Creator-philosopher Olodumare has created man for happiness and beauty. Creator-philosopher Olodumare is a happy Creator and so he has created man with a heart flowing with absolute happiness.

Yoruba Philosophy of Happiness and Religion: There is happiness in being a religious human being. And the fact that Yoruba people belong to the most religious people in the world, cannot be compromised or underestimated. They know about their philosophical beginning, when philosopher Oduduwa and his contemporaries took to reminiscing about how Ile-Ife would be governed and made liveable for one and all. It will be true to say that it is the knowledge of, and respect for their philosophical beginning that makes them always a happy people—philosophically and religiously.

Happiness is a personal blessing, as religion is a personal decision. Happiness is a personal right of every individual as religion is a right of every individual. One can derive one's happiness from any kind of religion whether that religion is conducted in one's house or in a house earmarked for Creator-philosopher God. To the religionists, happiness and everything on the surface the earth is through the benevolence of the Creator-Philosopher Oduduwa, the King of kings and the Lord of lords, and only the ingrate will think otherwise.

From the oral culture to the written culture, the Yoruba philosophers always say that a religious person is expected to be very humble and tolerant like a spiritualist. Religious people are not supposed to be fanatic. They are not supposed to be ostentatious.

Happiness is the lot of the people who love and worship the highest Spirit, God with a contrite heart. All the doors leading to rationality must be closed to religious bigots, if happiness must be respected and thrive conspicuously and insightfully.

A true believer does not *hate me* because my religion is different from his. A true believer who is awaiting salvation does not *hate me* just because my skin-dashiki is God-made of different hues.

A true believer in the Creator-philosopher of heaven and earth, the omnipresent, the omnipotent and the omniscient, should be happy, peaceful and loving, if only he is not a false heart. A true believer should avoid inflicting physical or spiritual pain on others, let alone shedding blood. He/she should not use his/her clerical position to molest the innocents. For neither the flagellation nor the penance can give birth to happiness even if the flagellant pays the victim oodles of naira.

Chapter 22

A New Dawn—Part One

That culture is the totality of man cannot be disregarded. That people in every community, settlement, village, town or a country have cultures of their own, is incontrovertible. Thus culture, the totality of man, can be regarded the sublime identity of man.

The movement towards African Political/Cultural Enlightenment started in earnest during the second half of the 20th century when most of the African countries started taking back the seeds and cotyledons of their freedom from their colonial masters. The age of emancipation has been born.

The success, rather the rise of the African Political/Cultural Enlightenment led to the founding of the Organization of African Unity (OAU), 1963 which is today known as African Union (AU), 2002.

It will be helpful, and indeed meaningful if this book remains a catalyst to a new dawn in respect of the Cultural Enlightenment of the Yoruba people, constructing three triangular doors, each of which leads to philosophy, religion and literature, as embodied in the Book of Enlightenment which is otherwise known as Ifa-Ife, containing the power of words and praises and curses about life and death. It has been said, it is being said that it is the sole book whose spirit rebelled against slavery, then staying alive and kicking in all the continents of the world where there is an anachronistic imprint of commercial and domestic slavery.

One thing we may quickly and unequivocally remember is that **Ife** is synonymous with life, and vice versa. Some keepers of traditions have argued rather favourably that life is derived from **Ife.** Let's leave the question of how the world came into being in the hands of the evolutionists and creationists who love to kick the question back and forth like a football without scoring. A second look at **Ife** and life shows a remarkable similarity betwixt **Ife** and life. The question the keepers of the traditions are asking is: Does **Ife** symbolize life? "Aye," which is translated to be the world, is a three-letter word like **Ife**. If one takes the joy to remove "l" from life, what remains is **Ife.**

On the other hand, if one joyfully writes "l" and puts it behind **Ife,** the upshot will be life. Thus life and **Ife** can sit comfortably at the shaky, three legged table, and ogling immortality during the crepuscular hours of the night, and looking at each other during the diurnal hours, as kith and kin, shaking hands in the realm of consanguinity, endorsed by immortality.

While Samuel Ajayi Crowther (1809-1891) was struggling to convert the Book of Enlightenment into the Holy Writ in the 19th century, some of the keepers of traditions were not slow or reluctant to ask him why he did not convert the Book of Enlightenment into a written form and make its copies available to the Holy See and to the Church of England in order for them to read and confirm that there is little or no difference between the worldview of the Book of Enlightenment and the worldview of the Old Testament of the Holy Writ.

Another thing that distinctly separates the Yoruba's Book of Enlightenment from the Cultural Enlightenment of other African countries, and indeed other parts of the world is ori—head. Ever since the Cultural Enlightenment has been passed from generation to generation, the keepers of traditions have been cudgelling their brains to see whether there is any part of the body that is more fundamental, more indispensable, more important than ori, the faculty/head. There is none. That is taken to be the answer, in its verisimilitude. To the Elders or the keepers of traditions, as the heart is the motor of the body, so also the head is the flagship of the body—spiritually and corporeally.

From the head of the household to the head of a farmland to the head of a village to the head of a township to the palace of an Oba, head has always been an indispensable part of the body in respect of the Yoruba thought. The thought of how life should be spent by a head or an Oba was like narrating a legend at a period when legends were considered the keys in the custody of a head. Today, social behavior like smoking of cigarettes, often referred to by some chain-smokers as "social civilization" has reduced the quintessence of a head from being the most important department of our cultural philosophy.

The Book of Enlightenment comprehends and rightly too that **ori** is the determiner of one's life. But the Book cannot ascertain or departmentalize whether **ori** is purposeless as soon as the self/soul leaves the body, and the lifeless body, perceived as a log of wood.

Today, as it was in the days of yore, when **ori** is faulty, the entire body is faulty. When the head—**ori** is correct, sound, respectful and creative, the whole body is correct, sound, respectful and creative. The Book of Enlightenment lets us know that **ori** is being allotted the largest amount of praises every day. Also, it is not unlikely to find itself defensive and sorrowful inside the box of inanities. The good things that are credited to **ori,** the good things that **ori** enjoys, the good things that are allotted to **ori,** depend on the owner of the head, the **ori**. Our prayers then, on a daily basis is, *"May our heads, in the name of Olodumare always be in the right position of being correct, sound, respectful and creative. Ase."*

Chapter 23

A New Dawn—Part Two

Perceptively, the aura of the Book of Enlightenment, the upshot of the act of reasoning, is the candle that lights the tunnel in the way leading to the meaning of life. The cultural Book of Enlightenment lets us know that the meaning of life resides in creativity and mobility/movement. You can visualize the meaning of life from the cooking of your soup to the dreaming of an idea that ultimately leads to the production of a book. Also, you can feel the meaning of life in your movement/mobility, say from your bedroom to your sitting room. The beating of your heart and the working of your brain attest to creativity, one component to the meaning of life. As said earlier, movement/mobility is part of a meaningful life and no life is meaningful without mobility/movement. In everything one does, there is always a meaning of life—creativity and mobility/movement.

The Cultural Enlightenment, from the Yoruba's perspective embraces philosophy, literature and religion of the people known as the Bringers of Light by the ancient terra-cotta artists, and by the born-again wordsmiths and the keepers of traditions who refer to it as the Book of Enlightenment in which Ile-Ife, the holy city and its Ifa-Ife Divination is the fountainhead.

The Stages of Cultural Movement in Respect of Enlightenment: The stages of Cultural Movement in respect of Enlightenment in Yoruba land can be partitioned into four stages. The first stage is presumed to have commenced from around 700 AD to 12th century. This is the period when the holy city of Ile-Ife was enjoying its pre-eminence, the height of artistic production in terms of the aesthetic terracotta, and the period when the nine sons of Oduduwa founded the city-states of Benin, Ila-Orangun, Ketu, Popo, Owu, Oyo, and Sabe, Abeokuta and Ijebu-Ode were later added to the list.

The second stage started around 12th century to 1914 when the Southern and the Northern territories of the land known as Nigeria today, were amalgamated in 1914 by Lord Frederick Luggard, from United Kingdom. It was the period in which the Oyo Empire (1400-

1905) is said to be one of the most powerful, resourceful and pragmatic empires in Africa. Additionally, it is the period when Dr. Samuel Ajayi Crowther (circa 1807-1891) became the first African Anglican Bishop. It was the period when Dr. Samuel Johnson (1846-1901) completed the writing of the History of the Yoruba.

The third stage started from circa 1914 to the middle of the 20th century. This is the period when the keepers of traditions, spearheaded by Sir King Adesoji Aderemi and Chief Obafemi Awolowo and their elite contemporaries, such as Chief Samuel Ladoke Akintola, Adegoke Adelabu, established and supported the Unity of Cultural cum Political Enlightenment, otherwise known as Egbe Omo Oduduwa. It was the birth of Yoruba Realism. Also, it is the period when the African countries began the movements toward their political emancipation from their colonial overlords.

The fourth and the last but not the least stage commenced from 1950s to the present. It was the period when Oshogbo School of Arts Movement was born, vide chapter sixteen of this book. The major avant-garde painter-artists in the Movement are Susanne Wenger, Prince Twins Seven Seven, Chief Jimoh Buraimoh, Ajibike Ogunyemi and a host of others. Within this period, there are also avant-garde writer-playwrights and dramatists. The writer-playwrights include Wole Soynka, Femi Euba and Ola Rotimi: and D.O. Fagunwa and Amos Tutuola who were full-fledged writers. The dramatists and playwrights include Hubert Ogunde, Duro Ladipo, Kola Ogunmola, Oyin Adejobi and many others.

There are two schools of thought regarding Yoruba folk or Cultural Enlightenment. The first school of thought belongs to the writers (fiction and nonfiction) who think and feel that Yoruba philosophy is too oral-ancient to stand on its own and by its own: that it's like a three-legged table, tumbling and falling at anytime.
They infer that Yoruba philosophy is a drop of water in the mighty Atlantic. And because it is a mere drop of water in the Ocean, it must be and should be a pocket in the body-dashiki of African Cultural Philosophy. They dream and presuppose that African philosophers should continue to be borrowers of Western philosophies. They also maintain that as long as the born-again churches preach West-religious-philosophy, it stands to reason for them to stick to the West and carve a niche in the temple of fame. Are they the learned ones who are guilty of colonial mentality, for continuously honouring themselves as the limpets of colonialism,

according to Fela Kuti, the anti-colonial maestro? Do we have a non sequitur here—from a logical point of view?

The second school of thought sees the light of the sun from another horizontal angle. They believe that not only should African Cultural Philosophy be a contemporary issue, it should be taught in a number of Western colleges and universities. Additionally, it should be an urgent focus in each African country as long as that country is independent and a member of the United Nations.

Brainstorming-wisely, they assert that it is right time for the present scholars and intellectuals to start to establish an indelible imprint for the present and for the future generations. Placing side by side the principles and expediencies of a writer, they verbalize that as long as John Locke, Bertrand Russell, Ludwig Wittgenstein, Jean-Jacques Rousseau, et cetera, have been the sun and enlightenment unto the Western culture, so must they be the sun and the enlightenment unto the African culture. As Afro-centric scholars and intellectuals, spearheaded by Molefi Asante, have been the sun and the enlightenment unto the wake-up-call, in respect of the African Cultural Philosophy, so must they listen to their theories on which reasoning is based—the premise—explicating the major and the minor premises. As W.E. B. Dubois, William Tubman, Kwame Nkrumah, Herbert Macaulay, Ahmed Sekou Toure, King Idris, Ahmadou Ahidjo, Modibo Keita, Sir Milton Margai, Silvanus Olympio, Hubert Marga, Habib Bourguiba, Ismail al-Azhan, Francois Tobalbaye, Patrice Lumumba, Felix Houphouet-Boigny, Chief Obafemi Awolowo, Julius Nyeyere, Leopold Senghor, Moktar Ould Daddah, Maguib Mahfouz, Gamal Abdel Nasser, Emperor Halle Selassie, Jomo Kenyatta, Kenneth Kaunda, Milton Obote, Nnamdi Azikwe, Wole Soyinka, Chinua Achebe, Ngugi wa Thiong'o, Anthony K. Appiah, Maulana Karenga, Nadine Gordimer, Maya Angelou, Derek Walcott, Camara Laye, Kola Abimbola, Wande Abimbola, Henry Louis Gates Jr, Toni Morrison, Malcolm X, have been the sun and enlightenment unto the African literary/political philosophy, so must they follow their footsteps, on the way to knowledge, accompanied by divinity-philosopher Ogun who will be clearing the way so that no one stumbles or falls.

The Independence Bridge has been built for over fifty years. Why must the majority still be walking under the Bridge, while a few are walking upon the same Bridge with the jaded pre-independence rulers?

We must not forget that Africans across the board possessed ancient Books of Enlightenment but when their European next of kin came from behind the waves, they disparaged those books and then trashed them, alas! In their search for a new light of knowledge, Africans are presently turning to the valuable wreckages of their ancient Books of Enlightenment, some of which have to be debunked in the midst of a more powerful one. Today, only a few books such as IFA-Ife Divination Book of Enlightenment survived the disparagement in the hands of our overseas kith and kin. If there should be any Book of Knowledge or Book of Enlightenment that survives the savages and ravages of history, that Book of Knowledge should be IFA-Ife Divination, comprising anthropology, cosmogony, cosmology, ethnology, ethnography, literature, mathematics, philosophy, psychology, religion, sociology and other fields of human interests. What we are discoursing today should be postulated as a development that would eventually open up new vistas.

Weaver-Philosopher: Let's listen to how a young woman (who loved to dress like a Saracenic woman) became a bucolic weaver-philosopher. Long, long time ago, a woman by name Tete went to fetch water in Toro village, between Ile-Ife and Oyo. On her way home, she sat upon a pollarded tree, resting her limbs. Soon, she saw a weaver-bird building her nest. As she was transfixed by the dexterity of her legs and her beak, she noticed nearby a spider building its web. She was exceedingly amazed to behold how a tiny insect was able to spin its web within a short period of time. Consequently, she began to ruminate upon the importance of every creature on the surface of the earth. Every creature has a part to play, she thought. Life became a mystery to her. Death on the other hand, became a log of wood (the end of the mystery) after life must have departed from the body.

With emotional tears in her eyes, she got home, with her head full of questions, unanswered. Now she was deeply involved in the act of reasoning, supporting her chins with her left palm. When her parents asked her why she was tearful, she proceeded to narrate what the weaver-bird and the spider had miraculously accomplished to surprise and charm her. Additionally, she said, "I am reasoning in order to widen my horizons, as our people increase in numbers, for the voice of the ancient philosopher is to reason well and to expand reasonably. If these tiny creatures of things could think and reason with their tiny heads, how much more a human being with a much larger head, who is delivered from the womb of life." Her parents let her know that life is full of inscrutable phenomena, adding that every creature is imbued with knowledge and love of life. In conclusion, they said, "Brightness in a child is noticeable from infancy. Conversely, a child who will grow up to be smart, shows that smartness while it still is a child."

Days later, Tete started to learn how to weave. This is how she became the first basket-weaver in Toro. This is how she became a bucolic philosopher and whenever people asked her how she acquired her knowledge of weaving, she would say with felicity that any lore that widens people's horizons and presents food for thought is the beginning of philosophy.

The Aura of Yoruba Cultural Enlightenment—philosophy, religion and literature, the three principal fields which are embodied in the sublimity of IFA-Ife Divination are the sine qua non when it comes to Yoruba culture. Apart from these three fields of learning, there are others such as history, mathematics, anthropology, sociology, psychology, cosmology and cosmogony.

All said and done, we must not discard the fact that if literate culture had been in existence on the African continent when the Europeans were thinking of where to go for the sale of their creative novel ideas—religion, philosophy and literature, they would not have gone to Africa as conquerors and disparagers, rather they could have gone as sharers of what they have known and shared it with their African counterparts.

Chapter 24

The Way to Enlightenment

The way to enlightenment is the ultimate aim of everyone who believes that there is life after death. Even those who do not subscribe to the notion that there is life after death, do need still to walk the way leading to enlightenment as explicated by the nineteenth-century language and folk philosopher Bishop Dr. Samuel Ajayi Crowther. From the Yoruba's perspective, every person who can trace his or her family tree to the holy city of Ile-Ife believes in life after demise.

Let's now expound on the way of enlightenment as a vista for rumination. The way of enlightenment is a slow process in life. Because it is a slow process, only a few people have found it so easily, even if it is not far from their reach.

In his journey to enlightenment, man will encounter many things—good or bad, evil and uplifting spirits. If care is not taken, man may not know which to choose from. When man chooses good, and what is considered to be good, he may still have some bad traits in him. If he chooses the uplifting thing, he may still have an evil spirit in him. But the gradual in-filling of enlightenment helps man master and suppress negative or retrogressive things in him. Step by step, as he carefully makes use of his good head, he will continue to move into it. It is then, only it is then he can tell one and all that he has found the way to enlightenment.

Yoruba narrative philosophy is a long-awaited discourse that opens up new vistas. The vistas are numerous but only one way that leads to these numerous vistas of enlightenment. Whether one is called a narrative writer, or a creative writer, or a literary writer, one must find one's way to the discourse that opens up new vistas. While treading the path, one can either be called a creative writer or a narrative/folk philosopher.

Let us point out four luminaries in this respect, who have strived hardest to find the way of enlightenment and to enlightenment and thus have advanced Yoruba narrative/folk philosophy. (Those whose work appeared in the 19th century are essentially idealists, while those whose work started in the 20th century are fundamentally realists). The first person that readily comes to mind is Reverend Dr. Ajayi Crowther, a freed slave who came back to Yoruba land preaching the Gospel of salvation from the Holy Bible after he himself had been baptized a Christian, and forsaken Yoruba system of reasoning and worshipping. By translating the English Bible into Yoruba in 1840s, he made a lot of Yoruba living in the cities and towns literate. Additionally, he helped in re-alphabetizing the Yoruba language in 1842s. The translation of the Holy Writ tremendously helped the Yoruba city-dwellers to compose in Yoruba. It enabled them to read and understand that the records of events in the Old Testament are similar to the dos and don'ts in the Yoruba Book of Enlightenment, the book of **love and wisdom**. The first Anglican African Bishop and the first linguist, Dr. Crowther travelled to many parts of the present-day Nigeria and other territories in West Africa. As he was dethroning Yoruba religion in one hand, and promoting Christianity in another hand, he was indirectly projecting and promoting Yoruba cultural philosophy. However, he did not derive his enlightenment from philosophy and its act of reasoning but from religion (mainly Christian) and its passionate emotions.

The second luminary is D.O. Fagunwa (1903-1963) whose five novels reminisce about his extra-ordinary hunting experiences in a cosmos inundated with metaphysical imaginations of diverse creatures. Versed in the nine attributes (love, justice, morality, prudence, valour, honour, honesty, temperance and fortitude) of the Yoruba people, he was a master describer who was fascinated with aesthetics of contradictions. Unarguably, he is the doyen of Yoruba folk/cultural philosophy. His passion for metaphorical allegories cannot be underrated.

The third luminary is Samuel Johnson (1846-1901). As my investigation reveals, Dr. Samuel Johnson was the father of classical pacificism and liberalism that worked along the seaboard of West African countries, especially in Yoruba land. Son of a recaptured slave, he was a clergyman, historian and idealist. He was one of the most influential Enlightenment Thinkers during his time. His work had great impact on Yoruba proto-historical, political, sociological and educational thought. From all accounts, his writing had influenced hundreds of returning slaves from North and South Americas, including West Indies. The most consequential among his writing is entitled, **"A History of Yoruba(s) from the Earliest Times to the Beginning of the British Protectorate."** The book was posthumously published. The book served as enlightenment for the Yoruba in

Africa and the Yoruba in Diaspora. This informative (albeit not comprehensive enough) book has always served as an eye-opener to the students of Fourah Bay College, founded in 1827, and which many returning slaves used to attend.

Due to his pacifist and liberalist propensities, he was able to redress the Ibadan-Ijaye war of 1860 to 1862 and the Ekiti Parapo war that erupted in 1877. All these shooting wars occurred during the darkest period of Yoruba's desperate search for enlightenment.

His theory of human kindness, **love and wisdom** reinforced Yoruba cardinal virtues and moral integrity, figuring eminently and prominently in the works of later historians, sociologists, religionists, educationists, philosophers, pacifists and liberalists who ascribe to the exposition that head (ori) is the fountainhead of human consciousness.

The last but not the least luminary is Professor Wole Soyinka whose corpora have opened up new vistas of enlightenment in the realm of narrative philosophy, with some elements of spiritual science. His corpora of poetry, novels, dramas and memoirs brought a new sun to the Yoruba folk/cultural philosophy in Africa and in Diaspora. The new sun became brightest in 1986 when he was awarded the Nobel Prize for literature. His oeuvre always portrays some elements of cockney humours, metaphors, ironies, euphemisms and syllogisms, adding lustre, euphonies, and food for reflection. A believer in the theory of pacifism, liberalism and narrative philosophy, he holds to the notion that as good literature quickens imagination, so also it becomes the foundation of pleasure. The first narrative philosopher to embrace divinity Ogun as his Muse, Professor Soyinka is a prolific avant-garde writer who is considered Enlightenment thinker and a veritable Bringer of shining Light to Yoruba culture in particular and to African culture in general. Since 1986, the award of his Nobel Prize in literature has continued to revolutionize the thinking of the Africans in general and the Yoruba in particular. He is an upholder and projector of the nine attributes of the land.

Let us now consider a philosophical skit which could easily be found in Soyinka's oeuvre. There was a small town in the vicinity of the Old Oyo Empire. The women in this town were noted for producing twin children. In this town, there was a two-year old horse with two different coats of colours—white from his midriff to the head and black from his tail to the midriff. The steed always bragged that he would forever remain a virgin, that no human being would ever make him a beast of burden. When he was four years old, a young-looking man (in his seventies) whose head-hair was as white as snow and whose goatee beard was as creamy as milk approached him and said, "Dear horse, I will like to hire you for a ride."

"You can't do that," answered the horse. "I am a virgin and I want to remain a virgin for the rest of my life. In short, I need no one to sit upon my back."

"All the horses are beasts of burden," said the white head-haired man with a confident smile. "You are a horse, therefore you are a beast of burden."

The virgin steed, the beautiful beast of burden sighed and neighed rather disappointingly for about three minutes and then said to the old but young-looking septuagenarian man, "You are syllogistically correct from head to toe. It's true that all the horses are the beasts of burden. What cannot be chewed must be swallowed or regurgitated/spat. This is the manifest destiny which Creator-Philosopher Olodumare has bestowed upon my head, the definition of my entire body."

His 1962 telephone conversation with his London Landlady is considered the best narrative skit of its kind. The imagery that one could be talking to his or her landlady/landlord from one continent to another is still manifest in the minds and hearts of the world.

Every now and then, one could easily feel or even see his love of words, his power of words and the aesthetics of his narrative philosophy in his works—poetry, dramas, novels and memoirs. His rhetoric speech, while accepting the Nobel Prize Award for literature in 1986 is a case in point, never to be forgotten. In that acceptance speech of his, *"This Past Must Address Its Present,"* Professor Soyinka chronicled the past, the present and even the likely future events of the world and demanded justice for all in general and for Nelson Mandela in particular. *"This Past Must Address Its Present,"* eloquent and downright, is arguably said to be the best Nobel Prize Award acceptance speech or Nobel Prize lecture of its kind ever since the first Nobel Prize Award for Literature was awarded in Stockholm, Sweden in 1901. Two years after the award of the Nobel Prize in literature, Mandela's Earth and Other Poems was published in 1988. A few years later, the world commenced to reflect on his loving call for justice as contained in his Nobel Prize

Award speech and his passionate call for justice in his poetry book—Mandela's Earth and Other Poems. As his call for justice echoed and re-echoed throughout the nooks and crannies of the world, the Apartheid Government policy and their sympathizers began to fall in love with reason which eventually graduated into action that knocked down in pieces the prison gates. What is the upshot of the tearing down of the prison gates? The upshot is that Nelson Mandela was set free—in—1990 after twenty-seven fat years behind bars in his own Earth. A remarkably fit septuagenarian with an affable, imperturbable demeanour, Wole Soyinka with his classical beard, and the rest of the loving and amicable world would continue to remember 1990 till the end of the tide and time.

This is what Pa Reuben Ojagbuwa Ogunyemi once said, "Man is perpetually seeking something every day. But enlightenment is the least thing he seeks on a daily basis. What he seeks is what he gets. But sometimes, he gets less than what he seeks. This happens whenever there are obstructions limiting his ability. He cannot do much about this in so far as his mind is not constructed like the person with little or no obstruction. Nor his mind is imbued with the same destiny. The Way of Enlightenment is a spiritual phenomenon. It is the hardest thing to obtain, keep and nurture."

Chapter 25

The Effects of Psychology on Yoruba Thought

One of Divinity-Philosopher Orunmila's distinct areas of expertise is psychology, believing that psychology is the knowledge of the human mind and its functions, especially those affecting the behaviour or the attitude of a person or a group of persons. Philosopher-Divinity Orunmila is the cultivator of psychology, an indispensable component of IFA divination, the Book of Enlightenment or The Body of Knowledge. *The Treasury of African Folklore* (1996) by Harold Courlander sheds the light on how IFA did spread from Ife throughout the Yoruba country to other West African cultures.

With all the eyes on perception, the effects of psychology on Yoruba thought can even be couched as the effects of divination on Yoruba thought, because divination is as the same as psychology in Yoruba land. But because the former is the title of this chapter, we will stick to the former. Cognizant of the fact that a diviner is the same as the psychologist in the eyes of the Yoruba, the Yoruba people always seek the help of the diviner whenever they find or perceive anything worrying or bothering them physically, and especially spiritually. Every diviner holds the notion that he has answers to many human problems. In short, a diviner thinks he has the power to heal or cure the mind or the soul. Thus *"come to me, I am your healer,"* is the diviner's slogan. Thus a diviner sees himself as an indispensable figure of a human being in the society.

Now then, let's consider the case of what happened some thirty-five years ago in a littoral village, called Modele. Tade was five years old. He was the first son of Mr. And Mrs. Jakoba. One day, he came in from the backyard playground where he had been playing with his age-group friends. About five hours later, Tade developed a stomach-ache. Very worried about his first stomach ache ever since he was born, Mr. and Mrs. Jakoba, started praying in the name of Jesus Christ for his healing.

Soon, the boy slept soundly. But on waking up, the ache began to torment him again. As the new converts to the Gospel of Salvation, husband and wife began to pray again, almost ceaselessly. And this continued from the first day of the incident to the third day. As the gorgeous sun was bidding the world goodbye on the third day, Chief Modo, a renowned keeper of traditions, advised Mr. and Mrs. Jakoba to consult the diviner/psychologist Kako, the sole diviner/psychologist in the littoral village, Modele.

Two hours of performing his act of divination, Kako was able to determine the cause of Tade's persistent stomach-ache—Tade had drunk a cup of water from a pot of rainwater in the compound. And inside his cup of water was a dead bumble bee.

An hour later, Tade went to the toilet and regurgitated the dead bubble bee. As he was coming out of the toilet, he smiled broadly. The stomach-ache had packed and gone. The parents were immediately relieved of their anxiety. They smiled and hugged the psychologist/diviner. They were exceedingly flushed with joy.

Since that day, they believed that Jesus Christ, the Son of Creator-Philosopher Olodumare, has the power to heal directly and indirectly. For them, Jesus Christ had healed their only son indirectly. Husband and wife now confessed how strong the power of divination/psychology had invariably been in their heads, except that they were not bold enough to vociferate it, due to their conversion from the old salvation to the new salvation.

In whatever situation in which a Yoruba person finds him/self, he/she will never abandon his/her head, the fountainhead of the act of thinking. In this narrative, we have perceptively observed that psychology and philosophy cannot but use the head in whatever they seek to achieve or accomplish, even if psychology always has upper hand. This is the conventional wisdom.

This is yet another short narrative, showing the effects of psychology on Yoruba thought and how both the psychology and philosophy do work amicably under the umbrella of the same culture.

Jinja was one of the women employed by the Department of Fisheries, Lagos State Ministry of Agriculture. Being a fishmonger, Lagos Bar Beach was where she sold her fishes of every description to her customers. One swelteringly hot day, she came home complaining of headache to Dada, her husband. Dada told her to rest her limbs, adding that a sound sleep presupposes a mind at rest. But Lola, her mother-in-law said that she should consult a diviner/psychology in order to diagnostically determine the elfin nuisance of her headache. First, she was held hostage by shilly-shally. But later, she agreed to consult the diviner/psychology. Her decision to consult a diviner/psychologist is a direct effect upon the act of reasoning, the path her husband was asking her to tread. For, staying in the sun in a swelteringly hot day can cause a headache. Whenever that happens, what the body needs is to rest or sleep after which the headache will disappear.

Chapter 26

The Characteristics of Yoruba Pragmatism

Every Yoruba person is taught how to be economical and to eat and remember his/her fellow citizens, near or far. He/she is taught the essence of the present and the essence of the future. He/she is often reminded that the past is a sage while the present is a page. What we must continue to remember is that every Yoruba person regards polite greetings as a kind of attribute. He is circumspect too. As every Yoruba is circumspect, so also he/she is pragmatic. He or she subscribes to the notion that if yielded to pragmatism, man can properly or wisely use his head to achieve the best in life. We may want to examine those qualities/characteristics, the day to day attributes that accrue to Yoruba pragmatism.

Natural and Cardinal Virtues: There are seven main natural virtues and nine cardinal virtues that are the characteristics of Yoruba pragmatism. The seven natural virtues are prudence, justice, temperance, valour, honour, fortitude and love. The nine natural virtues are love, morality, prudence, justice, temperance, valour, honour, honesty and fortitude. The cardinal virtues define the Yoruba man as his moral/ethical values define him. Let's look at them one by one.

Prudence: Prudence as applied to Yoruba pragmatism means the act of avoiding undesired consequences or the act of doing something good in the name of discretion. Prudence is an important characteristic in the body of pragmatism.

Justice: Justice in this respect, and as it affects the Yoruba society, is the exercise of authority in the maintenance of right, just conduct and fairness.

Temperance: Temperance is an important natural virtue in Yoruba life. Every Yoruba person endeavours to abstain from alcohol. If he/she ever drinks at all, he/she is conscious of what happened to philosopher Obatala or Orisa-Nla who got drunk while he was sent by the Creator-philosopher to the earth to create Ile-Ife.

Valour: Valour is a wall built around Yoruba city-states. It is shown very often in their folk tales. Bravery is the benchmark of how Yoruba interprets the world. That philosopher Oduduwa built Ile-Ife out of valour is incontrovertible.

Honour: Honour is an indispensable attribute in Yoruba pragmatism. Yoruba people give honour to their personal heads as they give it to their leaders, especially their de jure kings.

Morality and Wisdom: It is wisdom that seriously defines the Book of Enlightenment. Yoruba pragmatism cannot exist without wisdom. Every Yoruba person is being reminded to be displaying wisdom every day in order not to perish before the numbers of his days are complete on the surface of the earth. Pragmatically, if a Yoruba man will stumble and fall down, he will stand up gingerly and look back at the cause of his fall. Looking back to examine the cause of his stumble and fall, shows how pragmatic he is. However, it is morality that perches like a cap upon wisdom. While a school of moral philosophers will assert that morality is the father of wisdom, some folk philosophers often argue that wisdom is antecedent to morality. The good news is that both are the attributes/characteristics of Yoruba pragmatism.

Honesty: Honesty is an indispensable attribute in Yoruba Book of Enlightenment, the book of **love and wisdom.** Yoruba people will not stop at rebuking cheating, fraudulence and dishonesty, the antonyms of honesty.

Fortitude: Yoruba people always ask Creator-philosopher Olodumare to give them calm courage, self-control in the face of pain, suffering, danger, disappointment, calamity or difficulty. A great deal of fortitude was displayed by D.O. Fagunwa in his narrative philosophy.

Love: Love is the pre-eminent phenomenon that defines the act of reasoning in the human society. It is the Alpha and Omega in whatever Yoruba people do. It occupies a very important chapter in the Book of Enlightenment. Hence the Book of Enlightenment is being referred to as the book of **love and wisdom.** Love, an important characteristic in Yoruba thought, is also an important natural virtue which is like a nature cure when properly utilized.

Chapter 27

The Effects of Paradoxes on Yoruba Philosophy

The effects of paradoxes on Yoruba philosophy are like a hay of embarrassments, if only courtesy or decency will forbid me (as I regard myself as an infinitesimal branch in the process of reasoning) to nail them to the board as the hays of confusion. The Yoruba man has (ori) head, right? The answer is a monosyllabic yes. The Yoruba man believes in his head as the definition of his entire body, yes. But during the Yoruba civil wars of the 18th and the 19th centuries, the Yoruba man did lose the quintessence, the import and the pragmatism of his head as evocative emotions of dishonour pushed him into several bloody civil wars. Where is the head of this circumspect creature of Olodumare? Why should he allow himself to succumb to the nadir of his existence? Answers may not be found easily. Additionally, we may not be certain as to how to juxtapose the effects of paradoxes relating to Yoruba philosophy. Definitely, and without an open-door quandary, there are many paradoxes that may be confirmed true and pragmatic as we wait patiently for the rain to fall ere the rays of sunshine emerge.

Many, many years ago, Queen Oshun, one of the principal philosophers, let the Yoruba land comprehend the theory that *manner or character begets beauty—iwalewa*. This is the reasoned supposition on the lips of a small number of the Yoruba men and women, while going to bed and while waking up. In order to honour this very important theory from one of the ancient philosophers, the small number of the Yoruba scions regarded character as the linchpin in any relationship, for no man wanted to marry a woman just because of her beauty, and no woman wanted to marry a man just because of his handsomeness.

However, there are suppurating evidences that things have changed today. Many Yoruba men and women thought the statement was a paradoxical one. Philosopher Oshun had contradicted herself, many would argue. They pointed out that the facial beauty and pulchritude is what attracts a male to a female and a female to a male, and not the character which is being affected by moods on a daily basis. Theoretically, *character begets beauty* is good to hear or listen to in discussions, in songs, in stories, in heroic deeds and in adages. It sounds eloquently and ethically too, but practically many people in Yoruba land are no longer subscribing to it. Yet many continue to enjoy the use of it.

Yoruba people utter and revel in many paradoxes: some as railleries and some as cockney humours. But despite their effects on Yoruba folk philosophy, the Yoruba people never stop believing that philosophy is the act of reasoning, coming from ori, the head/faculty, the definition of the entire body.

Yet another paradox which is common in the land and which affects Yoruba philosophy is the following statement: *Ise l'ogun ise.* This statement means working is the medicine for destitution. The statement was seen as unclear and contradictory. The ordinary Yoruba person does not come to terms with how working will ever serve as a medicine for destitution. Thus it takes some time before people begin to hug the statement. Again, it has its own effects on the act of thinking.

The most common paradox in recent years is the following: It takes a village to raise a child but my two children do not feel the presence of the village in their lives because they always come to the village only during the weekends. This sentence may sound contradictory because the two children only visit the village during the weekends. It might take a while before it becomes a common sense in the heart of anyone with a head, but as times goes on, it will be seen in its entirety as a non-contradictory sentence. Does this affect the thinking of a Yoruba philosopher in anyway? Yes, it does. Does it penetrate the heart and mind of every thinker? Yes, it does. Is it a supposition which both the intellectual and the scholar can ruminate over? Time will tell, as I am on the side of optimism.

This is the paradox which I know as I was growing up. Life is a place to cry in order to smile over crying as many times as we can. This paradox has a daily effect on Yoruba philosophy because of the word, life which is what we need as we engage in the act of reasoning.

Aye ni ajo sugbon orun n'ile. This translates to mean, Life is a sojourn, heaven is but a home. It can also be phrased in another way like this: Life is a temporary place but heaven is the permanent home. Since time immemorial, this statement has been a commonplace on the lips of Yoruba people, old and young, men and women. This is sole the paradox every culture vulture uses or points to whenever there is a discussion about life and death. Every folk philosopher believes that there is no death without life, and that there is no life without death. The savant tongue of a philosopher subscribes to the fact that life and death complements each other. He lets us know that any creature on the surface of the earth is on a temporary basis. Life is a place where there is no room for permanency but temporariness. Only when a person returns to heaven will he/she find a permanent abode.

In every chapter of Ifa-Ife Divination, the Book of Enlightenment, the source of **love and wisdom,** references are directly or indirectly made to this paradox. In some instances, philosopher Orunmila has compared life to a market place which one visits on a sojourn basis, returning home when shopping is done. The perceptive effects of this paradox are what immortality is to Creator-Philosopher Olodumare, as what mortality is to man.

Chapter 28

The Impacts of Proverbs on Yoruba Thought

The impacts of proverbs on Yoruba thought are like a chain of perceptions tying the proto-history of the Yoruba land to the present. They are like metaphorical allegories binding together anecdotal aphorisms. They are the beams of the sunshine and the moonlight. They are like the blood coursing through the veins of the Yoruba people. Because a Yoruba person needs a proverb every day, he/she is often called an honourable head with a proverb beneath his/her metaphorical tongue. The Yoruba man believes that a proverb is the salt of a word or a sentence. A proverb is a horse that races between heaven and earth. A proverb enlivens the head or the faculty, the domain of the act of reasoning. He cannot perceive how a sentence can be picturesque without a proverb. These are the suppurating evidences that demonstrate that proverbs have palpable impacts on Yoruba thought. Proverbs are the taproots of the Yoruba sentences. They are the chains that lead one to perceive life and understand life as the brainchild of the act of reasoning.

"The promise of the rain had begun. It has been pelting down now for seven hours. The sun has come out and the moon and the stars will be visible as soon as the day yields to the darkling." This is the utterance of Ijapa, the past master of the Yoruba folk philosophies and folktales.

The following narrative is an accretion that proves the fact that proverbs have day to day impacts on Yoruba thought. One day, Ijapa decided to embark on a short journey to Motoro to buy a gourd of palm wine, his favourite unadulterated drink. As he set out, he quickly adjured the road not to become his driver. That was minutes after he had verbalized the utterance above. About fifteen minutes later, he reached the precincts of Motoro. He began to scratch his head as he was thinking of what proverb he would say on entering the town. He was cognizant of what he had to do— answer every question proverbially. He had known a couple of friends who had visited Motoro in the past, and penalized for not knowing how to answer questions proverbially. How were his friends penalized? First, they were carried shoulder-high like heroes. Second, they were asked to farm for the keepers of traditions for three days after which they were set free, looking wiser than before.

Actually, one cannot infer that Ijapa does not have a repertoire of adages, maxims or saws in his head. He has, and possibly more than any other keeper of traditions or a philosopher in the land. When least expected, he had a paradoxical sleep, and waking up from the paradoxical sleep, and beholding Motoro Mountain which was clearly defined against the primary colours of the eastern sky, the following proverb emerged from his faculty: *"He who commits an atrocious act gives the person to whom it is committed strength."* With that in his head, he took some steps across the border into the town. A few yards before he reached the best tapster in the town, a fellow customer asked him whether a stutterer would ever call baba. He smiled and said, "No matter how long it will take, a stammerer/stutterer will call baba." In order to demonstrate to his fellow customer that he was not a dunderhead, a cretin or a dolt when it comes to the knowledge of the proverbs in the land, he said, "For a wise (head), a few words are adequate for comprehension."

On finishing his drink in thirty guttural gulps, he heaved a sigh of relief, characteristic of a connoisseur of palm wine and then began to wonder why Yoruba land is flooded with so many proverbs that are likened to the salt, "because it is my perception and here I speak for every son and daughter of Oduduwa that if one should consider the importance of the salt in our lives, we should also consider the import of fire in our lives, which is dangerous (nonetheless a friend of the seekers of love and wisdom) but which serves as the head of the kitchen as the human head serves as the definition of the body. This unequivocally demonstrates the fact that there are many contradictions in our kitchens. My spouse once likened a man to fire, while she compared a woman to the salt of the earth. I don't want to expatiate on this. I will leave this as a head of another discourse which life and all its ramifications may force me to exposition as I continue to run away from the good-for-nothing tail to the good-for-something head."

No sooner he completed his monologue than he looked behind him and saw his doting wife waiting for him with another gourd of palm wine in hand, telling him that to be happy, man must be good and to be good, man must be happy. She had bought the gourd of palm wine from which he would drink like a fish till the end of time. "My doting wife is in the midst of my felicity, for my felicity is incomplete without my wife and hers is incomplete without mine."

As a sudden perception of what might become his fate as a drinker crossed his mind, he commenced to remember many ancient and consequential proverbs—one after the other. He has become a proverb himself, another tassel to his hat of primary colours.

Chapter 29

The Philosophical Aphorisms

Yoruba land abounds in philosophical aphorisms. They are short, wise sayings, similar to proverbs, developed during the oral history of the land. Some aphorisms are expressed directly, while some are expressed indirectly. Either directly or indirectly, a Yoruba person who is wise in knowledge of Yoruba folk ways and folk lore will understand the philosophical aphorisms whenever they are spoken, or written.

The followings are some of them and they are capable of turning a numskull into a wise head.

Other creatures do not hurt man: it is because when man starts to hurt them, man starts to complain.

You dare not hate me, for no one hates the earth without treading upon it, for no one hates the water without drinking it, for no one hates the air without inhaling it. I am a component of these natural elements.

In order not to love and lose, set your eyes upon the day you'll pass on, for those who have loved and lost would be among those who would put your sand into the earth.

The world is as true or as false as the world elects to believe it.

If not for the forbidden fruit that ended in the gullets of Adam and Eve, the world could have found a full-fledged unconditional love.

Do not weep like a latchkey child, do something like a *Man*. Fela did not weep while doing those musical stunts of his, which he believed the on-going generation must not forget.

I do not kiss easily but whenever I do, peace within salvation comes out of fire.

I do not battle ordinarily but whenever I do, the earth gives birth to the mother of all battles.

Wars occur when the parties in conflict are bereft of civilization of rationality and compromise.

The philosophy, religion and literature of Ifa-Ife Divination survived during the turbulent waves of slavery and colonization because it is the only *covenant of hope* given to Africa by Creator-Philosopher Olodumare.

The burden of proof between fiction and nonfiction is always found between illusion and disillusion.

Fears and superstitions often lead to the death of uninitiated compound of a man.

A gentleman never fights with his hat on. Otherwise he'll lose it. In order to become a gentleman, my parents always ask me to wear my hat.

Any lore that widens people's horizon and presents food for thought is the beginning of philosophy.

There is always inadequacy in whatever man does. The inadequacy lingers on until man is able to find out the source of that which he has done.

If you say Africa belongs to the East, it is a joke. If you say it belongs to the West, you're not falling betwixt two stools.

Every idea is a thought as every thought is a dot.

Deeper than what man knows is a lot of what he does not know.

It is not possible to learn what no one knows.

A sound sleep presupposes a mind at rest. But if a leader cannot solve the power-failure in his beloved country, his mind is a rest-upon-failure.

By not knowing what's knowable when knowing is worth knowing, means knowledge is acquirable for whose mind is ready for it.

There is a proverb and philosophy in every name that proudly points to the creativeenergies of the ancestors.

Philosophy starts where the vestiges of slavery and colonization end.

Writers can only become wordsmiths without borders if only the countries and their borders put a finger on world literatures or multiculturalism.

Africa and Africans have been on the back burner for so long, now the continent can be on the front burner if only one of its countries is *allowed* to become a permanent member of the Security Council of the United Nations.

I walked through the ruins of invisibility in a broad daylight but I was rescued by the promptness of visibility during the midnight hours.

If there is anything to be learned by a non-African who has been reluctant to learn something about Africa, this is now the right century to learn it, for it is always possible to learn when there is something to learn.

Ame-fri-ca? has stood up to become a military and an economic super power: who will stand up to become a moral— (spiritually/philosophically) super power as the innocents are no longer molested by the pulpit?

Rather than chew a kola-nut of riches and *wahala* from the altar of irrationality and be famous, I will prefer to chew a kola-nut of riches from the altar of rationality and be non-famous.

Betwixt the major and the minor premises, I may find myself in a crossroad. But if the lot falls on me to choose one, I will fall for the minor premise to define me, epithetically.

Friendship is a grain of paradise that never withers, but on developing into love, that love becomes a universal mystery, to be understood only by people with mysterious minds.

Happiness is a lifetime treasure—a spring water that never dries.

Will it be regarded a slap on God's face anytime man defies to utilize the talent given to him by Creator-Philosopher Olodumare?

The sun knows when to rise and set. The moon knows when to phase. Any leader who does not know how to utilize the resources at his/her disposal, he/she is the most educated doltish leader on earth.

The earth is a creation of beauty and happiness. In order to appreciate this beauty and happiness, we need to appreciate the nature that speaks volumes to our beauty and happiness.

The natural thirst that is never quenched is the thirst for unconditional love.

Vanity is likened to the wind that strikes hardest the rock without a mark worthy of glory.

Man must be a creature of all seasons to understand the vagaries of human emotions.

If one adheres to one's tenor, one's tenet is almost established.

Man is the most worrisome creature. He is the most worrisome creature because he depends wholly on other non-human creatures for his survival.

It is the mind that interprets what the eyes behold, for without the mind, the eyes will be likened to a blurred mirror.

Life is a whirligig. And man's philosophy of happiness is found or evidently apparent in the whirligig of time, inasmuch as man is answerable to his five senses—sight, hearing, smell, taste, and touch, as he grows every day to make a mark in the world.

As long as man has ori (head in Yoruba), man has a body of philosophy, for ori (head) is the substrate onto which other parts of the body are answerable to.

I am working with time and refuse time to brutalize my life and bury my body, without my soul.

Good literature quickens imagination, gladdens the heart, and adds fullness to the meaning of life, to be found in the aesthetics of contradictions, alive in our seeing, hearing, smelling, tasting and touching.

The beauty I behold in an angel is less than my desire to invest in that beauty because that beauty may not be on the same par with her character.

Amongst the thistles, there is a beautiful thing to behold that can be a sight for sore eyes.

Even the brightest halo of success does not always perch upon the most diligent.

The foes fell so low –so woefully low that all attempts to rescue them seem to have been suspended.

May kindness adorn your life and make me part of that kind adornment.

Reasons not to understand the mysteries of the world are the same reasons why no one understands the crow of a chanticleer.

I opened my heart to the water of peace, to the air of life, to the mother nature of love so as comprehend the whistling sound of the wind amongst the willows.

I have long established in my heart that a contrite heart should rise above all the vestiges of perfidies if that heart is truly contrite.

A wordsmith whose work (writing on philosophy) is teachable and learnable is a teacher. It does not matter whether his/her students are in a private or public setting, campus-based or online.

Life does not start with speaking, it starts with thinking, a limb in the act of reasoning, courtesy of the head.

The more you know your history and become part of it, the better you will feel.

Man must be happy to be good. Conversely, man must be good to be happy.

I will not close my womb or break away from the wisdom, inherent in the keepers of traditions until all my children born in Diaspora in the 21st century begin to bear some African names—honouring their long pedigrees, accentuating their enlightenment, dignifying their regal freedoms and sweetening their birth water.

Let the mind be the reader and let the head be the interpreter of what the mind reads.

Each time I step out of my paradise-like hole, I learn the act of living through cognition, and the act of departure, which occurs whenever living has overstayed its tenure.

Chapter 30

The Colourful House of Ethics

In his numerous pronouncements, which today had become his magnum opus, Divinity-Philosopher Oduduwa lets us know that morality is the taproot and the fruit of religion, while character (iwa) is the faith associated with morality. Additionally, he would remind his subjects that the codes of morality or the ethical codes in Yoruba land are so high and precious. And because they are so high and precious, all the scions of the land should uphold them as jealously as they could, so as not to become an object of ridicule. The colourful house of ethics in Yoruba land is as old as Ile-Ife. In other words, the Yoruba people have known ethics since the myth that created the world. From their nimble-minded divinities, they have learnt that ethics is a branch of philosophy in which the society evaluates a particular course of moral actions. They have realized that ethics is a system of moral principles. As a matter of course, they are convinced that ethics deals roundly with what is morally good and bad, right and wrong.

Like many principles, apparent in our existence, ethics is a two-way phenomenon. The following is credited to philosopher Oduduwa who once said, "Children are indispensable in our culture. It is evident that a child's hand cannot reach the high shelf. It is also evident that an Elder's hand cannot enter the gourd. Therefore, for a culture to prosper, children should play their part and the Elders, the keepers of traditions, should continue to play their part, as they continue to initiate our children into the realm of happiness, wisdom and the ingredients of moral integrity and rectitude."

Yoruba land has always been a polytheistic society. That is they believe or worship more than one deity who is answerable to the Supreme Deity. All their deities pay their allegiance to that Supreme Deity, Olodumare, the philosopher Creator of heaven and earth. Their act of reasoning let them know their dos and don'ts come from Olodumare via the intermediary divinities. Therefore, their concept of God has every chapter and verse to perpetuate what is taken to be the rationality and the norm of morality. Morality is therefore both the taproot and the grain of paradise, as found in the act of reasoning. The two are inseparable. And no one attempts to s-e-p-a-r-a-t-e them.

Good and bad, right and wrong are like a tabernacle with two front doors. While good and bad share the same entrance, right and wrong must go through the same door. No matter when and how they labor to go in, the two pairs must meet each other in the middle of the tabernacle. They must meet at the centre because the Creator–Philosopher is always theocentric. He is the acme of the universe as the head (ori) is the definition of the body. In Yoruba land, any one born of woman must meet at the centre, the altar. The altar in this sense is the womb of the community, under the auspices of the keepers of traditions who pay their homage to the ethical values and the **love and wisdom** in the **IFA**-Ife Divination, the Book of Enlightenment. The Creator is the highest Divinity in the centre of morality, and in the centre lies one's harvest, consequences of one's words and deeds. Because we cannot separate morality from philosophy or from religion, every Yoruba is a believer in philosophy, as he or she is a believer in religion, at least in the olden days, if not now. And because he/she is a believer, he/she is duty-bound to adhere to what the Creator-Philosopher sanctions to be good or bad, right or wrong.

We have seen that it is good to be healthy, happy and to be successful and so on. Also, we have noticed that every soul wants to bask in the grace or glory of Creator-Philosopher Olodumare. You want to grow old, you want to be safe, you want to ward off evils living in the powers of darkness and overcome difficulties. All is philosophically good and bold. These possible desires (nay negative) are the good and the right things every Yoruba person strives for. In order to be healthy, happy and prosperous, one is obliged to do the right thing, knowing rationally that there are rewards for the good and punishments for the bad. One doesn't have to kill before one knows that killing is bad and unethical. Yoruba scions say that if you don't know what it is to be in pains, put your fingers in a fire. Another apt or fitting aphorism that tells us to be wary the way we treat others is this. "*A dani loro f'agbara ko ni.*" This translates to mean, "*He who commits an atrocious act gives the person to whom it is committed strength.*" In everything, as in all things, there is always requital for good or evil.

It is the same Creator-Philosopher who dispenses rewards for good and punishments for bad that encourages obedience, and repudiates disobedience. Therefore, morality/ethics demands that we obey the rules and regulations as laid down by the loving-kindness of the highest Supreme Being, for the Yoruba people not only think of the present world we are living in, they rationalize very much also of the Hereafter.

The most important features of the Yoruba ethics is not obedience, disobedience, reward or punishment. It is **Iwa** (character). Noble character is the most important mirror that acts like a reflection of the body. Noble character is the sun that shines; it is the moon that shimmers. It is the head that dictates every action of the body. It is that very quality that distinguishes man from a quadruped like an addax or gnu. Noble character is the real God's image in man, the very sense why the Yoruba say *"we are created in the image and the mirror of Creator-Philosopher Olorun."* Noble character transcends anything man possesses on earth. It is true to know that Yoruba land builds its moral education on noble character, for it is character which the Author of Life judges before one's soul could be consigned to him. To the Yoruba, and for the Yoruba, man's wealth on earth depends on his character, hence Olodumare stresses pragmatically that character must be the primary content in the colourful house of ethics.

The following are the principal constituents which lead to the noble character, the constituents of happiness.

1: Abstinence from falsehood
2: Abstinence from malevolence
3: Abstinence from stealing or from robbery
4: Cultivating the habit of telling the truth
5: Cultivating the spirit of loving-kindness
6: Cultivating the spirit of hospitality
7: Abstinence from selfishness
8: Giving honour and due respect to old age
9: Protecting women as the better halves
10: Abstinence from hypocrisy
11: Chastity rather than un-chastity should be encouraged in womanhood
12: Avoid treading the path of pride and dishonour.

The Yoruba's colourful house of ethics is like the philosophical calabash bowl of ethos. From this calabash bowl ethos, one can find the quintessence of life. It is handed down from the Creator-philosopher to his beloved messenger-philosopher Oduduwa, the founder of the holy city, Ile-Ife, as we have read in chapters one and eleven of this book. For generations, Yoruba, as a people, have not only adhered to this colourful house of ethics (the embodiment of their happiness), they have also offered the divine souls their hands of fellowship and milk of human kindness, accentuated by esprit de corps.

> Noble character (Iwa) makes it easy for
> A village to raise its children
> Never withers, the grains of paradise
> Planted by noble character

> Like a touch, it lights the lives of our children,
> Who are lighting the world, in their natural skin colours.

Iwa ni esin: Noble character is a religion or a faith. That is, a religion forms a good character. While the act of reasoning—philosophy (the brainchild of religion), opens the faculty to the how? And why? Noble character reflects in the ethos—the attitudes and behaviours of the believers.

It is incomprehensible and could be perceived as preposterous to know that more than a whit (more than a little bit) has been happening lately to Yoruba house of ethics. One of the principal constituents that lead to noble character is rudely attacked. Thus the calabash of morality is chipping away with the dawn of each day. Which one of those constituents are we talking about? We are talking about stealing or robbery in number three above. Every Yoruba person who does not believe that philosophy precedes religion is likely to lapse into thievishness today. In the past the act of reasoning would prevent anyone from stealing things that did not belong to him/her. Retrospectively, this is like a slap on the face of the pioneer and father of Yoruba idealism and philosophy, respectively.

Natural and Cardinal Virtues: There are two types of virtues or attributes that are reflected in Yoruba philosophy and religion. Natural virtues are the first known attributes in Yoruba act of reasoning. They were first introduced by Oduduwa and his contemporary philosophers. They are love, morality, justice, honour, valour, prudence and temperance. During and after the birth of Yoruba religion, a set of attributes, known as cardinal virtues was introduced to the land. These attributes are love, morality, justice, honour, valour, prudence, temperance, honesty and fortitude. They all belong to the colourful house of ethics. The most consequential of these nine virtues are morality and love.

Chapter 31

The Religion-Philosophy of Samuel Ajayi Crowther (1807-1891)

Samuel Ajayi Crowther was consecrated the first Anglican African Bishop in 1864 when Yoruba land was beginning to take the will for the need. He was informed and transformed by the knowledge of Yoruba culture—folk philosophy, religion and literature. Cognizant of Yoruba morality, he emphasized on character (iwa) as the seed of Life, which makes Life a joy because character is pleasing to the Author of Life—Creator-Philosopher Olodumare. Additionally, he was an idealist, a linguist of many African languages, including Latin and Greek. He was absolutely prepared to enlighten all the citizens of the land, religiously, philosophically, sociologically, economically and politically. Translating the English Bible into Yoruba Bible in 1880; makes him the first ecclesiast to do so on the African continent. Today, all the religio-philosophers in Yoruba land have learned and continued to learn and follow his footsteps. A positive thinker of excellent character, he was erudite, pragmatic and circumspect. His emulative pragmatism amazed his bishopric colleagues in Africa and in overseas. Many wondered how a basket weaver, an ex-slave could be so diligent, humble and flexible.

With the courtesy of folk philosophy, as well as by the virtue of narrative or folk philosophy, let's listen to how *Ajayi Crowther's Piano* by this author has shed light on him as the nineteenth-century folk and language philosopher, religio-philosopher, missionary and abolitionist after he had become a venerated Bishop in 1864, the same year he was awarded Doctor of Divinity by the Oxford University.

The sun was just scratching and removing the wisps of clouds from its path when Bishop Crowther woke up with a stretch and a yawn. A positive thinker, he believed that life is worth-living to the fullest. He had studied classics. He had studied European philosophy. He did not know what next he had to study but African philosophy in general and Yoruba philosophy in particular. So in fairness to his faculty and the sense of belonging, to which he had been faithful, he had devoted the last months of his life to Yoruba narrative/folk philosophy. This is the time to do so. A time when there were so many cross-purposes caused by his overseas bishopric colleagues. It was God's good time in which he intuited that his overseas bishopric colleagues wanted to divest him of his vestments.

In his exchange of correspondences with Karl Marx (1818-1883), a few moons after completing **The Role of Religion, Philosophy and Literature in Advancing Yoruba Language,** his magnum opus, he argued that the ethics of rulership in Yoruba land in which a ruling house would sway its absolute authority over its domestics could be likened to the bourgeoisie versus the proletariat or the working class in Europe which was the fundamental focus of Karl Marx. Would the small fingers ever carry out their revolution against the big fingers? Prior to his death in 1883, Karl Marx could not conceal his exultation that he was one of the few European philosophers who knew a whit of truth (courtesy of Ajayi Crowther) about Yoruba folk philosophy.

According to the Yoruba ancient saw, a road can never be straight from the beginning to the end without a bend. Today, that aphorism is hardly true. A road can be straight from the beginning to the end without a bend. But a road can never be straight if the road chooses to become a driver. And this opens to two schools of argumentative discourses. Additionally, taken from another perspective, we may liken a road to life which never progresses (straight) without smooth and rough edges. There are always joys and tears as life progresses.

Meeting the Elders and keepers of traditions from the north to the south, and from the east to the west of the land, it quickly occurred to him that Yoruba folk philosophy is full of aphorisms. He was made to understand that a folk philosophy is the cultural philosophy of a people depicting their cardinal virtues, such as morality, love, temperance, prudence, honor, honesty, bravery, justice and fortitude. He learnt from the ancients that Yoruba philosophy is a narrative, folk, or cultural philosophy, explicating and pointing to the knowledge of the causes and the nature of things, affecting the corporeal and the spiritual world and its wellness. According to him, philosophy helps in exercising the minds, especially when dialoguing.

Ajayi's Philosophy of Mathematics: Even if Bishop Ajayi Crowther did resign as the Bishop whose evangelization brought conversion to all the citizens in the coastal settlements and towns of West Africa, his door always remained ajar to those seeking his spiritual guidance, wisdom, knowledge and love. He once convinced his students with a demonstrative theory that 4 plus 4 equals 9. This is how he proved the theory. He brought from his dashiki pocket two ropes of equal length. Each rope had four knots. Then he decided to have one single rope and he commenced to tie the ropes. On tying the ropes, he had added a new knot, making 9 knots altogether. So his theory had practically been proved. Mathematically, he would expound that **30** is a common multiple of 2, 3, 5, 6, 10 and 15, while **28** is a multiple of 7. His penchant for mathematics explained why he believed that mathematics is everything in life so far as there are additions, subtractions, divisions and multiplications in our daily life.

In some of his cockney humors that embodied major and minor premises, during which time he would love to play his pianoforte, some girls would begin to dance. And to those who were not dancing because of shyness, he would say: *All the girls know how to walk and dance: you are girls, therefore, you must know how to walk and dance.* Here, he succeeded in shedding light on both major premise and minor premise.

In his teaching of Yoruba folk philosophy to the youths, he added the following to the repertoire of Yoruba narrative/folk philosophy: Once upon a time, there was a village where the village girls had to walk a long distance to fetch water from a misfit stream that never dried in spite of a year-old drought in the village. Jokayi was a village girl who went to fetch water after she had been told not to bother to go because of her swollen thumb. Her response was that all the water fetchers came from a village and because she came from a village, she must become a water fetcher, stretching the value of major and minor premises.

It happened one day, during one of his lectures, and when least expected, one of his auditors stood up, announced his name as Labijo and asked, "Could the Bishop let us know why his beloved wife go by the name Lai Philosopher?"

"Thank you very much," said the Bishop. "This is the second time I would be asked the question. In each time, I would hold the brief for my spouse. Next time, if the question arises again, I would ask my wife to answer the question herself. She is called Lai Philosopher because she could humbly and joyfully trace her pedigrees to the artist-philosophers of the land. The cognomen is symbiotically regarded as her pseudonym. Labijo, are you satisfied with my explanation?"

"Yes, I am sir," said Labijo with a nod of contentment.

After this, Rosa, an overgrown Creole damsel with a green-white-green bandanna, whose pinched mouth was in contrast to her wide, luscious and fleshy lips, stood up and said in a deliciously dulcet voice, "In some of his philosophical homilies, our progenitor lets us understand that everyone should go for philosophy because philosophy enhances the mind and widens one's horizons. Could the Bishop expatiate on this?"

Bishop Ajayi Crowther wiped his brow with his milk-white handkerchief and rejoined that our progenitor was trying to pinch out the lateral buds in philosophy. He added, "Certainly, philosophy enhances the faculty. It opens our minds to small and big ideas, especially when dialoguing or when an exchange of views (arguments) is involved. Due to their ceaseless search for wisdom, philosophers are expected to be hatchers and bearers of reasoning and knowledge, capable of sanitizing the world, liberating the mind and allowing the human race achieve its potential—scientifically, spiritually and corporeally."

Then Joke's tiny and pusillanimous voice sang in the air and said, "How could terracotta artists ascertain that the foreign archaeologists are not misdating their artworks? Secondly, could you tell us what Y-O-R-U-B-A stands for?"

Bishop Ajayi Crowther harrumphed and said, "According to my light, there is no way the terracotta artists could tell, especially when the dating was done in their absence. If they were to be here today, they would probably challenge those archaeologists and authenticate that some of their pre-dynastic artworks were over 10, 000 years old. You see, many of the foreign archaeologists could not imagine that the Yoruba artists had the genius, the precocity to produce such exquisite naturalistic civilization. This is the core problem, the amazing superiority of one naturalistic civilization over the other.

"Your second question falls under speculative philosophy. In short, Yoruba stands for a monotheistic unity as instructed by Creator-Philosopher Olodumare, and morally upheld, and thusly explained by Divinity-Philosopher Oduduwa:

"**Y:** Yes, we believe in thee
O: Oh Olodumare
R: Redeem us from
U: Upper to our entire
B: Bodies
A: Amen/Ase."

Oduduwa's philosophy of the golden rule had turned domestic slaves into domestics or household attendants. And his philosophy of neighbourliness tore apart the ancient practices of sacrificing human beings (as in the Old Testament) as immolations to Creator-Philosopher Olodumare through deities.

Giving credit to King/Divinity-Philosopher Oduduwa, and appreciating his philosophical mind, he laid emphasis on ori—head as the most important part of the body, the definition of the body, the substrate unto which other parts of the body are answerable. He theorized that in order for the scions of the land to believe in their philosophy, they should understand themselves, and to believe in their philosophy, and in order to believe in their philosophy, they must themselves be in some degree philosophers.

Chapter 32

Philosophy of Yoruba Language

Language and literature deal with words. Because both of them deal with words, they do butt each other. But the butting of heads has somehow subsided to a whit. And so the butting has not been destructive. But a few cross-purposes were noted and regarded as anachronisms. In this day and age, language and literature have stopped butting their heads with each other. While language is the system, literature is the field within that system. But how do we define language? We can define language as the system of communication spoken or written, consisting of words in a structured and conventional way. How do we define literature? Literature can be defined as anything written or oral, covering all the fields of learning.

Language is very crucial in whatever we want to communicate. According to the nineteenth-century religion-philosopher Bishop Dr. Samuel Ajayi Crowther (1807-1891), father of modern Yoruba language philosophy, and according to other language lovers in the world in general and in Yoruba-land in particular, language has more than one aim or purpose and it is used differently in different contexts. During his academic stay in Oxford, Dr. Samuel Ajayi Crowther pointed out that "I weave," is a whole different linguistic deal from saying "I sculpt." He added that "I sculpt," is not the same thing as weaving, but verbalized that "I weave," is the same thing as sculpting. This type of language among ordinary language philosophers may be difficult to comprehend because Dr. Samuel Ajayi Crowther himself was once a weaver before he rose from that humble beginning to the height of his destiny and the acme of his scholarship.

(Thomas Cathcart has demonstrated in his book, *Plato and Platypus Walk into a Bar*, that philosophy and language can elicit some kind of cockney humours and air of felicity. The author lets us know that both philosophy and language can lead to the construction and payoff of jokes and the construction and payoff of philosophical concepts are made of the same stuff.) Aphoristically, we may add to this by saying that things that are equal to the same are equal to one another.

Let's Consider the Following as Pioneered by Bishop (Dr.) Samuel Ajayi Crowther: When a Yoruba language philosopher rejoins and says to an Elder, the keeper of traditions, "Pa, I understand you beyond what you have verbalized or what you intend to say." He can also put it this way, "Pa, I surely know where you are heading with your sentence."

In order to fully grasp the reality which is what the language philosopher purposes to achieve, the language philosopher finds the fullness of life. The Elder may praise the language philosopher for being smart. He/she may infer that half a word suffices for the wise. And that wise is **omoluwabi**—character-conscious person. As an intellectual, a language philosopher who is supposed to be engaged in critical study, thought and reflection about the reality of the society, and then proposes solutions for the normative problems of the society must be cognizant of the fact that a word or language is like an egg, once dropped, it breaks into fragments and cannot be pieced together to be the same again.

Here is a simple but important illustration. I love Creator-Philosopher Olodumare/God to love human beings is not the same as I love good to love human beings. But some traditional or language philosophers will argue that the goal and the intention is the same since Creator-Philosopher Olodumare is good and to love good is to love Creator-Philosopher Olodumare, as there is no good without the love of Creator-Philosopher Olodumare.

This is another clash of the language whose aim or objective is the same: Tulasi and Babami planned to enter one of the Pearly Gates. Tulasi was the first to arrive. Instead of entering the Pearly Gate, he simply sat down waiting for the door to open by itself. But when Babami came for the same purpose, he taught Tulasi what to do. The following is the dialogue between the seekers of immortality by the door of one of the Pearly Gates.

Tulasi: So I must wait all this long for the Pearly Gates to open.

Babami: What are you doing here?

Tulasi: Waiting for the voice of God to open the door leading to the Pearly Gates.

Babami: You don't need all that wait. Just push the door open. If you love God that is what you need to do: the par for the course.

Tulasi: I love God and human beings too.

Babami: Let's go. We need not argue over the construction of the language.

What we must continue to remember is that language philosophers seek to understand the way language represents reality. In this respect, we may want to expatiate upon the truths of facts and the truths of imaginations, as shown below.

Here is a case in which two language philosophers subscribed to the truth of fact and the truth of imagination as they padded towards a blind alley. One accepted that the alley was indeed blind but the other could not bring himself to accept the reality/truth that the alley was indeed blind because he could climb over the fence and continue padding along. Some of the confusions we do find in our spoken and written words occur because language philosophers represent realities differently. And we don't know how often truths of facts and truths of imaginations play into each other.

A: *Mo ti de ile ayo, nibiti awaon alayo tin se ayo.* This is translated to: I have reached a home/house of happiness, where happy people regale in happiness.

B: *Mo ti de ile ife, nibiti awon onife ti nse ife.* This is translated into: I have reached a house/home of love, where loving people celebrate love.

In A and B, we see how a language philosopher or a philosopher of language seeks to use **"where."** The interrogative adverb helps him/her to understand the way language represents reality in fullness. The nature of the house/home and the content of the character of the home/house helps him or her to better understand how language represents reality, and this is made possible and explicit by the use of where, an interrogative adverb. This is a finite reality within realities because human understanding is finite.

Conclusion

According to my father, "The world of the enslaved and the colonized people is handicapped." The most handicapped of their personality is psychology, followed by philosophy. The former colonized and enslaved people they know will have to depend on their masters for a long, long time to come before they could free themselves from the historical world of their masters.

When the Europeans came to their various lands to divide and rule, they came with one absolute idea at the backs of their minds—the idea to plant their political, philosophy and psychological systems in the hearts and souls of the people they were enslaving or colonizing. They succeeded. Their success can be seen or felt everywhere today. See what is happening in India, Brazil and Nigeria, for example. These three countries belong to the first ten most populous countries in the world, colonized by Britain and Portugal, respectively.

From the oral to the written accounts, it is not common to see a domestic servant or slave rise above his master. This is the case today amongst the peoples whose pedigrees had once been boxed in slavery or colonialism. They have lost their tongues. They have lost their orientation. They have lost their roots and riches. Their world is handicapped, period. They have been elevated to the position of a domestic and to rise to the apex of their former riches and determinism will take another millennium.

With little or no references to the psychological bruises of the past, the former enslavers and colonizers refer to them as poor people, knowingly forgetting that they are the causes of their poor conditions. But what they cannot or must not forget, either pretentiously or unpretentiously is their language (part of the totality of man) which they have used in capturing and manipulating the enslaved and the colonized people and which the enslaved and colonized people are using till today.

For many years, indeed for many centuries, the Holy Bible has been regarded by the three monotheistic luminaries—Christianity, Islam and Judaism—as a divinely inspired treatise that shows evidence of Olodumare's pre-eminence (omnipotence, omnipresence and omniscience) and manifestation. But with the rise of Philosopher Obafemi Awolowo (popularly called Chief Awo) and a few other intellectuals and scholars, the Holy Book is revealed as being composed by human beings who after their thorough research believe the world should have one universal God to be worshipped in truth and in spirit, as opposed to worshipping God through gods and goddesses, ancestors and other visible and invisible phenomena which had been worshipped since the time of the Early Man.

Their research is so downright that it is very hard to replace the Holy Bible from its pre-eminence when it comes to religion, philosophy, literature, history, anthropology and mathematics which all these inspired ancient writers have put together in its pages, from Genesis to Revelation.

Hurrah! Philosophy has loosened itself from the stranglehold of religion. And one can predict or rationalize with certainty that as more and more people are interested in African philosophies: as more and more researches are being carried out, efforts should now be made to carve out carefully the philosophy of each country instead of lumping them together under that mammoth land mass, called Africa. Often times, prominent philosophers are left out.

Additionally, African philosophy will invariably be a limb borrowed from European philosophy if our researchers do not address, discourse, emphasize and bring to the front burner the folk philosophy—the people's philosophy, known long before the advent of the occupiers.

It is no fallacy when we say Africans made an egregious mistake by not defending themselves with weapons of mass disorientation during the time their lands were besieged and occupied. They forgot that any creature—tree, fish, bird, quadruped, has a natural weapon to ward off an unwanted intruder. Man has no such natural weapon, hence man has devised means to protect himself so that he can be on the same par with other creatures.

Those Europeans who arrived as anthropologists even carried dangerous weapons. Most of these European anthropologists came from tribal Europe and imposed upon Africans their tribal ways of life. What existed in Africa before their imposition are chiefdoms, according to the keepers of traditions. They pooh-poohed Africans as *primitive* or *tribal* because *primitive* or *tribal* is what they experienced or knew before coming to Africa to use such misnomers.

"Let's travel to the much-discussed distant exotic lands. As we travel, we shall find out how their cultures are similar or different from our past cultures, for traveling is a form of education." Thus each European who was able to travel to Africa in the days of colonialism is highly regarded—educationally and experientially.

As made explicit earlier, Yoruba culture from the proto-history to the present, consists of folk/cultural philosophy, autochthonous religion and folk tales. They are embodied in Ifa-Ife Divination, known as the tripartite Book of Enlightenment in Yoruba land and in Diaspora.

Yoruba philosophy is a witness of two epochs. The first epoch is an epoch-making history in cosmology and mythology. This is also an epoch-making history in oral philosophy in oral culture during which time Oduduwa was the sole philosopher, the head, the Bringer of Light, and a prominent diviner. He theorized about the visible and invisible worlds, reminiscing about the cosmology, cosmogony, and the mythological creatures in the visible and invisible worlds.

The second epoch is the epoch of metaphysical philosophy. This commenced in the 19th century when the land was becoming literate through the diligence and pragmatism of Dr. Bishop Ajayi Crowther, the first Anglican Bishop.

Although religion is often considered first in Yoruba culture, nonetheless, it is philosophy, the thought of man and the reasoning of the mind that actually leads the faculty to the creation and the practice of religion. Thus philosophy is antecedent to religion.

Today, the academic and the non-academic people are becoming more and more interested in Yoruba philosophy. Thus more and more researches are being carried out on Yoruba philosophy, as more and more books are being written on it—embossing its mark and advancing its research amongst non-African thinkers and political scientists who are beginning to open their doors to other cultures, widening their views.

From the Yoruba's perspective, as embodied in the folk memory, and Ifa-Ife, the tripartite Book of Enlightenment, a folk philosophy is a narrative philosophy, explicating and pointing to the knowledge of the causes and the nature of things, affecting the corporeal and the spiritual universe—and its wellness.

Pragmatically, the Yoruba land is a land rich in hundreds of philosophical aphorisms and lore. This explains why the Yoruba people believe and adhere to the fact that any lore that widens people's horizons and presents food for thought, is the beginning of philosophy. Yes, it is the beginning of philosophy, we will say in one voice, for Yoruba philosophy or the act of reasoning has been in the dark since the departure of Divinity-Philosopher Oduduwa. Let's turn on the light and the dark will flee and disappear, for sure.

It is hoped that this book will set free one and all from the bondage of religion. We will be manumitted and then recognize that philosophy is the act of reasoning as deposited in our heads and religion is the passion as deposited in our hearts. That passion must have bruised our hearts so much that we invariably feel that without religion we will be delivered into the hands of fear, and that fear will in turn deliver us into the hands of death.

The progress made so far is the progress emanating from reason to rise and develop our faculties, for no one will ever say that his/her reason comes from acquiring wealth. Reason has made such progress a food for thought. And as more and more colleges and universities are producing graduates in Yoruba philosophy, they will surely spread the notion that philosophy is antecedent to religion. It is then, it is only then they will commence to munch from the seeds of enlightenment. Partaking from the seeds of enlightenment will enable them to tread the path constructed by reasoning and not a kind of passion coated with evocative emotions.

We may, if hard pressed, rationally submit that it is a plausible scenario to embrace the notion that philosopher Oduduwa will continue to occupy the number one position on the list of Yoruba ancient thinkers. Like his symbiotic contemporaries, he is not an additive inverse who is added to a real number that is expected to produce or result into zero.

Many of the leading lights on folk philosophy, most notably Oduduwa, Dr. Samuel Johnson, D. O. Fagunwa, Amos Tutuola, who were downright believers in the new and old cardinal virtues and values, do not want the Yoruba faith and philosophy to perish. (What Oduduwa produced before he paid his debt to nature is philosophy, which later gave birth to religion, as noted in chapter one).

Conclusion

Many questions are arising today which the young and old are beginning to be asking. They include the following: How long has religion been encroached on philosophy? How long has philosophy been moping inside the box of religion? How long have the scholars and intellectuals been discoursing, recording and theorizing without taking a stand or holding brief for philosophy? Were the Yoruba wars fought because of the religious and philosophical differences? Have there been tensions and suspicions on both sides—philosophy and religion?

How many Yoruba faith-healers and diviners and believers in the **love and wisdom** in the Book of Enlightenment were persecuted during the encroachment of the alien faiths—Christianity and Islam? There may be no record, as an evidence, but if and when a record is found, it will be non-consequential and obsolete. But a record of how the boards of divination and other diviners' paraphernalia were pooh-poohed or disdained can readily be made available, albeit orally.

If only temporization or procrastination can be eschewed, our heads (ori) will rejoice as reason will dominate our heads/faculties. Verily, we will bear our light and we will not wait for others to carry it for us.

One more thing is remaining. That one more thing is very crucial if we want the seeds of philosophy to grow and become the seeds of enlightenment in this 21st century. The Yoruba need to desist from asking the following preposterous question: **Omo ta ni o?** This translates to mean **whose child are you?** This is the question on the lips of so many Yoruba during the Yoruba wars of the 19th centuries, the period of Yoruba renaissance during which time the luminaries in the names of Bishop Ajayi Crowther, Dr. Samuel Johnson, Herbert Macaulay and others brought a new wheel of enlightenment to the land. This question is not only preposterous but also embarrassing. It is but a misnomer. It is an affront to Oduduwa, the preeminent philosopher of the milk-and-honey-flowing land who had livingly enjoined every scion of this land of milk and honey to always and morally carry a decent tongue beneath his or her tongue. Now that peace is reigning supreme in the land, now that we recognize that king/Divinity-Philosopher Oduduwa is the father of the land, now that we see ourselves as the descendants of Oduduwa in the past, in the present and in the future scenarios, now that we know that each and every one of us is either a prince or a princess, now that reason has prevailed over evocative emotions of faith, now that we recognize Ile-Ife as the sole holy city in the land, we should stop asking such an absurd question, for asking such a ridiculous question demonstrates that the bad spirit of belligerence is still in our blood. We are the citizens of Yoruba land, munching the same fruit of freedom and equality. To dream of the second coming of philosopher Oduduwa for the purpose of telling us the exposition of the question is like praying for the second coming of the Son of man, who is also a philosopher in his own right. Let's inter, **"Whose child are you?"** once and for all. But before we inter it or excommunicate it like a pariah, let us change the embarrassing question into **"Who is the father of Yoruba folk philosophy?"**

The supra, as subtle as it is, comes to one encapsulation. And that encapsulation is that Yoruba philosophy has succeeded in proclaiming itself as the leader of Yoruba culture. From the oral culture of its distant past to its vibrant present and buoyed by its scholarly discourses, Yoruba philosophy is best understood as a folk philosophy, a set of narratives and cultural practices that attempt to explain the causes and the nature of things affecting the corporeal and the spiritual universe.

The Yoruba people, who number more than 30 million on the African continent and many millions in their Diaspora, inhabit a world of myths, allegories, poetry, and the love and wisdom of the Ifa divination system. Those are just a few of the components of Yoruba culture, the genesis of which is the holy city of Ile-Ife, Nigeria. They serve to remind the Yoruba of a past that has survived through oral tradition. From that foundation have Yoruba philosophy religion, and literature developed, all of which blend ancient truths and divine moralities with reason.

Prominent Yoruba scholars, intellectuals, leaders, and others—among them Samuel Adjai Crowther, Obafemi Awolowo, Wole Soyinka, Wande Abimbola, Sophie Oluwole, Toyin Falola, Lusiah Teish, Abiola Irele, Stephen Adebanji Akintoye, Kola Abimbola, Biodun Jeyifo, Rowland Abiodun and Jacob Olupona—have analyzed and weighed the theory that the ancient hero and deity Oduduwa is the founder of the Yoruba nation, the bringer of light to the Yoruba people, and the pioneer of Yoruba philosophy. This discussion is a continuing one, and it is vital to understanding Yoruba philosophy.

Yoruba philosophy is rich in aphorisms and proverbs. It is also committed to a search for love and wisdom, which is evident in the first novel published in the Yoruba language—D.O. Fagunwa's Ogboju Ode Ninu Igbo Irunmale (1938). In his novel, as in many of his other literary works, Fagunwa blended fantastic fables with folk philosophy and religion, and it reflects the admixture of happy and unhappy imaginings he found within himself. E. Bolaji Idowu took a similar focus in Olódùmaré: God in Yoruba Belief, a work of theology; its research was carried out in 1955, and the book was published in 1962. More than any book of or about the Yoruba in the 20th century, Olódùmaré succeeded in combining religion with philosophy and literature. It makes clear that any lore that widens people's horizons and presents food for thought is the beginning of philosophy. Olódùmaré also underscores that Yoruba philosophy is a folk philosophy that valorizes the Yoruba people's cardinal virtues—namely, love, morality, temperance, honesty, honour, bravery, justice, prudence, and fortitude.

The word for head in Yoruba—ori—carries physical and spiritual connotations that cannot be separated. The ori defines the body; other parts of the body are answerable to it. The ori holds the body's knowledge and is its destiny. Yoruba philosophy cannot exist without an ori. In a similar vein, Yoruba philosophy can be considered antecedent to Yoruba religion, in the same manner that every idea comes from the head before going into action.

IFA-Ife Divination may not be common in other African philosophies, but it is for the Yoruba people an oasis of wisdom, love, and morality. It is a fulcrum that is independent of Western or Asian philosophy. Complex and indispensable, **IFA**-Ife Divination is an integral component of Yoruba culture. **IFA**-Ife Divination is made explicit through its Babaláwo, he who is versed in the knowledge and wisdom of the unknown—a philosopher steeped in his love for nature, in the use of herbs, and in the ways of the countryside. For Yoruba culture to be analytically meaningful, there must be **IFA**-Ife Divination, just as there must be the ori. Thus, a Yoruba writer is dependent on that fulcrum. Someone who writes on Yoruba religion can thus be called a religio-philosopher. Similar conclusions follow: someone who writes on Yoruba literature can be identified as a literary philosopher. Someone who writes on Yoruba philosophy can be referred to as a philosopher even if his or her work is imbued with elements of religion and literature. But the word philosopher itself is a complicated one, torn as it is between a sense of the Western-trained philosopher and of the Babaláwo. Wande Abimbola embodies those complexities, and his book Ifá Will Mend

Our Broken World (1997) demonstrates that, if one truly knows **IFA**-Ife Divination, one will easily find peace of mind and success in life.

The ori is the foundation of Yoruba philosophy, and a Yoruba philosopher will be reluctant to separate it from destiny, just as a Yoruba religio-philosopher will feel reluctant to separate himself from divination. Through **IFA**-Ife Divination, the ori and its essence appear in every spoken and unspoken word of the Yoruba people. To them and for them, the ori is the definition of the entire body. It is the foundation, the fulcrum, the taproot.

About the Metaphorical Allegorist, Fabulist and Philosopher Ijapa

Emerging from a stygian corner, Ijapa has identified himself as the folk hero and the fabled protagonist of antiquity in Yoruba folktales, and not a reptilian imagination of a stunt creature. For if a man is everything as Ijapa is everything that has been beguiling our children for generations, therefore Ijapa cannot be relegated to anything less than a man created in the image and the likeness of Creator-Philosopher Olodumare.

Said Ijapa, "I will pull myself from the darkling to the light. I will pull myself from bathos to sublime. I will prove myself (and let the burden of proof roll like a philosophical gourd to the threshold of one and all) that I am **not** a four-legged protagonist but a human protagonist like you, versed in metaphorical allegories."

Selected Bibliography

Abimbola, Kola (2006) Yoruba Culture: A Philosophical Account, Iroko Academic Publishers, Birmingham, United Kingdom.

Abimbola, Wande (2003) Ifa Will Mend Our Broken World, Aim Books, Boston, MA, United States.

Appiah, Kwame Anthony (2010) The Honor Code, W.W. Norton, New York, US, London United Kingdom.

Asante, Molefi Kete (!987) The Afrocentric Idea, Temple University Press, Philadelphia, USA.

Awolowo, Obafemi (1981) Voice of Reason, Fagbamigbe Publishers, Akure, Nigeria

Beiser, Frederick C (1987) The Fate of Reason, Harvard University Press, United States and United Kingdom.

Berlin, Isaiah (2000) The Power of Ideas, Princeton University Press, New Jersey, USA and UK

Butterworth, John; Thwaites, Geoff (2005) Cambridge University Press, Cambridge, USA and UK.

Cahn, Steven (Ed) (2011) Thinking About Logic, Westview Press, Boulder, Colorado, USA.

Cathcart, Thomas (2006) Plato and Platypus, Walk into a Bar...Harry N. Abrams Inc, New York, New York.

Cather, Willa (1893-1902) Articles and Reviews: published in a Book-format (1970) The World and the Parish, University of Nebraska Press, Nebraska, United states.

Courlander, Harold (1996) A Treasury of African Folklore, Marlowe & Company, New York, New York.

Deleuze, Gilles; Guattari, Felix (1994) What Is Philosophy? Columbia University Press, New York, USA.

Epega, A. Afolabi (2003), IFA: The Ancient Wisdom, Athelia A. Epega, New York. USA.

Eze, E. Chukwudi (Ed.), (1997), Post-Colonial African Philosophy, Blackwell Publishers, Oxford, United Kingdom

Eze, E. Chuckwudi (Ed), (1998), African Philosophy (An Anthology), Blackwell Publishers, Oxford, United Kingdom

Fagunwa, D.O (1950), Ogboju-Ode Ninu Igbo Irunmale, Thomas Nelson and Sons, London, UK

Feibleman, James K (1973), Understanding Philosophy, Horizon Press, New York, United States

Gyegye, Kwame (1987) African Philosophical Thought (revised edition), Temple University Press, Philadelphia, United States

Hacking, Ian (2002) Historical Ontology, Harvard University Press, Cambridge, USA and UK.

Halbertal, Moshe (2012) On Sacrifice, Princeton University Press, New Jersey, USA and UK

Hountondji, Paulin (1983), African Philosophy, Myth and Reality, Indiana University Press, Indian, United states

Karenga, Maulana (2004) Kawaida Theory: An African Communitarian Philosophy, University of Sankore Press, Los Angeles, United States.

Klein, Daniel (2006) Plato and Platypus, Walk into a Bar...Harry N. Abrams Inc, New York, New York.

Makinde, Moses Akin (2002) Awolowo as a Philosopher, Obafemi Awolowo University Press, Ile-Ife, Nigeria

----------------(1984) African Philosophy, Culture and traditional Medicine, Center for International Studies, Ohio University, Athens, United states.

Nkrumah, Kwame (1964), Consciencism, Panaf Books Ltd, London, United Kingdom

Nyerere, Julius (1974), Man and Development, Oxford University Press, United Kingdom

Ogunyemi, Yemi D. (2010), The Oral traditions in Ile-Ife, Academica Press, Palo Alto, United States

------------(2009), The Literary/Political Philosophy of Wole Soyinka, Frederick, United States

------------(2003), The Aura of Yoruba Philosophy, Religion and Literature, Diaspora Press of America, Boston, United States

------------(1998), Introduction to Yoruba Philosophy, Religion and Literature, Athelia Henrietta Press, New York, United States.

--------------(1998), The Covenant of the Earth, Athelia Henrietta Press, New York, United States

Oluponna, Jacob (2011) City of 201 Gods: Ile-Ife in Time, Space and the Imagination, University of California Press, Los Angeles, United States

Pinker, Steven (2002) The Blank Slate, Penguin Books, New York, United States

--------------(2009) How the Mind Works, W.W. Norton and Company, New York, USA
and London, UK.

Soyinka, Wole (1976), Myth, Literature and the African World, Cambridge University Press, New York, United States

------------------(2012), Of Africa, Yale University Press, New Haven, United States.

Thorton, John (1992, 1998) Africa and Africans in the Making of the Atlantic World, 1400-1800, Cambridge University Press, New York, United States

Wiredu, Kwasi (1983), Philosophy and African Culture, Cambridge University Press, New York, United States

References

Proto-History Philosophers

Divinity **Esu:** He was a great philosopher who subscribed to the aesthetics of contradictions. He belonged to the Divine Hall of the Yoruba pantheon.

Divinity **Obatala:** Philosopher Obatala or Orisa-Nla was a popular philosopher during the period of creation. He is versed in human anatomy. He belonged to the Divine Hall of the Yoruba pantheon.

Divinity **Oduduwa:** Oduduwa was a pacifist, liberalist, transcendentalist, a great reasoner/thinker who planted the seeds of enlightenment and founded the holy city of Ile-Ife. Thus he is the father of Yoruba folk philosophy. He belonged to the Divine Hall of the Yoruba pantheon.

Divinity **Ogun:** Philosopher Ogun was the classical commander-in-chief of iron and steel. He believes in the theory that there are good things in fighting as there are opportunities in tragedies. A fleet-footed man, he always sets out at dawn. He belonged to the Divine Hall of the Yoruba pantheon.

Divinity **Olokun:** He is an important philosopher who is in charge of waters. He belonged to the Divine Hall of the Yoruba pantheon.

Divinity **Orunmila:** He is a knowledgeable philosopher and psychologist and the brainchild of, or cultivator of **IFA-Divination**, an integral part of the Book of Enlightenment/the Body of Knowledge, containing love and wisdom. He is a natural healer and member of the Divine Hall of the Yoruba pantheon.

Divinity **Oshosi:** He is versed in hunting and the art of hunting. He was a sharp shooter who never failed to find his hunted or quarries. He is credited to have introduced hunting to Yoruba land.

Divinity **Oshun:** She is one of the youngest female philosophers. She characterizes character, beauty, sweet waters and productivity. She identifies herself with River Oshun, a river said to be a blessing to mothers and mothers-to-be. She is a member of the Divine Hall of the Yoruba pantheon.

Divinity **Oya:** She is foremost amongst the Yoruba female philosophers. She identifies herself with River Niger. She is a member of the Divine Hall of the Yoruba pantheon.

Divinity **Sango:** He was the philosopher who represents fire, lightning and thunder. He belonged to the Divine Hall of the Yoruba pantheon.

Divinity **Soponna:** Philosopher Soponna typifies destruction upon malevolence. He acts and fights for whosoever needs his help and that person must possess a contrite heart. He is a member of the Divine Hall of the Yoruba pantheon.

Divinity **Yemoja:** She is a respectable female philosopher who represents the ocean, the essence of motherhood and a protector of children worldwide. She belonged to the Divine Hall of the Yoruba pantheon.

Post-Oral Philosophers

Chief Moshood Abiola (1937-1998): He was a philanthropist, liberalist and a political philosopher.

Sir King Adesoji Aderemi (1889-1980): He was a discreet, respectable and peace-loving traditional king of the holy city of Ile-Ife and political philosopher. He was a social democrat, pacifist and liberalist. He vouchsafed for the fundamental unity that put an end to the schisms that hitherto existed among the royal houses in Nigeria.

Oba Efuntola Adefunmi (1928-2005) Oba Adefunmi was a lover of Yoruba/African royal values. He was the first African-American to be coroneted a king by a Yoruba royal authority outside of Yorubaland. In order to bring closest to the hearts of African-Americans in Diaspora, he founded the Oyotunji African Kingdom (as a New World Yoruba initiative) in 1970.

Adegoke Adelabu (1915-1958): A writer, a journalist and the first chairman of Ibadan District Council. He was a charismatic pacifist.

Chief Samuel Ladoke Akintola(1910-1966): A national and international orator, and a gifted user of Yoruba proverbs and aphorisms. He was both a liberalist and pacifist.

Chief Obafemi Awolowo (1909-1987): A dynamic political philosopher who made Western Nigerian civil service one of the best in the world. He was considered a social democrat, a revolutionary, pacifist and liberalist. He is a scenarist, often referred to as the President Nigeria never had.

Beier, Ulli (1922-2011): He was a well-travelled scholar, researcher, writer and artist. Ulli Beier was a connoisseur of the Yoruba literature, religion, philosophy and artefacts. Together with dramatist Duro Ladipo, he founded Mbari-Mbayo Centre in Ibadan-Oshogbo in 1962. And in 1982, he founded and directed the Iwalewa House, an art centre at the Bayreuth University, Germany.

Chief Tai Bola (1898-1989): A local historian, liberalist, pacifist, philosopher and keeper of traditions

Bishop (Dr.) Samuel Ajayi Crowther (1807-1891), he was the first nineteenth-century language and idealist/folk philosopher. The first Anglican African Bishop of the Niger Territory, he translated the English Bible into Yoruba language. He was, according to our record, the first religion philosopher of the land. Additionally, he was a pacifist, an abolitionist, a missionary who was on the vanguard of, and belonged to the Way of Enlightenment that emerged after the Yoruba wars in the 19th century.

D.O. Fagunwa (1903-1963): A writer and narrative, folk philosopher. He was the first Yoruba folk philosopher, employing metaphysics or naturalism to tell his stories.

Dr. Samuel Johnson (1846-1901): An influential classical Enlightenment thinker, he was a pacifist, liberalist, philosopher and historian. He was the first person to complete the historical writing of Yorubaland—A History of the Yoruba(s), published in 1921. He belonged to the Way of Enlightenment that emerged after the Yoruba wars.

Duro Ladipo (1931-1978) A popular international playwright and the author of **Oba ko so**—the king did not hang. **Oba ko so** is a melodramatic play of how the famous king Sango was presumed dead but alive and kicking, as he became king of Thunder and Lightning. He was often referred to as a playwright whose mouth emitted fire while acting.

Herbert Macaulay (1864-1946): Doyen of Lagos politics, he was an astute political philosopher and pacifist. He essayed to turn the fears and scars of the Yoruba wars into intrepidity, the irascibility into rationality and the defeated into valiant survivors. These pacific efforts of his enabled him to found in 1944, a viable political party in Nigeria—National Council of Nigeria and Cameroons (NCNC), together with Dr. Nnamdi Azikwe. Also, he was the founding visionary of the Nigerian National Democratic Party (NNDP) in 1923, the first political party in the united Nigeria. He belonged to the Way of Enlightenment that was rapidly taking root after the Yoruba wars.

Hubert Ogunde (1916-1990) A pacifist, liberalist and prolific artist, he was an actor, playwright, theatre manager and musician who founded Ogunde Concert Party in 1945, the first professional theatrical company in Nigeria. He was the doyen of modern Yoruba /Nigerian playwright and dramatist.

Kola Ogunmola (1925-1973) He was the founder of Ogunmola Travelling Theatre in 1947. A gifted dramatist, actor, mime, director and playwright, he staged the musical version of Amos Tutuola's The Palm wine Drinker which was performed at the first Pan-African Culture Congress in Algiers in 1969.

Ajibike Ogunyemi: He is one of the many men who worked with Susanne Wenger to make Oshun Grove the artistic statement it is today. A prolific sculptural artist, Ogunyemi's work is known throughout Oshun state.

Twin Seven-Seven (1944-2011) Member of the Oshogbo School of Art Movement, Twin Seven-Seven began his art career in the 1960s in the workshops conducted by Ulli Beier and Georgina Beier in Oshogbo. A versatile and gifted artist, he was designated UNESCO Artist for Peace in 2005, in recognition of his contributions to the promotion of dialogue and understanding amongst peoples, particularly in Africa and in Diaspora.

Wole Soyinka: A liberalist and political philosopher. In embracing pacifism, he took delight in political activism, displaying an exceptionally discreet/tactful bravery. Soyinka is a multi-talented avant-garde litterateur. He was the winner of the Nobel Prize for literature in 1986, the first wordsmith of African descent to be so honoured.

Chief Susanne Wenger (1915-2009) An exceptional artist, pacifist, liberalist and philosopher (a connoisseur of Yoruba cultural values and cardinal virtues), Susanne Wenger is instrumental to the formation of the New Sacred Art Movement otherwise known as the Oshogbo School of Art Movement. Due to her devotion, her wisdom and love for sculptural art and culture of the Yorubaland, the Oshun Oshogbo Sacred Grove was declared a UNESCO World Heritage Site in 2005.

Index

A

Abeokuta, 161
Abiola, 220
Abiola, Chief Moshood
    Olawale, 214
Accra, 61, 62, 63, 118
Achebe, Chinua, 163
Addis-Ababa, 64, 66, 118
Adefunmi, King Efuntola,
    130, 220
Adejobi, Oyin, 162
Adelabu, Chief Adegoke, 162,
    220
Aderemi, Sir Oba Adesoji,
    162, 220
Ahidjo, Ahmadou, 163
Ajayi, Bishop Crowther, 15,
    xxi, 5, 11, 158, 162, 167,
    168, 199, 200, 201, 202,
    205, 206, 211, 213, 221
Akintola, Chief Samuel
    Ladoke, 162, 220
Al-Azhan, Ismail, 163
Angelou, Maya, 163
Asante, Kete Molefi, 163, 217
Atlantic Yoruba Kingdom, 43
Awolowo, Chief Obafemi, 8,
    1, 11, 100, 131, 162, 163,
    210, 214, 217, 218, 220

B

Beier, Ulli, 8, 130, 221, 222
Benin, 44, 48, 161
Bourguiba, Habib, 163
Braimoh, Jimoh, 130

D

Daddah, Ould Moktar, 163
Dubois, W.E.B, 163

E

Egbe Omo Oduduwa, 131,
    162
Eko Atlantic City, 47, 48, 51,
    53, 55, 97
Euba, Femi, 162

F

Fagunwa, D.O., xx, xxi, 11,
    135, 136, 162, 168, 178,
    212, 215, 217, 221
Fourah Bay College, 169

G

Gates, Jr, Henry Louis, 163
Gordimer, Nadine, 163

H

Houphouet-Boigny, Felix,
    163

I

Ibadan, 48, 120, 130, 169, 220,
    221
Idris, King, 163

Ijapa, xxi, xxvii, 120, 128, 138,
    139, 140, 143, 144, 145,
    146, 147, 148, 183, 184, 216
Ijebu-Ode, 107, 161
Ila-Orangun, 161
Ile-Ife, xix, xx, xxiv, xxv, xxvii,
    1, 8, 15, 19, 31, 34, 35, 37,
    41, 43, 44, 45, 46, 94, 107,
    112, 113, 114, 133, 135,
    144, 146, 151, 154, 161,
    164, 167, 178, 193, 196,
    214, 218, 219, 220
Ipepe, 44, 46, 48, 55, 56
Iwalewa, 43, 44, 46, 58, 59,
    152
Iwalewa House, 130, 221

J

Johnson, Dr. Samuel, xxi,
    162, 168, 212, 213, 221

K

Karenga, Maulana, 163, 218
Kaunda, Kenneth, 163
Keita, Modiba, 163
Kenyatta, Jomo, 163
Ketu, 101, 103, 161
Kuti, Fela, 163
Kuti, Ransome Funmilayo,
    xxvi

L

Lagos, xxvii, 43, 44, 45, 48, 49,
    50, 51, 53, 54, 82, 97, 104,
    105, 107, 118, 120, 130,
    153, 174, 221
Laye, Camara, 163
Locke, John, 163
Luggard, Frederick, 161
Lumumba, Patrice, 163

M

Macaulay, Herbert, xxvi, 163,
    213, 221
Mahfouz, Maguib, 163

Mahin, 44
Mandela, Nelson, 170, 171
Marga, Hubert, 163
Margai, Sir Milton, 163
Mi Rivera, xx, 63, 64, 66, 67,
    68, 69, 72, 74, 78, 79, 80,
    81, 82, 83, 84, 85, 86, 87,
    88, 90, 91, 92, 94, 95, 96,
    100, 107, 111, 112, 113,
    114, 115, 116, 117, 118,
    119, 122, 123
Moremi, 34, 46, 66, 101, 144,
    151
Morrison, Toni, 163

N

Nasser, Gamal Abdel, 63, 64,
    163
Nyerere, Julius, 218

O

Obasanjo, Olusengun, xxvii
Obote, Milton, 163
Ogunyemi, Ajibike, 162, 222
Ogunyemi, Chief Reuben O,
    133
Old Oyo Empire, 39, 169
Olympio, Sylvanus, 163
Omolara, 44, 45, 46, 47, 48,
    49, 51, 52, 53, 55, 56, 57,
    58, 59
Owu, 161
Oyo, 34, 39, 161, 164
Oyotunji African Kingdom,
    130, 220

P

Popo, 161
Prince Iwa, 43
Princess Ewa, 43

R

Rotimi, Ola, 162
Rousseau, Jean-Jacques, 163

S

Sabe, 161
Selassie, Emperor Halle, 62, 64, 163
Senghor, Leopold, 163
Soyinka, Wole, xxi, xxvii, 143, 163, 169, 170, 171, 214, 218, 222, 229

T

Thiong'o, Ngugi wa, 163
Tobalbaye, Francois, 163
Toure, Ahmed Sekou, 163
Tutuola, Amos, 162, 212, 222

U

Ugbo, 43, 44

W

Walcott, Derek, 163
Wenger, Susanne, 8, 130, 162, 222
Wittgenstein, Ludwig, 163

X

X, Malcolm, 163

Y

Yoruba-land, 4, xxv, 205

By the Same Author

Novels

The Melodrama of The Last Word
The Myths of the Coffee Boys
The Dreams of Joy
Sweet Mother
The Talking River
The Literary Philosophy for the Year 2000
The Voice of The Earth
My Gazar With My Geisha
The Last Cowrie Queen

Novelettes/Novellas

My Sworn Friend
The Death of a Would-be Title-holder
Pursuit of Wisdom

Short Stories

The Chief Who Married 35 Wives
The Yellow House
Follow Me
Aduke is a Singer, Mama
Okobaba and the Nine Angels
Tortoise, the Storyteller
Waiting for the Dry Season
Vendetta
The Story That Never Ends
My Beautiful Sister
Letters From Our Empire
The Floating Bungalow

Poetry

The Covenant of the Earth
The African Soul
The New Talking Drum
The Dawn of Tomorrow
M-A-S-T-A-M-A-N-D-A
The Anthologies of the Diaspora
The Danger of a Single Rejection
Codes of Morality

Children's Stories

The Source of River Koku
How Dogs Become Friends of Men
Tortoise—The Wisest Creature
January—December Lyrics
A Hut Never Hurts
Why Giraffes Have Long Necks
Why a Cock Cannot Crow
The Belling of the Wild Cat
How Catty-Coo Chases Mousy-Loo
Jumbo and Piggy
Butti and Moti
How Zebras Got Their Black and White Stripes
My First Dream
How the Tortoise Survived the Famine in Ogba
The Muddy Glade
Why Dada Was Called Ho, Ho, Ho.
How Kati Became A Swimmer
The Missing Child
How Kemi and Layo Started Schooling
The Postman and His Son
Tortoise, My Friend
Why Grasshopper Hop
Time for Competition
The House an Elephant Built
A Day with A Hunter

My Daddy's Sweet Potatoes
How Hoody & Hoofy Became
Soccer Players
Mama, Let Me Be Me
Why and How the Elephant Got his Huge Ears
The Ostrich and the Boomerang
Long Live the Queen
My Neighbor's Diary
Why Jako Shoots without Missing
The Bee that Keeps Her Promise
The Song of a River

Actualities

Literatures of the African Diaspora
Introduction to Yoruba Philosophy, Religion & Literature
Path to Ifetherapy & Its Healing Poems
The Literary/Political Philosophy of Wole Soyinka
Women In Europe
Media In Africa
Political Ideas for Peace & Development in Nigeria
The New Intellectuals for Peace & Development
My Contact With Africans & Africa (Editor)
The Writers and Politics
We Should All Be Philosophers
The Artist-Philosophers in Yoruba land
Yoruba Idealism

Drama

Three Plays
Obama, the Pragmatic President
(Subtitle: The Ankh of Progress)
King Oduduwa Visits Americas and Europe

www.ingramcontent.com/pod-product-compliance
Lightning Source LLC
Chambersburg PA
CBHW072141290426
44111CB00012B/1944